The
Globalization
Paradox

Also by Dani Rodrik

One Economics, Many Recipes: Globalization, Institutions, and Economic Growth

Has Globalization Gone Too Far?

The
Globalization
Paradox

Why Global Markets, States, and Democracy Can't Coexist

Dani Rodrik

UNIVERSITY PRESS

OXFORD
UNIVERSITY PRESS

Great Clarendon Street, Oxford OX2 6DP

Oxford University Press is a department of the University of Oxford.
It furthers the University's objective of excellence in research, scholarship,
and education by publishing worldwide in

Oxford New York

Auckland Cape Town Dar es Salaam Hong Kong Karachi
Kuala Lumpur Madrid Melbourne Mexico City Nairobi
New Delhi Shanghai Taipei Toronto

With offices in

Argentina Austria Brazil Chile Czech Republic France Greece
Guatemala Hungary Italy Japan Poland Portugal Singapore
South Korea Switzerland Thailand Turkey Ukraine Vietnam

© Dani Rodrik 2011

First published 2011
Published as *The Globalization Paradox: Democracy and the Future of the World Economy* by W.W. Norton, 2011

British Library Cataloguing in Publication Data

Data available

Printed in Great Britain
on acid-free paper by
Clays Ltd., St Ives Plc

ISBN 978-0-19-960333-6

3

To Çetin Doğan

An extraordinary man whose dignity, fortitude, and resolve will prevail over the great injustice he has been forced to endure.

CONTENTS

Recasting Globalization's Narrative

published a little book early in 1997 called *Has Globalization Gone Too Far?* A few months later, the economies of Thailand, Indonesia, South Korea, and other countries in Southeast Asia stood in tatters, casualties of a massive international financial whiplash. These countries had been growing rapidly for decades and had become the darlings of the international financial community and development experts. But all of a sudden international banks and investors decided they were no longer safe places to leave their money in. A precipitous withdrawal of funds ensued, currencies took a nose-dive, corporations and banks found themselves bankrupt, and the economies of the region collapsed. Thus was born the Asian financial crisis, which spread first to Russia, then to Brazil, and eventually to Argentina, bringing down with it Long-Term Capital Management (LTCM), the formidable and much-admired hedge fund, along the way.

I might have congratulated myself for my prescience and timing. My book eventually became a top seller for its publisher, the Washington-based Institute for International Economics (IIE), in part, I suppose, because of the IIE's reputation as a staunch advocate for globalization. It was a kind of a Nixon-in-China effect. Skepticism about globalization was more interesting when it came from a quarter where it was least expected. "A pro-globalization think tank publishes study by Harvard professor who warns globalization is not what it's cracked up to be"—now that is something worth paying attention to!

Alas, I was far from getting it right. My book was oblivious to the crisis brewing in financial markets. In fact, not only had I not foreseen the coming storm, I had decided to leave financial globalization—the trillions of dollars in currencies, securities, derivatives, and other financial assets exchanged globally on a daily basis—out of the book altogether. Instead, I had focused on the difficulties that international trade in goods was generating in labor markets and for social policies. I worried that the boom in international commerce and outsourcing would exacerbate inequality, accentuate labor market risks, and erode the social compact within nations. These conflicts need to be managed, I argued, through more extensive social programs and better international rules. I had decided to write the book because my colleagues in the economics profession were pooh-poohing such concerns and missing an opportunity to engage productively in the public debate. I believe I was right at the time, and the economics profession as a whole has since moved much closer to the views I expressed then. But the downside of *financial* globalization? That was not on my radar screen at the time.

In the years that followed the Asian financial crisis, my research increasingly turned toward understanding how financial globalization worked (or didn't). So when, ten years later, the International Monetary Fund asked me to prepare a study on this topic, I felt I was prepared. The article I wrote in 2007 with my co-author Arvind Subramanian was titled "Why Did Financial Globalization Disappoint?"[1] The promise of financial globalization was that it would help entrepreneurs raise funds and reallocate risk to more sophisticated investors better able to bear it. Developing nations would benefit the most, since they are cash-poor, subject to many shocks, and less able to diversify. That is not how things turned out.

The better performing countries—such as China—were not the countries receiving capital inflows but the ones that were *lending* to rich nations. Those who relied on international finance tended to do poorly. Our article tried to explain why unleashing global finance had not delivered the goods for the developing nations.

No sooner had we sent the article to the printer than the subprime mortgage crisis broke out and enveloped the United States. The housing bubble burst, prices of mortgage-backed assets collapsed, credit markets dried up, and within months Wall Street firms had committed collective suicide. The government had to step in, first in the United States and then in other advanced economies, with massive bailouts and takeovers of financial institutions. Financial globalization lay at the core of the crisis. The housing bubble and the huge edifice of risky derivatives it gave rise to were instigated by the excess saving of Asian nations and petrostates. That the crisis could spread so easily from Wall Street to other financial centers around the world was thanks to the commingling of balance sheets brought on by financial globalization. Once again, I had missed the bigger event unfolding just beyond the horizon.

I was hardly alone, of course. With very few exceptions economists were busy singing the praises of financial innovation instead of emphasizing the hazards created by the growth in what came to be known as the "shadow banking system," a hub of unregulated finance. Just as in the Asian financial crisis, they had overlooked the danger signs and ignored the risks.

Neither of the crises should have come as a total surprise. The Asian financial crisis was followed by reams of analysis which in the end all boiled down to this: it is dangerous for a government to try to hold on to the value of its currency when financial capital is free to move in and out of a country. You could not have been an economist in good standing and not have known this, well before the Thai baht took its plunge in August 1997. The subprime mortgage crisis has also generated a large literature, and in view of its magnitude and momentous implications, surely much more will be written. But some of the key conclusions are not hard to foresee: markets are prone to bubbles, unregulated leverage creates systemic risk, lack of transparency undermines confidence, and early intervention is crucial when financial markets are going belly-up. Didn't we know all this from as long ago as the famous tulip mania of the seventeenth century?

These crises transpired not because they were unpredictable but because they were *unpredicted*. Economists (and those who listen to them) had become overconfident in their preferred narrative of the moment: markets are efficient, financial innovation transfers risk to those best able to bear it, self-regulation works best, and government intervention is ineffective and harmful. They forgot that there were many other storylines that led in radically different directions. Hubris creates blind spots. Even though I had been a critic of financial globalization, I was not immune from this. Along with the rest of the economics profession I too was ready to believe that prudential regulations and central bank policies had erected sufficiently strong barriers against financial panics and meltdowns in the advanced economies, and that the remaining problem was to bring similar arrangements to developing countries. My subplots may have been somewhat different, but I was following the same grand narrative.

Doubts All Around

When countries on the periphery of the global system such as Thailand and Indonesia are overcome by crisis, we blame them for their failures and their inability to adjust to the system's rigors. When countries at the center are similarly engulfed, we blame the system and say it's time to fix it. The great financial crisis of 2008 that brought down Wall Street and humbled the United States along with other major industrial nations has already ushered in an era of newfound zeal for reform. It has raised serious questions about the sustainability of global capitalism, at least in the form that we have experienced in the last quarter century.

What might have prevented the financial crisis? Did the problem lie with unscrupulous mortgage lenders? Spendthrift borrowers? Faulty practices by credit rating agencies? Too much leverage on the part of financial institutions? The global savings glut? Too loose monetary policy by the Federal Reserve? Government guarantees for Fannie Mae and Freddie Mac? The U.S. Treasury's rescue of Bear Stearns and AIG? The U.S. Treasury's refusal to bail out Lehman Brothers? Greed? Moral hazard? Too little regulation? Too much regulation? The debate on these questions remains fierce and will no doubt continue for a long time.

In the bigger scheme of things, these questions interrogate mere details. More fundamentally, our basic narrative has lost its credibility and appeal. It will be quite some time before any policy maker can be persuaded that financial innovation is an overwhelming force for good, that financial markets are best policed through self-regulation, or that governments can expect to let large financial institutions pay for their own mistakes. We need a new narrative to shape the next stage of globalization. The more thoughtful that new narrative, the healthier our economies will be.

Global finance is not the only area that has run out of convincing story lines. In July 2008, as the subprime mortgage crisis was brewing, global negotiations aimed at reducing barriers to international trade collapsed amid much acrimony and finger-pointing. These talks, organized under the auspices of the World Trade Organization (WTO) and dubbed the "Doha Round," had been ongoing since 2001. For many anti-globalization groups, they had come to symbolize exploitation by multinational corporations of labor, poor farmers, and the environment. A frequent target of attack, in the end the talks were brought down for more mundane reasons. Developing countries led by India and China concluded that there was not enough on offer from the United States and the European Union for them to dismantle their own industrial and agricultural tariffs. Even though efforts to revive the talks continue, the WTO seems to have run out of ideas to boost its legitimacy and make itself relevant once again.

The world's trade regime differs from its financial counterpart in one important respect. Corrosion in the system of trade relations does not produce a blowup from one day to the next. When nations find the rules too constraining and no longer appropriate to their needs, they find ways of flouting them. The effects tend to be more subtle and show up over time in a gradual retreat from the cornerstone principles of multilateralism and non-discrimination.

Developing nations have always complained that the system is biased against their interests since it is the big boys that make the rules. A motley collection of anarchists, environmentalists, union interests, and progressives have also occasionally made common cause in their opposition to globalization for obvious reasons. But the real big news in recent years is that the rich countries are no longer too happy with the rules either. The rather dramatic decline in support for economic globalization in major countries like the United States reflects this new trend. The proportion of respondents in an NBC/*Wall Street Journal* poll saying globalization has been good for the U.S. economy has fallen precipitously, from 42 percent in June 2007 to 25 percent in March 2008. And surprisingly, the dismay has also begun to show up in an expanding list of mainstream economists who now question globalization's supposedly unmitigated virtues.

So we have the late Paul Samuelson, the author of the postwar era's landmark economics textbook, reminding his fellow economists that China's gains in globalization may well come at the expense of the United States; Paul Krugman, the 2008 Nobelist in Economics, arguing that trade with low-income countries is no longer too small to have an effect on inequality in rich nations; Alan Blinder, a former U.S. Federal Reserve vice chairman, worry-

ing that international outsourcing will cause unprecedented
dislocations for the U.S. labor force; Martin Wolf, the *Financial
Times* columnist and one of the most articulate advocates of globalization, expressing his disappointment with the way financial
globalization has turned out; and Larry Summers, the Clinton
administration's "Mr. Globalization" and economic adviser to
President Barack Obama, musing about the dangers of a race to
the bottom in national regulations and the need for international
labor standards.

While these worries hardly amount to the full frontal attack
mounted by the likes of Joseph Stiglitz, the Nobel Prize–winning
economist, they still constitute a remarkable shift in the intellectual climate. Moreover, even those who have not lost heart often
disagree vehemently about where they would like to see globalization go. For example, Jagdish Bhagwati, the distinguished free
trader, and Fred Bergsten, the director of the pro-globalization
Peterson Institute for International Economics, have both been
on the front lines arguing that critics vastly exaggerate globalization's ills and underappreciate its benefits. But their debates
on the merits of regional trade agreements—Bergsten for, Bhagwati against—are as heated as each one's disagreements with the
authors mentioned above.

None of these economists is against globalization, of course.
They do not want to reverse globalization, but to create new
institutions and compensation mechanisms—at home or
internationally—that will render globalization more effective,
more fair, and more sustainable. Their policy proposals are often
vague (when specified at all), and command little consensus. But
confrontation over globalization has clearly moved well beyond
the streets to the columns of the financial press and the rostrums
of mainstream think tanks.

The intellectual consensus that sustains our current model of
globalization had already begun to evaporate before the world
economy became engulfed in the great financial crash of 2008.

Today, the self-assured attitude of globalization's cheerleaders has all but disappeared, replaced by doubts, questions, and skepticism.

An Alternative Narrative

The world has seen globalization collapse once already. The gold standard era—with its free trade and free capital mobility—came to an abrupt end in 1914 and could not be resuscitated after World War I. Could we witness a similar global economic breakdown in the years to come?

The question is not fanciful. Although economic globalization has enabled unprecedented levels of prosperity in advanced countries and has been a boon to hundreds of millions of poor workers in China and elsewhere in Asia, it rests on shaky pillars. Unlike national markets, which tend to be supported by domestic regulatory and political institutions, global markets are only "weakly embedded." There is no global antitrust authority, no global lender of last resort, no global regulator, no global safety net, and, of course, no global democracy. In other words, global markets suffer from weak governance, and are therefore prone to instability, inefficiency, and weak popular legitimacy.

This imbalance between the national scope of governments and the global nature of markets forms the soft underbelly of globalization. A healthy global economic system necessitates a delicate compromise between these two. Give too much power to governments, and you have protectionism and autarky. Give markets too much freedom, and you have an unstable world economy with little social and political support from those it is supposed to help.

The first three decades after 1945 were governed by the Bretton Woods compromise, named after the eponymous New Hampshire resort where American, British, and other policy makers from Allied nations gathered in 1944 to design the post–World

War II economic system. The Bretton Woods regime was a shallow multilateralism that permitted policy makers to focus on domestic social and employment needs while enabling global trade to recover and flourish. The genius of the system was that it achieved a balance that served multiple objectives admirably well. Some of the most egregious restrictions on trade flows were removed, while leaving governments free to run their own independent economic policies and to erect their preferred versions of the welfare state. Developing countries, for their part, were allowed to pursue their particular growth strategies with limited external restraint. International capital flows remained tightly circumscribed. The Bretton Woods compromise was a roaring success: the industrial countries recovered and became prosperous while most developing nations experienced unprecedented levels of economic growth. The world economy flourished as never before.

The Bretton Woods monetary regime eventually proved unsustainable as capital became internationally more mobile and as the oil shocks of the 1970s hit the advanced economies hard. This regime was superseded in the 1980s and 1990s by a more ambitious agenda of economic liberalization and deep integration—an effort to establish what we may call hyperglobalization. Trade agreements now extended beyond their traditional focus on import restrictions and impinged on domestic policies; controls on international capital markets were removed; and developing nations came under severe pressure to open their markets to foreign trade and investment. In effect, economic globalization became an end in itself.

In pushing the postwar globalization model beyond its limits, economists and policy makers overlooked what had been the secret of its original success. The result was a series of disappointments. Financial globalization ended up promulgating instability rather than higher investment and more rapid growth. Within countries, globalization generated inequality and insecurity instead of lifting all boats. There were stupendous successes in this period—China and India in particular. But as we shall see, these were countries that chose to play the globalization game not by the new rules, but by Bretton Woods rules. Instead of opening themselves unconditionally to international trade and finance, they pursued mixed strategies with a heavy dose of state intervention to diversify their economies. Meanwhile countries that followed the more standard recipes—such as those in Latin America—languished. And thus globalization became a victim of its own earlier success.

Replacing our economic world on a safer footing requires a better understanding of the fragile balance between markets and governance. I will offer an alternative narrative in this book based on two simple ideas. First, markets and governments are complements, not substitutes. If you want more and better markets, you have to have more (and better) governance. Markets work best not where states are weakest, but where they are strong. Second, capitalism does not come with a unique model. Economic prosperity and stability can be achieved through different combinations of institutional arrangements in labor markets, finance, corporate governance, social welfare, and other areas. Nations are likely to—and indeed are entitled to—make varying choices among these arrangements depending on their needs and values.

Trite as they may sound as stated, these ideas have enormous implications for globalization and for democracy, and for how far we can take each in the presence of the other. Once you understand that markets require public institutions of governance and regulation in order to function well, and further, you accept that nations may have different preferences over the shape that those institutions and regulations should take, you have started to tell a story that leads you to radically different endings.

In particular, you begin to understand what I will call the fundamental political trilemma of the world economy: we cannot simultaneously pursue democracy, national determination, and economic globalization. If we want to push globalization further, we have to give up either the nation state or democratic politics.

If we want to maintain and deepen democracy, we have to choose between the nation state and international economic integration. And if we want to keep the nation state and self-determination, we have to choose between deepening democracy and deepening globalization. Our troubles have their roots in our reluctance to face up to these ineluctable choices.

Even though it is possible to advance both democracy and globalization, the trilemma suggests this requires the creation of a global political community that is vastly more ambitious than anything we have seen to date or are likely to experience soon. It would call for global rulemaking by democracy, supported by accountability mechanisms that go far beyond what we have at present. Democratic global governance of this sort is a chimera. There are too many differences among nation states, I shall argue, for their needs and preferences to be accommodated within common rules and institutions. Whatever global governance we can muster will support only a limited version of economic globalization. The great diversity that marks our current world renders hyperglobalization incompatible with democracy.

So we have to make some choices. Let me be clear about mine: democracy and national determination should trump hyperglobalization. *Democracies have the right to protect their social arrangements, and when this right clashes with the requirements of the global economy, it is the latter that should give way.*

You might think that this principle would be the end of globalization. Not so. I hope to convince you by the end of this book that reempowering national democracies will in fact place the world economy on a safer, healthier footing. And therein lies the ultimate paradox of globalization. A thin layer of international rules that leaves substantial room for maneuver by national governments is a *better* globalization. It can address globalization's ills while preserving its substantial economic benefits. We need smart globalization, not maximum globalization.

Economists Are Human, Too

Economists and policy advisers have exhibited myopia far too long toward the tensions and frailties that economic globalization generates. They have attributed every roadblock along the way to ignorance or, worse still, self-interested lobbying by protectionists of all kinds. They have paid insufficient attention to the legitimate clash among competing values and ideals that the single-minded pursuit of globalization accentuates. They have overlooked the link between well-functioning markets and purposeful state action. Their prescriptions have correspondingly done more harm than good at times. And they have missed countless opportunities to deploy the tools of their trade to better effect.

By necessity, then, this is also a book about economists and their ideas—about the tales they tell themselves and others. It explains how these tales have shaped our world, how they almost brought that world to an end, and how many of these economic ideas can now be used to erect a better global economic system. It is perhaps natural for an economist like me to think that ideas—and economists' ideas in particular—matter a whole lot. But I think it is hard to overstate the influence that these ideas have had in molding our understanding of the world around us, shaping the conversation among politicians and other decision makers, and constraining as well as expanding our choices. Political scientists, sociologists, historians, and others would no doubt claim equal credit for their professions. Policy choices are surely constrained by special interests and their political organization, by deeper societal trends, and by historical conditions. But by virtue of its technical wizardry and appearance of certitude, economic science has had the upper hand since at least the end of World War II. It has provided the language with which we discuss public policy and shaped the topology of our collective mental map. Keynes once famously said that "even the most practical man of affairs is usually in the thrall of the ideas of some long dead economist." I think he didn't put it nearly strongly enough. The ideas that have produced the policies of the last fifty years have emanated from economists who are (for the most part) very much alive.

Economists often get an unfair rap. They are perceived as market fundamentalists who care little about communities, social values, or public goals other than efficiency and economic growth. They promote material consumption, greed, and selfishness, it is said, over other ethical norms and socially cooperative behavior. The image of an economist most people carry in their head is that of Milton Friedman, preaching endlessly about the virtues of free markets and the perils of government intervention—in housing, education, health, employment, trade, and other areas. This is not an accurate picture at all. Economists use a variety of frameworks to analyze the world, some of which favor free markets and some of which don't. Much of economic research is in fact devoted to understanding the types of government intervention that can improve economic performance. Non-economic motives and socially cooperative behavior are increasingly part of what economists study.

The problem is not that economists are high priests of free market fundamentalism, but that they suffer from the same heuristic biases as regular people. They tend to exhibit groupthink and overconfidence, relying excessively on those pieces of evidence that support their preferred narrative of the moment, while dismissing others that don't fit as neatly. They follow fads and fashion, promoting different sets of ideas at different times. They place too much weight on recent experience and too little weight on more distant history. They tend to overfocus on remedies that will address the last crisis, while paying insufficient attention to tensions that may result in the next. They tend to attribute dissenting views to ignorance or self-interest rather than genuine differences in evaluating the underlying circumstances. They are clannish, drawing a big distinction between who's in and who's out (i.e., card-carrying members of the profession versus the rest). As with all possessors of specialized knowledge, they tend to get arrogant when outsiders encroach upon their field. In other words, economists are human. They behave as humans do—not as the fictional hyperrational, social welfare–maximizing planners that their own models sometimes rely on.

But economists are not just any other group. They are the architects of the intellectual environment within which domestic and international policy making takes place. They command respect and are listened to—ironically the more so the worse the economic situation. When economists get things wrong, as they occasionally do, they can do real damage.

When they get things right, however, their contribution to human welfare is huge. Behind some of the greatest economic successes of our time—the reconstruction of global trade in the postwar period or the rise of China and India—lie simple but powerful ideas relentlessly driven home by economists: trade is better than self-sufficiency, incentives matter, markets are an engine of growth. As I will show, there is much in economics that can and should be celebrated.

So this is not a simple morality play about good guys and bad guys. I have as little patience for briefs that hold economists responsible for the world's various ills as I do for self-congratulatory accounts by market fundamentalists. I will neither denigrate economists' ideas, nor be a cheerleader for them. I will instead show how they have been used and misused at different times, and how we can build on them to construct a better form of globalization—one that is more consistent with the values and aspirations of different nations as well as more resilient. To date, economics has been two parts wonder drug and one part snake oil. I hope this book will help the reader tell the difference.

The
Globalization
Paradox

Of Markets and States

Globalization in History's Mirror

On November 17, 1671, the regulars at Garraway's coffee-house, a popular hangout for London's shipowners, stock-brokers, and merchants, were greeted with an unusual announcement:

> On the fifth of December, ensuing, There Will Be Sold, in the Greate Hall of this Place, 3000 weight of Beaver Skins, comprised in thirty lotts, belonging to the Honourable, the Governour and Company of Merchants-Adventurers Trading into Hudson's Bay.

This sale of beaver fur was of more than passing interest to the clientele at Garraway's. Considered a source of the highest quality fur, beaver pelts were in great demand during the seventeenth century. Beaver was held in such high regard that in 1638 King Charles I had prohibited the use of any material other than beaver fur in hat making.

To the great consternation of the city's merchants, financiers, and nobility, London was a backwater where the fur trade was concerned. Most beaver fur originated from Russia and was sold through the Baltic and Black Sea ports to traders in major Continental cities such as Paris, Vienna, and Amsterdam. In addition, overhunting had resulted in a severe depletion of beaver stock and in high prices. London's wealthy had to content themselves with lower-quality fur that trickled in from the Continent or obtain their supplies directly from these cities at great expense. The public auction at Garraway's heralded a new era of plentiful, high-quality fur.[1]

How had the beaver furs found their way to Garraway's? Who or what was "the Governour and Company of Merchants-Adventurers Trading into Hudson's Bay"? There lies an interesting tale of globalization from another era.[2] This was a very different kind of globalization, to be sure. Yet look at it closely, and you learn quite a deal about what makes globalization possible—and what limits it.

The Age of Chartered Trading Companies

The series of events that landed the beaver furs at Garraway's had three unlikely protagonists. Two were brothers-in-law of French extraction with the colorful names of Pierre-Esprit Radisson and Médard Chouart, sieur des Groseilliers. Radisson and des Groseilliers were *coureurs des bois*, unauthorized adventurers and traders of furs in the northern reaches of Quebec in today's Canada. The French colonial regime in what was then called "New France" had established a profitable business buying beaver pelts from Native Americans. The natives would bring their supplies to trading posts established by the colonists and sell the beaver in exchange for firearms and brandy. In keeping with the economic philosophy of the day—mercantilism—this was all arranged as a monopoly, to generate the maximum profit for the French crown and its representatives.

Radisson and des Groseilliers's forays in the northern forests of the region, closer to the shores of Hudson's Bay, had led them to think they could greatly expand the existing supply of beaver furs by going deeper into the largely unexplored Native American territories. But the French colonial administration, too set in its established ways, would have none of it. The two adventurers were fined for trading without license and des Groseilliers landed in jail for a brief time.

Thwarted by their countrymen, the two brothers-in-law decided to change masters. In search of alternative sponsors, they traveled to London, where they were presented to King Charles II. Most important, they managed to attract the attention of Prince Rupert, the third protagonist of our story. Prince Rupert, born in Bohemia, was the nephew of Charles II and an adventurer of a different kind. He had fought in England, on the Continent, and in the Caribbean, and was also an amateur inventor and artist. Radisson and des Groseilliers's plan was to establish a sea route from England by traveling across the northern Atlantic into Hudson's Bay through the Hudson's Strait. This way they could bypass the French authorities and reach the Indian tribes directly from the north, an area as yet unclaimed by European governments. It was a risky and costly plan, for which they needed both royal protection and financial support. Prince Rupert was in a position to provide both.

On the morning of June 3, 1668, des Groseilliers set sail from London on the *Nonsuch*, a small vessel especially selected for its ability to travel inland, in a voyage financed by Prince Rupert and his entourage. He landed on the shores of Hudson's Bay four months later. (A second ship with Radisson on board had to return to England after encountering severe storms along the way.) Des Groseilliers and the crew wintered there, established contact with the Cree Indians, and returned to England in October 1669 on the *Nonsuch* with a good supply of beaver.[3]

Having demonstrated that their business plan worked, our three protagonists then did what anyone with a good head for business engaged in long-distance trade would have done at the time: lobby the king for monopoly rights. It didn't hurt of course that

Prince Rupert was family to Charles II. On May 2, 1670, the crown granted Prince Rupert and his partners a charter which established "the Governour and Company of Merchants-Adventurers Trading into Hudson's Bay." The company thereby created eventually came to be known as Hudson's Bay Company. It survives to this day as HBC, Canada's largest general retailer, which makes it also the world's oldest joint stock company.

The charter Charles II granted to Hudson's Bay Company is an extraordinary document that confers enormous powers on the company. The king begins by commending his "beloved cousin" Prince Rupert and his associates for having led the expedition to Hudson's Bay "at their own great cost" and for having discovered "considerable commodities," which will produce "great advantage to us and our Kingdom." He then grants sole trade and commerce of all those "seas, straits, bays, rivers, lakes, creeks, and sounds in whatsoever latitude they shall be" that lie within the entrance of Hudson's Strait, along with all the adjoining territory that does not already belong to another "Christian prince or state." But the charter does not stop there. Charles II then makes the company "the true and absolute lords and proprietors" of all the territories just described.[4]

In appreciation of the troubles that Prince Rupert and his associates (the "merchant-adventurers" who had risked their capital in the venture) had gone through, and in expectation of great benefits to the kingdom in the future, the company received not just monopoly trading privileges but also full property rights over the Hudson's Bay area. "Rupert's Land," an area covering all the rivers that drain into the Bay, came under the ownership of the company. The full dimensions of this territory weren't even known at the time since it hadn't been completely explored. It turned out that Charles II had just signed off a good chunk of today's Canada—an area that eventually would amount to roughly 40 percent of the country, or more than six times the size of France[5]—to a private company!

The king's charter made Hudson's Bay Company a government in all but name, administering a vast territory and ruling over the local Indians who had no choice in the matter. The company could fight wars, pass laws, and dispense justice. Needless to say, it was the sole arbiter of the fur trade in Rupert's Land, setting the conditions and prices of the exchange with the natives. In the nineteenth century, it even issued its own paper currency, which became legal tender in areas it controlled. The territorial control of the company did not end for some two hundred years, until 1870, at which point the company turned possession of Rupert's Land over to the Dominion of Canada in exchange for £300,000 ($34 million in today's money).[6]

The Canadian fur trade was comparatively small and the Hudson's Bay Company no more than a footnote in the extensive mercantile system of long-distance trade of the seventeenth and eighteenth centuries. The major trade routes lay elsewhere. There was of course the infamous Atlantic triangular trade, which carried slaves to the Americas in exchange for sugar, cotton, and tobacco (with the Europe-Africa leg providing an important connecting link). There was also the ever important trade with India and Southeast Asia, which could now bypass Venetian and Muslim intermediaries thanks to Vasco da Gama's passage of the Cape of Good Hope in 1497–98. In the three centuries following Columbus's and da Gama's discoveries, the world experienced a veritable boom in long-distance trade. According to one estimate, international trade rose at more than double the rate of world incomes in this period.[7]

The companies that made this trade possible were mostly chartered trading monopolies organized along lines similar to Hudson's Bay Company. Many have well-recognized names, such as the English East India Company and the Dutch East India Company, and many have left significant marks on history.

The most famous among them, the English East India Company, or the "Governor and Company of Merchants of London Trading into the East Indies," as it was originally called, was chartered in 1600 as a joint stock company. Its monopoly covered trade with the Indian subcontinent and China (including opium trade). As with the Hudson's Bay Company, its powers extended considerably beyond trade. It had a standing army, could make war, enter into treaties, mint its currency, and administer justice. It expanded its control over India through a series of armed confrontations with the Mughal Empire and alliances with local rulers. The East India Company performed a vast range of public functions, including investments in transport, irrigation, and public education. It eventually became a tax collector as well, administering a land tax on the local population to supplement its trading profits. Even though the company lost its trading monopoly in India in 1813, it continued to rule for several decades. Finally, it was abolished as a result of the Indian Mutiny of 1858, at which time control of India passed directly to the British crown.

These companies had their own flags, armies, magistrates, and currencies. Meanwhile they paid dividends to their shareholders back home. That trade and rule were so closely entwined may seem like an anachronism to modern observers—the peculiar feature of an era whose misconceptions about economics have long been set straight. The dominant economic philosophy of the seventeenth century was mercantilism, which advocated a close alliance between the sovereign and commercial interests. In hindsight, mercantilists had some truly cranky ideas, such as the view that economic well-being sprang from accumulating silver and other precious metals. They thought free trade should be confined to raw materials and industry reserved for domestic producers through high import tariffs. But they also believed in capitalism (as we would call it today) and in exports, which set them light-years ahead of many of their contemporaries. While the Dutch and the English were scouring the ends of the world for raw materials and markets, the Ottomans and the Chinese— by far the more powerful entities—had both withdrawn into a doomed quest for self-sufficiency.[8] The mercantilists' narrative of capitalism was based on the view that the state and commercial enterprise ought to serve the needs of each other. Economics was a tool of politics, and vice versa. International trade, in particular, had to be monopolized to exclude foreign powers and to reserve the benefits for the home country.

Today, we are likely to take our cue more from Adam Smith, whose *Wealth of Nations* (published in 1776) was a frontal attack on mercantilist thought and practice. Economic liberals, with Smith as their founding father, have a different narrative. They believe that economies flourish when markets are left free of state control. Competition, rather than monopoly, maximizes economic advantage. Protective barriers on trade—import tariffs and prohibitions—reduce competition and thus are a way of shooting oneself in the foot. State-business collaboration is just another name for corruption. Adam Smith did not deny that there was a role for government, but his vision was of a state restricted to national defense, protection of property rights, and administration of justice. In his view, mercantilism and the chartered monopolies were a drag on the development of national economies and of global commerce. According to this narrative, rapid economic growth and true globalization had to wait until the nineteenth century, when Adam Smith's ideas finally won the day.

This dichotomy between markets and states—between trade and rule—is false and hides more than it reveals. Market exchange, and especially long-distance trade, cannot exist without rules imposed from somewhere. The story of the Hudson's Bay Company reveals the close link between power and economic exchange in its naked simplicity. I want to trade with you, so you better play by my rules! We may think of later eras of globalization as more detached from state rules and power—and hence as more "pure." But that would be quite wrong. Power was exercised; just differently—and less obviously. Where there is globalization, there are rules. What they are, who imposes them, and how—those are the only real questions.

It is not that there are always malevolent powers lurking behind markets and globalization. We can have better or worse rules. But we need to discard the idea that markets work best when they are left to their own devices. Markets necessarily require non-market institutions in order to function. Using the Nobel Prizewinner Doug North's pithy definition, these institutions supply the "rules of the game" for markets. Their presence in turn begs the questions of how they are designed and whose interests they serve. When we confront these questions head-on, instead of assuming them away, we get a better handle on how to design market-supporting institutions. We are also led to some uncomfortable thoughts on the limits of economic globalization.

But let's first return to our chartered companies to understand the role that statelike powers played in fostering long-distance trade.

What It Takes to Reap the Benefits of Trade

It is a simple principle that every child knows, and then relearns in college economics courses: there are gains from trade whenever you have something that I value more than you do. Recast as trade between different parts of the world, this quickly becomes a tale of comparative advantage. Whatever a country has plenty of can be exchanged for things that it lacks. Cree Indians along Hudson's Bay certainly had plenty of beaver. But they were short of blankets, kettles, and of course the rifles and brandy that they didn't even know they needed before they encountered white men. Given the high demand for beaver fur in Europe, the potential gains from intercontinental trade were huge.

In textbook renditions of trade, this would be just about the end of the story. In the real world, things are not that simple. Look at the obstacles that our triumvirate of heroes and their associates had to overcome. They had to engage in a dangerous venture—with risks to both purse and life—to reach the Indians through a new, maritime route. They had to build and man trading posts along Hudson's Bay under severe weather conditions. They had to explore the areas inland and make connections with the Indians. They had to open and maintain channels of communication, build trust, and convince the Indians of their peaceful intentions. They had to do the "market research" to figure out what the Indians would buy in return for fur. Above all else, they had to provide a safe and secure environment within which trade could be carried out. That in turn required laws and regulations, backed up by force (if needed).

In other words, they had to invest in the infrastructure of trade—transport, logistics, communications, trust, law and order, contract enforcement—before trade could actually take place. Our "merchant-adventurers" *had* to carry out statelike functions, because trade would have been impossible in their absence.

The bargain that a sovereign struck with private companies under mercantilism was essentially this: You, the company, pay for the institutional infrastructure, and in return I will allow you to make monopoly profits from the resulting trade. This quid pro quo was well understood, and sometimes quite explicit. As early as 1468, the Portuguese granted Fernão Gomes a monopoly of trade with Africa for five years on the condition that "he extend the exploration of the coast southwards by one hundred leagues (a little over three hundred miles) each year."[9] In 1680, when the monopoly of the Royal African Company in Britain's slave trade was challenged, the advocates for the company defended it in terms that were quite explicit about the "public" functions performed by the enterprise: the slave trade required the construction of forts along the West African coast at an expense that was too great for private traders; the trade had to be defended from attacks by other nations; maintenance of forts and warships required exclusive control; private traders upset local rulers by attempting to enslave "all and sundry, even Negroes of high rank"; and so on.[10] Unfortunately for the company, these arguments did not prevent the monopoly from being repealed in 1698. The slave trade was far too profitable for it to remain the exclusive preserve of a single company.

When the Hudson's Bay Company was charged by its opponents with underpaying American Indians for beaver pelts, it argued that those low prices were only fair given the difficulties of commerce in the North American wilds. It is true, the company said, that Indians were asked to pay high prices for English goods while being paid little for the furs. But this was common practice for "civilized traders all the world over, [when] dealing with ignorant and dependent tribes." After all, "the risks of life and limb and goods in remote regions are great, and great profits must be made to meet them."[11]

Ultimately, someone has to shoulder the responsibility for peace, security, and the framework of laws and regulations that makes trade possible. What distinguishes mercantilism from later versions of capitalism is that the job fell by and large on private entities. When private companies could no longer perform those tasks—either because they became too weak or competition from other nations undercut their rents—the crown had to intervene. Asked by a House of Commons committee in 1857 about the likely consequences of abolishing the special privileges of Hudson's Bay Company, a leading politician and former director of the company put it plainly: this would be of no consequence as long as "Canada shall bear the expense of governing [the territory ceded by the company] and maintaining a good police and preventing the introduction, so far as they can, of competition within the fur trade."[12] The company may not have been happy to see its monopoly go, but it could live with it as long as the prerequisites for doing business were henceforth to be supplied (and paid for) by the Canadian state.

The abolition of the East India Company following the Indian Mutiny of 1858, and its replacement by direct colonial rule from London, provides another perfect example of the transition. When the private firm and its armies were no longer up to the task, the sovereign had to step in with his own, more effective powers of persuasion.

Overcoming Transaction Costs

A contemporary economist would summarize the argument thus far by saying that the role played by the Hudson's Bay Company, the East India Company, and other chartered trading companies was to reduce the "transaction costs" in international trade to enable some degree of economic globalization. It is worth spending some time on this concept, as it holds the key to understanding globalization—what restricts or deepens it—and will recur throughout our discussion.

Economists like to think that the propensity to "truck, barter, and trade," in Adam Smith's evocative (but careful)[13] phrasing, is such an ingrained element of human nature that it makes "free trade" the natural order of things. They even have coined a general term for different types of friction that prevent mutually beneficial trade or render it more difficult: "transaction costs." Transaction costs are in fact rampant in the real world, and if we fail to see them all around us it is only because modern economies have developed so many effective institutional responses to overcome them.

Think of all the things that we take for granted that are absolutely essential for trade to take place. There must be some way—a marketplace, bazaar, trade fair, an electronic exchange—to bring the two parties to a transaction together. There must be a modicum of peace and security for them to engage in trade without risk to life and liberty or concern for theft. There must be a common language for the parties to understand each other. In any form of exchange other than barter, there must be a trusted medium of exchange (a currency). All the relevant attributes of the good or service being exchanged (for example, its durability and quality) must be fully observable. There must be sufficient trust between the two parties. The seller must have (and be able to demonstrate) clear property rights over the goods being sold and must have the ability to transfer these rights to the seller. Any contract that the two sides enter into must be enforceable in a court of law or through other arrangements. The parties must be able to take on future commitments ("I will pay you so much upon the delivery of . . . ") and do so credibly. There must be protection against third parties trying to block the exchange or impede it. I could keep going, but the point is probably clear.

Sometimes these requirements do not raise major hurdles for trade. If you have two cookies and I have two glasses of lemonade, we could easily carry out a trade that would leave both of us better off. At other times, the trade relies on an extensive network of institutional prerequisites. Apple and its subcontractors in China must necessarily operate in a contract-rich environment involving a long list of specific bilateral commitments. When Citigroup makes a loan to a firm in a developing nation, it relies on a combination of the borrower's reputation, the strength of laws in the host country, and the likelihood of international sanctions as a precondition for agreeing to the deal. When something goes wrong in these relationships—a Chinese subcontractor passes on the iPhone's proprietary designs to a competitor or Citigroup's borrower refuses to service his debt obligations—there may be precious little that the aggrieved parties can do. The fear that such things can and will go wrong acts as a considerable deterrent to the transactions in the first place. In economists' language, these are trades with potentially quite significant transaction costs.

Institutions—at least those that support markets—are social arrangements designed to reduce such transaction costs. These institutions come in three forms: long-term relationships based on reciprocity and trust; belief systems; and third-party enforcement.

The first of these generate cooperation through repeated interaction over time. For example, a supplier is deterred from cheating his customer because he worries that he would lose future business. The customer in turn chooses not to shortchange the supplier because it would be costly to switch suppliers and build a long-term relationship with a new firm. As the relationship builds, trust increases, and it becomes possible to contemplate larger ventures. These self-supporting processes do not rely on any formal legal structures or organizational backstops. They predominate in developing nations where such structures are weak.

Second, trade can be supported through belief systems or ideologies. The fruit seller doesn't sell a traveler rotten fruit because "that would simply be wrong." A country may choose not to raise tariffs or restrict capital flows because "that is not the way things are done." Perhaps these actors truly internalize the reasons for their actions. Perhaps they fear being ostracized by their communities—tribe, caste, religious group, ethnic group, or "community of nations," as the case may be—if they are seen to defy prevailing norms of good behavior. Wherever they may come from, widely held views on the appropriateness of different courses of actions may discipline parties to an exchange and support a level of honesty and cooperation that might be difficult to achieve otherwise.

Repeated interaction and community norms work best when markets are mostly local and small scale, when people do not move around much, and when the goods and services traded are simple, standardized, and don't have to travel over long distances. But as economies grow and geographical mobility increases, the need for clear and extensive rules and more reliable enforcement becomes paramount. The only countries that have managed to become rich under capitalism are those that have erected an extensive set of *formal* institutions that govern markets: tax systems that pay for public goods such as national defense and infrastructure, legal regimes that establish and protect property rights, courts that enforce contracts, police forces to sanction violators, bureaucrats who design and administer economic regulations, central banks that ensure monetary and financial stability, and so on. In the language of the economist, these are institutions of "third-party enforcement." The rules of the game are enforced by a formal, typically governmental apparatus. You pay your taxes in part because you want better roads and schools, but I suspect you would pay a lot less if it weren't for the tax collector.

When we look at the size of the government across different societies, we uncover a rather amazing fact. With very few exceptions, the more developed an economy, the greater the share of its resources that is consumed by the public sector. Governments are bigger and stronger not in the world's poorest economies but in its most advanced economies. The correlation between government size and per capita income is remarkably tight. Rich countries have better functioning markets *and* larger governments when compared to poor ones. All this may be surprising at first sight, but the preceding discussion helps us understand what is going on. Markets are most developed and most effective in generating wealth when they are backed by solid governmental institutions. *Markets and states are complements,* not substitutes, as simplistic economic accounts would often have it.

Trade and Governments

This point was brought home to me in quite an unexpected way some years back. The government plays such a pervasive role in modern society that many social scientists, myself among them, find it impossible not to be obsessed by it. One day I was sitting in my office wondering why shrinking the public sector had proved so difficult despite the clamor for "small government" from conservative politicians when an article by the Yale political scientist David Cameron crossed my desk.[14]

Cameron was interested in the following question: Why had the public sector expanded so rapidly in the major advanced economies in the decades following World War II? Even though Cameron focused only on the post-1945 experience, this was in fact a trend that went further back in history. Around 1870, the share of government expenditures in the economies of today's advanced economies averaged around 11 percent. By 1920, this share had almost doubled, to 20 percent. It increased further, to 28 percent, in 1960. By the time of Cameron's study it stood at more than 40 percent, and has continued to rise since then.[15] The increase has not been uniform across different countries. Governments are considerably smaller today in the United States, Japan, and Australia (with expenditure shares below 35 percent) than they are in Sweden or The Netherlands (55–60 percent), with most of the other European countries in between. Cameron wanted to understand the sources of this difference.

His conclusion, based on a study of eighteen advanced nations, was that openness to international trade had been a major contributor. Governments had grown the largest in those economies that were the most exposed to international markets. Some countries are naturally more sheltered from the forces of international competition, either because they are large or because they are distant from their major trading partners. This is exactly the case of the small government economies on our list (the United States, Japan, and Australia). Small economies close to their trading partners, by contrast, engage in much more trade and have larger public sectors (such as in Sweden and The Netherlands).

This is a highly counterintuitive argument if you are used to thinking that markets can prosper only where the state does not intrude. I knew of course that more advanced economies have larger public sectors, but the Cameron claim was something else: he argued that the variation in the size of the public sector among equally rich economies could be explained by the importance of trade to their economies.

I must confess that I was suspicious about Cameron's result; economists tend to be a skeptical bunch, especially when faced with statistical work by other social scientists. My first reaction to the article was: this cannot be true. The sample is too small (only eighteen countries). The effect is driven by country size rather than exposure to international trade per se. There are many other confounding effects that the analysis has not taken into account. And so on.

I decided to check for myself. I downloaded some data and began to look at how government size lines up against economic openness. I first scrutinized the advanced countries that Cameron had focused on. I used different data sources and varying time periods, but to my surprise the Cameron result held up. Then I expanded the analysis to developing nations, looking at more than a hundred countries for which data were available. Again, the picture was the same. Finally, I tried to make the result disappear by controlling for everything that I could think of—country size, geography, demography, income level, urbanization, and many other factors besides. Whichever way I cut the data, I found a strong positive correlation between a nation's exposure to international trade and the size of its government.

Where was this correlation coming from? I considered many possible explanations, but none survived my battery of tests. In the end the evidence seemed to point strongly toward the social insurance motive. People demand compensation against risk when their economies are more exposed to international economic forces; and governments respond by erecting broader safety nets, either through social programs or through public employment (more typical in poor nations). This was essentially the same argument that Cameron had made, and it clearly went beyond the small set of rich countries he had considered. I had stumbled on one of the fundamental truths of economics that no one in graduate school had ever told me about: If you want markets to expand, you need governments to do the same.[16]

This need for expansion isn't just because governments are necessary to establish peace and security, protect property rights, enforce contracts, and manage the macroeconomy. It is also because they are needed to preserve the legitimacy of markets by protecting people from the risks and insecurities markets bring with them.

The recent subprime mortgage crisis and deep recession provide a good example. Why didn't the world economy fall off the same protectionist cliff that it did in the Great Depression of the 1930s? In the decades since, modern industrial societies have erected a wide array of social protections—unemployment compensation, adjustment assistance and other labor market interventions, health insurance, family support—that mitigate demand for cruder forms of protection such as sheltering the economy behind high tariff walls. The welfare state is the flip side of the open economy. Markets and states are complements in more ways than one.

Globalization's Love-and-Hate Relationship with the State

Now we can begin to appreciate how greatly international commerce differs from domestic economic transactions. If you and I are citizens of the same country, we operate under an identical set of legal rules and benefit from the public goods that our government provides. If we are citizens of different countries, none of this is necessarily true. There is no international entity that guarantees peace and safety, passes laws and enforces them, pays for public goods, or ensures economic stability and security. In view of the differences in culture and distances that separate nations, informal institutions such as reciprocity and norms typically do not induce much cooperation either. The market-supporting institutions that do exist are local and vary across nations. As a result, *international trade and finance entail inherently higher transaction costs than domestic exchanges.*

But there is more. The higher transaction costs are not just due to the absence of the requisite international institutions. Domestic arrangements geared to the needs of national markets also impede global commerce frequently. National rules inhibit globalization. The most obvious examples include government-imposed tariffs on trade or regulations that restrict international lending or borrowing. Whatever domestic purpose such restrictions may serve—social and political stability, encouragement of domestic entrepreneurship, or pure cronyism—they constitute clear transaction costs on international exchanges. The taxes that finance social safety nets and other public investments can also necessitate some restrictions on international exchange in order to prevent footloose professionals or capitalists from evading them.

In addition, many domestic regulations and standards discourage cross-border transactions, even when they are not primarily aimed at raising barriers to trade. Differences in national currencies, legal practices, banking regulations, labor market rules, food safety standards, and many other areas raise the costs of doing business internationally. "For us to remain competitive," Jeffrey Immelt, CEO of General Electric, complained in 2005, "we simply cannot navigate a regulatory maze that forces us to tweak and modulate every product and process to suit individual regulatory regimes at their whim."[17] Governments help reduce transaction costs within national boundaries, but they are a source of friction in trade *between* nations.

International markets operate outside the formal institutional framework of sovereign entities and therefore, absent special arrangements, are deprived of the support of those frameworks. Equally important, international markets operate across the institutional boundaries demarcating states and their jurisdictions. These two facts—the absence of an overall institutional framework for global markets and the tensions such markets generate between local institutions—are fundamental to understanding economic globalization. They help us think our way through the challenges of globalization and appreciate its limits. We return to them throughout the book.

Thus the difficulties the Hudson's Bay Company and its contemporaries faced while carrying out long-distance exchange were not specific to the seventeenth century or to trade in fur, spices, and other favored commodities of the time. International trade *is* different and requires special institutional arrangements. For all its faults, the chartered trading monopoly was a successful institutional innovation—aligned with the politics and economics of the time—that overcame many of the transaction costs specific to intercontinental trade. It spurred private entities to invest in knowledge, security, and contract enforcement, and thus made ongoing trade possible.

Of course, not all participants in the trade benefited equally. The prices received by the Cree Indians, for example, were unconscionably low.[18] The slave trade was an abomination. Over time, companies became more interested in maintaining their monopoly profits than in expanding trade networks. The co-dependence that developed between states and private companies helped neither the quality of governance nor economic performance over the long run. Adam Smith was right to question whether chartered monopolies contributed positively to the national balance sheet in the end. But as Smith's ideas gained ground and Britain and other leading powers dissolved the monopolies, the fundamental problem remained: how to render international trade and finance cheap and safe. The transaction costs inherent in the international economy would continue to haunt traders, financiers, and politicians.

Globalization's Conundrum

Markets have demanding prerequisites—and global markets even more so. Markets for basic foodstuffs, say, and other necessities, can work pretty well on their own in small communities where people know each other and interact repetitively. A small cabal of businessmen and financiers can enforce trade and exchange when they share a common belief system. Anything bigger, more wide-ranging, and ultimately sustainable requires a large cast of supporting institutions: property rules to establish ownership, courts to enforce contracts, trading regulations to protect buyers and sellers, a police force to punish cheaters, macro-policy frameworks to manage and smooth the business cycle, prudential standards and supervision to maintain financial stability, a lender-of-last-resort to prevent financial panics, health, safety, labor, and environmental standards to ensure compliance with public norms, compensation schemes to placate the losers (when markets leave some in the cold, as they often do), social insurance to provide some insulation against market risks, and taxes to finance all these functions.

In short, markets are not self-creating, self-regulating, self-stabilizing, or self-legitimizing. Every well-functioning market economy blends state and market, laissez-faire and intervention. The precise mix depends on each nation's preferences, its international position, and its historical trajectory. But no country has figured out how to develop without placing substantial responsibilities on its public sector.

If states are indispensable to the operation of national markets, they are also the main obstacle to the establishment of global markets. As we will see, their practices are the very source of the transaction costs that globalization has to surmount. That is the central conundrum of globalization: can't do without states, can't do with them!

Hence global markets are doubly problematic: they lack the institutional underpinnings of national markets and they fall *between* existing institutional boundaries. This dual curse leaves economic globalization fragile and full of transaction costs, even in the absence of direct restrictions on trade and cross-border finance. It renders the quest for a perfect globalization a fool's errand.

The mercantilists' chartered trading companies offered one solution to these dilemmas. Thanks to their statelike enforcement powers, these companies imposed their own rules over foreign populations in distant lands. However, they became less effective over time as they proved unable to handle restless local populations and the mercantilist narrative lost its appeal. The nineteenth century—the first era of true globalization—would have to rely on different mechanisms.

2

The Rise and Fall of the First Great Globalization

During the seventeenth and eighteenth centuries, world trade had expanded at a steady clip of around 1 percent per year, outpacing the rise in world incomes but not greatly so. Starting sometime in the early part of the nineteenth century, world trade began to grow by leaps and bounds, registering an unprecedented rate of almost 4 percent per annum for the century as a whole.[1] Transaction costs that impede long-distance trade—due to transportation and communication difficulties, government restrictions, or risks to life and property—began to decline precipitously. Capital flows boomed and most of the world's economies became financially more integrated than ever before. This was also an era of vast flows of people between continents, with working-class Europeans migrating en masse to the Americas and other lands of recent settlement. For these reasons, most economic historians consider the long century before 1914 the first era of globalization. Indeed, by many measures the world economy only recently surpassed the 1913 levels of globalization in trade and finance. In terms of labor mobility, the world has still to catch up.

Trade and Institutions During the Nineteenth Century

What made this era of globalization possible? Standard accounts identify three important changes in this period. First, new technologies in the form of steamships, railroads, canals, and the telegraph revolutionized international transport and communications and greatly reduced trade costs starting in the early part of the nineteenth century. Second, the economic narrative changed as the ideas of free market economists like Adam Smith and David Ricardo finally got some traction. This led the governments of the world's major economies to substantially relax the restrictions they placed on trade in the form of import taxes (tariffs) and explicit prohibitions. Finally, from the 1870s on, the widespread adoption of the gold standard enabled capital to move internationally without fear of arbitrary changes in currency values or other financial hiccups.

Yet these cannot be the end of the story. As we saw in the last chapter, the transaction costs in the world economy extend beyond transport, tariffs, and currency instability. The standard accounts omit two vitally important institutions specific to the nineteenth century. These institutions enabled a deeper globalization than had been possible to date and echo the market-supporting arrangements we encountered earlier.

The first of these was a convergence in belief systems among the period's key economic decision makers. Economic liberalism and the rules of the gold standard connected policy makers in different nations and led them to coalesce around practices that minimized transaction costs in trade and finance. Where this narrative held sway—as in Britain and among the world's major central banks throughout the entire period—globalization remained safe. Where it was absent or dissolved over time—as with trade policy in Continental Europe after the 1870s—globalization lost ground.

The second institution was imperialism. Whether of the formal or informal kind, imperialism was a mechanism for imposing trade-friendly rules, a type of "third-party enforcement," with the governments of the advanced countries as the enforcer. Imperialist policies deployed the political and military power of the major countries to bring the rest of the world into line whenever possible. Hence they provided an important backstop to globalization being derailed in the peripheral parts of the world economy—Latin America, Asia, and the Middle East—and could be used to render these regions safe for international trade and finance.

This chapter explains how the nineteenth-century version of globalization emerged and how domestic politics led to its unraveling. We begin our tour with trade policies and turn to the gold standard next.

The (Limited) Victory of Free Trade

Free trade beliefs were ascendant throughout the nineteenth century, thanks to the efforts of economists such as David Ricardo and John Stuart Mill who built on Adam Smith's insights to show how unrestricted trade is beneficial to all countries taking part in it. As we shall see in the next chapter, these ideas were elegant, powerful, and could be stated with logical precision. But their influence varied across countries and over time. Even though we think of the nineteenth century as an era of free trade, Britain is the only large economy that maintained open trade policies for any length of time. The United States put up very steep tariffs on manufactured imports during the Civil War and kept them high throughout the century. The major Continental powers in Europe were unhesitant converts to free trade only for a short period during the 1860s and 1870s.

The crucial date in nineteenth-century tariff history is 1846, the year that Britain abolished Napoleonic Wars–era tariffs on imports of grains. These so-called "Corn Laws" were at the center of political struggles in early nineteenth-century Britain, as they pitted rural interests against urban interests. Here "corn" was synonymous with grains, and the tariffs in question covered all food and cereal imports. Landlords wanted high tariffs that kept food prices high and raised their incomes. Urban manufacturers, increasingly powerful as the effects of the Industrial Revolution diffused through London, Manchester, and other cities, wanted to abolish the tariffs to reduce the cost of living. That reduction, as Karl Marx among others would argue, would allow capitalists to pay even lower wages to their workers. This debate galvanized British society and politics, with forces for and against the Corn Laws engaged in what appeared to be a bitter fight over a few import taxes, but was really about who would rule Britain and prosper in years to come. The well-known magazine *The Economist* is a product of this era, founded by opponents of the Corn Laws to spread and popularize free trade views, a role which it continues to perform today. In the end, the ascendant manufacturing interests won the day: they had both the intellectual arguments and the forces of the Industrial Revolution on their side.

Once the Corn Laws were abolished in Britain, the dominant economic power of the day, the pressure was on for other European countries to follow suit. Many perceived the reform as a political and economic success in Britain. Economic commentators on the Continent pointed with awe to the large increase in Britain's commerce and output since the repeal—although of course it was really the Industrial Revolution that deserved the bulk of the credit. Britain's apparent success did not necessarily make trade liberalization easier in other countries. As the emperor Louis-Napoléon Bonaparte put it to the British MP and free trade proselytizer Richard Cobden, "I am charmed and flattered at the idea of performing a similar work in my country; but it is very difficult in France to make reforms; we make revolutions in France, not reforms."[2] However, there was one political expedient to which

free trade–minded leaders have resorted ever since: reduce trade
barriers in exchange for another country doing the same, and
then present liberalization to the opposition as a necessary "concession" made to get the other party to open their markets.

The result was the Cobden-Chevalier treaty of 1860, which
committed Britain to reduce its duties on French spirits in return
for France reducing its tariffs on British manufactured goods.
This was followed by a series of similar treaties signed with other
Continental countries. An important innovation in the Cobden-
Chevalier treaty was the most-favored-nation (MFN) clause. The
clause required that the original signatories also receive any tariff reduction one of them subsequently grants to third countries.
This network of trade treaties became an important instrument of
tariff reduction throughout Europe during the 1860s and 1870s.
By the mid-1870s, most prohibitions on trade had disappeared
and average tariffs on manufacturing stood at low single digits
in Britain, Germany, The Netherlands, Sweden, and Switzerland,
and in the low teens in France and Italy, down from levels that
were a multiple of these rates.[3]

Free trade did not win everywhere. The fight over the Corn Laws
illustrates a theme we will have plenty of occasion to return to:
because trade policies have important consequences for income
distribution, they get entangled in much broader political con-
tests. The economist may decry the artificiality—and therefore
pointlessness—of the transaction costs that government-imposed
trade barriers create, but the argument does not always carry the
day when there are strong political interests or economic arguments that go in the opposite direction. In case you think those
political pressures and economic arguments always derive from
narrow self-interest and obscurantist doctrines—the story of the
repeal of the Corn Laws is often held up as a victory of progressive
ideas and liberalism over traditional nobility and authoritarian
institutions—consider the experience of the United States.

As different as the United States' political makeup was from

Britain's during the early part of the nineteenth century, the two countries had one thing in common: tariff controversies stood at the center of national politics. As one exasperated Pennsylvania legislator would later reflect, "man is an animal that makes tariff speeches."[4] Trade policies fed directly into the most important social and political cleavage in the country, between South and North. The slaveholding South was organized around an export economy based on tobacco and cotton. The free states of the North relied on a nascent manufacturing base that lagged behind Britain in productivity and struggled to compete with cheaper imports. The South depended on international trade for its prosperity. The North wanted protection from imports, at least until it could catch up.[5]

The Civil War of 1861–66 was fought as much over the future of American trade policy as it was fought over slavery. As soon as the war started, Abraham Lincoln raised U.S. tariffs, and trade protection was increased further following the North's victory. Import tariffs on manufactured goods averaged 45 percent in the decade after 1866 and never fell much below that level until World War I. By any standard, the United States was a highly protectionist country during the late nineteenth century. Coincidentally or not—the debate continues—this was also the period during which it caught up with and then surpassed Britain's industrial prowess.

We will return to the relationship between trade policy and economic growth later. For now, what is interesting about the U.S. experience is that it represents a case where free trade was decidedly not in the service of a "progressive" political cause. As the distinguished political scientist Robert Keohane has written, "pursuing the logic of the market had tragic effects in the long run. The economic impact on the South of growth without diversification or industrialization was harmful enough. Much more serious were the social and political results of making cotton king: slavery was entrenched and civil war became increasingly likely."[6] Whatever its other economic consequences, free trade in nineteenth-century America would have further reinforced and strengthened slavery as a social and political institution. The damage that it would have done to the development of political institutions of the country can only be guessed at, but the picture is unlikely to have been a pretty one.[7]

The lesson is clear: depending on where a country stands in the world economy and how trade policies align with its social and political cleavages, free trade can be a progressive or a regressive force. Britain was the industrial powerhouse of the world in the mid-nineteenth century and liberal trade policies favored manufacturing interests and the middle classes. The United States was an industrial laggard with a cost advantage in slavery-based plantation activities, where liberal trade policies would have benefited repressive, agrarian interests. Free trade and "good politics" don't always go together.

Meanwhile, on the European Continent second thoughts about free trade did not take long to make their appearance. An important trigger, as often happens, was a long economic recession that started in the 1870s and hit farmers especially hard. The transport revolutions and tariff cuts resulted in an influx of grains from the New World and sharply lower prices. Everywhere on the Continent agricultural interests clamored for protection, often making common cause with industrialists who were reeling under competition from the more advanced British producers (and increasingly from American exporters too). In Bismarck's Germany, this led to the famous "marriage of iron and rye," a coalition between agriculturalists and industrialists that produced sharply higher tariffs from the end of the 1870s onward. Always a savvy political operative, Bismarck rationalized the new policy by complaining that Germany had become the dumping ground of other countries' excess production. France and other Continental powers followed suit with their own high tariffs, and the general trend toward tightening of trade restrictions continued until the onset of World War I.

By 1913, average import tariffs in the Continent on manufactures had doubled to almost 20 percent.[8]

There was a paradoxical aspect, from the standpoint of the liberal economic narrative, to this increase in protection in late nineteenth-century Europe. As the economic historian Paul Bairoch notes, not only did trade volumes increase quite rapidly after 1890, so did incomes, especially in those countries that put up trade barriers.[9] This experience, just like that of the post–Civil War United States, casts more doubt on a simple relationship between policies of free trade and economic growth. We will return to the subject later in the context of our discussion of the Bretton Woods regime and the effects of globalization on today's developing countries.

It was only in Britain that the protectionist slippery slope was resisted in the decades before World War I, despite pressure from "fair traders" who wanted to retaliate against the high tariffs on British exports in the rest of Europe.[10] It wasn't just that free trade ideology dominated the public discourse to a much greater extent in Britain, "protectionism" having become a derogatory term to browbeat your opponents with. It was also that Britain's strong trade position in manufacturing rendered tariffs a rather pointless and redundant policy. When Prime Minister William Gladstone mocked those who sought retaliation in trade policy, he appealed to both factors. What in the world does "Fair Trade" mean? he asked. "Well, gentlemen," he responded, using an argument that would be repeated endlessly by free traders henceforth, "I must say it bears a suspicious likeness to our old friend Protection."[11] This was plain old protectionism trying to make itself look more attractive by assuming a new name.

Gladstone pointed out that Britain stood to gain little from retaliation since its imports of manufactured goods were so much smaller than its exports. Tariffs imposed on such a tiny base would have little punitive power. Britain's large trade surplus, Gladstone pronounced, made free trade the better policy for the country. A contemporary economist would cringe at Gladstone's mercantilist argument, which suggests that a country benefits from trade only insofar as it runs a trade surplus.[12] No matter. Britain's dominance in manufactures helped it avoid a protectionist cascade.

If among advanced countries free trade relied on a difficult and fragile balance between a shared ideology and a constellation of political interests at home, in the rest of the world it was imposed mostly from the outside. In Asia, European imperialism guaranteed that the rights of foreigners were protected, contracts enforced, disputes adjudicated under European countries' rules, exporters and investors welcomed, debts repaid, infrastructure investments undertaken, locals pacified, nascent nationalist ambitions thwarted, and so on—neutralizing the long list of transaction costs that could impede international commerce. Recall how the East India Company was superseded by the British Raj when the former proved unable to handle local insurgency, or how the Hudson's Bay Company's police powers were handed over to the Dominion of Canada. The British Empire brought law and order to societies that lacked them, argues the Harvard historian Niall Ferguson: "no organization in history has done more to promote the free movement of goods, capital and labor," he writes, "than the British Empire in the nineteenth and early twentieth centuries."[13]

One does not need to buy into Ferguson's glowing take on the British Empire to agree with his assertion that imperialism was a tremendously powerful force for economic globalization. A recent statistical study found that two countries that were members of the same empire had twice the volume of trade between them compared to trade with others outside the empire, holding as many things constant as is feasible in this kind of quantitative work. The reason? "[E]mpires increased trade by lowering transactions costs and by establishing trade policies that promoted trade within empires." The specific instances of reduced transaction costs that the study's authors are able to quantify are the use of a common language, the presence of a common currency, the monetizing of recently acquired colonies, and preferential trade arrangements.[14]

It would be a mistake to think such effects were confined to cases where metropolitan powers exerted direct imperial rule. Imperialism came in both formal and informal variants. Britain, France, the United States (which eventually got into the game), and the other powers did not always have to extend direct rule to bend other regions to their will. The threat of military force and political pressure were often adequate. In a classic article entitled "The Imperialism of Free Trade," John Gallagher and Ronald Robinson show that there was a continuum between informal influence and formal rule, with the latter employed only as the last resort when conditions were too unsettled and unruly to achieve the desired effects through local rulers.[15]

A prime instrument of informal influence was the trade treaty. If the locals proved insufficiently in awe of Smith and Ricardo's ideas, gunships standing at the ready could always provide the necessary persuasion. So Britain signed a treaty with Ottoman Turkey in 1838 that forced the country to restrict import duties to a maximum of 5 percent and abolish import prohibitions and monopolies. The British also fought the so-called "Opium War" with China in 1839–42 to open up the country to imports of opium and other goods exported from the British Empire. Commodore Matthew C. Perry signed a treaty with Japan on behalf of the United States in 1854 to open the country to foreign shipping and trade. These and other similar treaties would impose ceilings on import duties (one-sided, of course), restrict the ability of the less powerful countries to conduct their trade policies independently, grant foreign traders legal privileges, and enforce foreigners' access to ports.

Thus, despite the unmistakable explosion in trade, the globalization of the nineteenth century was not based as much on free trade as it is often portrayed. Policies of empire—formal or informal—clearly promoted trade, but they were based on the naked exercise of power by the metropolitan countries and hardly represented "free trade" in the true sense of the term. And if one leaves Britain aside, liberalism scored only limited victories in the domestic trade policies of major economies. Some countries (such as the United States) never truly espoused free trade policies, while others (such as the European Continental powers) reverted back to higher levels of protection after a couple of decades. Domestic politics rarely proved conducive to free trade for long stretches, except where economic supremacy guaranteed relative immunity from import competition. Thanks to the transport revolution and the rise in incomes, there was plenty of globalization—more probably than at any other time in history with the exception of the last few decades. But this globalization rested on awkward and fragile institutional pillars, a set of prerequisites unlikely to be replicated.

The Gold Standard and Financial Globalization

What was true of the trade regime was even truer of the financial and monetary regime that governed nineteenth-century globalization, the gold standard. Discipline enforced through imperialist practices was once again crucial to uphold free capital flows. And the belief system that underpinned the gold standard and sustained financial globalization between 1870 and 1914 would not survive the mortal blows received from the Great Depression and the revolution in economic thought that John Maynard Keynes wrought.

The gold standard rested on a few simple rules. Each national currency had its gold parity, which pegged its value rigidly to gold. For example, the British pound sterling was defined as 113 grains of pure gold and the U.S. dollar as 23.22 grains.[16] The central bank of each nation stood ready to convert national currencies to gold at these parities. Accordingly, exchange rates between currencies were also irrevocably fixed; one British pound equaled 113/23.22 or 4.87 dollars. Money could flow freely across countries, and be exchanged at the fixed rates determined by the gold parities.

The rules meant that changes in the domestic supply of money were tightly linked to movements in gold reserves. A country with a deficit on its foreign balance of payments would lose gold to its trade partners, and experience a reduction in its money supply. These gold flows would in turn trigger corrections in economic conditions which economists call the "automatic adjustment mechanism." In a deficit country, tight money and credit would result in a combination of rising interest rates and falling domestic prices. These in turn would lead to reduced spending and improved trade competitiveness, restoring equilibrium on external payments.

Under gold standard rules, governments had no ability to muck around with monetary policy to alter domestic credit conditions, because domestic money supplies were solely determined by gold and capital flows across national borders. In principle, central bankers had little to do besides issuing or retiring domestic currency as the level of gold in their vaults fluctuated. The system had clear, universal, and non-discretionary rules. The financial regime minimized transaction costs across national boundaries. Financiers and investors had to contend with neither surprises nor controls at the border.

In practice, central bankers had some room to maneuver and departed from these "rules of the game" on occasion. In particular, a country with a trade deficit could delay or avoid a rise in interest rates if there were compensating private capital flows coming in from abroad. But the availability of these "stabilizing" flows of capital depended critically on the credibility of central banks' commitment to the gold parity. Markets assumed that governments would eventually defend the parities come hell or high water. They did so because that was the *belief system* that governed central bank behavior at the time. The maintenance of the gold standard had absolute priority in the conduct of monetary policy both because the system came to be viewed as the foundation of monetary stability and because there were no competing objectives—such as full employment or economic growth—in the conduct of monetary policy. Ideas mattered, here as elsewhere. The notion that active monetary and fiscal policies could systematically smooth business cycles or that currency devaluation could help reduce trade imbalances—these were yet to come, or heretical at best. There was no widely believed or well-articulated conception of how governments could stabilize demand, output, or employment.

Unlike trade policy makers, central bankers were insulated from the push and pull of domestic politics and could operate autonomously. Barry Eichengreen, one of our most astute historians of financial globalization, hits it right on the nail: central banks' ability to maintain free capital flows and fixed exchange rates in the face of economic shocks "rested on limits on the political pressure that could be brought to bear on [them] to pursue other objectives incompatible with the defense of gold convertibility."[17] The central banks of the leading powers—Britain, France, and most others—were in fact privately owned and had no public function besides the issue of legal tender. The United States did not acquire a public institution acting as a central bank until 1913, when the Federal Reserve Act created the Federal Reserve System. Central bankers in different nations operated as members of a club, with greater affinity for each other than for their domestic brethren drawn from worlds outside finance.[18] In the words of Eichengreen, the gold standard was a "socially constructed institution."[19]

The financial globalization experienced by the world economy in the decades before World War I was nothing short of extraordinary. In a passage that is reproduced in almost every book on globalization, the predominant economist of the twentieth century John Maynard Keynes would nostalgically reminisce in 1919 about how the inhabitant of London could invest his wealth freely in any part of the world without any hindrance or worry that he may be deprived of the fruits of that investment.[20] This was a period when the world's financial markets operated with the least amount of transaction costs. Interest rates in London, New York, and the major financial centers of Europe moved as one—as if they were joined as part of one single market. Capital flowed freely and in huge quantities from where it was plentiful (Britain in particular) to where it was scarce (the New World in particular). Unlike in the case of free trade, there was no retreat from gold and from free capital flows before World War I intervened—despite considerable clamor for departing from the gold standard during the 1870s and 1880s. Such heights of financial globalization were not to be scaled again until very recently.

The durability of the institution was severely tested in the 1870s when a shortage of gold resulted, as the rules of the gold standard demanded, in tight credit conditions and price deflation in both Europe and the United States. Most hard hit were farmers, for whom the high interest rates in the face of falling prices were crushing. There was much clamor for a return to a bimetallic standard, which would have allowed governments to monetize silver and increase the money supply. The revolt reached its apogee in the United States, where William Jennings Bryan, three-time Democratic candidate for president, gave his famous "You shall not crucify mankind upon a cross of gold" speech at the 1896 Democratic National Convention.[21] The central banks stood firm and the gold standard held. Ultimately what probably saved the gold standard was that price deflation came to an end once the gold discoveries in South Africa after 1886 led to an increase in the market supply.

As we have seen, among the major economic powers of the day financial globalization was the product of convergent beliefs within a close-knit club of central bankers who made all the important decisions. Among the countries on the periphery of the global economy in Latin America, Middle East, and Asia, monetary orthodoxy ruled as well—even though not many of them made a full-fledged transition to the gold standard. The more serious problem in world finance was how to ensure that sovereign entities, and borrowers within them, would repay their debts.

It is a perennial problem and the bane of international finance. When a domestic borrower refuses to repay, the aggrieved lender can go to court and attach the borrower's assets, and expect the judgment to be enforced by the domestic authorities. When a debtor in a foreign land will not pay, the lender has few options. There is no international court to pass judgment and no international police to enforce that decision. Essentially the only check on the borrower is the likely loss in reputation and the potential cost of being shut out of international credit markets for a period of time.[22] Despite these costs to reputation, history shows that defaulters eventually reenter international financial markets. Several implications follow. First, the borrower might default on his international obligations not just when he is *unable* to pay, but also when he is simply *unwilling* to pay—a much lower threshold. Second, anticipating this, a rational and forward-looking bank or bond holder is unlikely to engage in much international lending, or will do so only at a high premium. Alternatively, there will be boom-and-bust cycles driven by shortsighted lending followed by subsequent default. The market for international finance cannot thrive unless there are credible mechanisms for enforcing repayment.

As with trade treaties, it was a big help to have gunboats and imperial rule as enforcers of debt contracts. The British capitalist who invested in Indian railways knew that the British Raj was there to guarantee the safety of his investment: "so long as he was guaranteed five per cent on the revenues of India," one British official remarked, "it was immaterial to him whether the funds which he lent were thrown into the Hooghly or converted into bricks and mortar."[23] When the Ottoman Empire defaulted on its obligations to mostly British and French bond holders in 1875, the

Europeans prevailed on the weakened Sultan to let them set up an extraterritorial agency to collect Ottoman tax revenues. The Ottoman Public Debt Administration (which began operations in 1881) became a vast bureaucracy within the Ottoman state with the primary purpose of paying foreign creditors. When nationalist agitation in Egypt threatened British financial interests in 1882, the British invaded the country to "restore political stability" and ensure that foreign debts would continue to be repaid. At the time, the prime minister, William Gladstone, had a sizable chunk of his wealth invested in Egyptian obligations so in this case the link between financial globalization and military power was particularly transparent.[24] Britain eventually ended up governing Egypt directly, even though its early intentions had been much more limited.

The United States itself had a checkered history of honoring debts, with many of the states having defaulted throughout the nineteenth century, so it is ironic that the Americans eventually became the debt enforcers in the western hemisphere. Theodore Roosevelt made it clear in 1904 (in the so-called "Roosevelt Corollary" to the Monroe Doctrine) that the United States would ensure that Latin American countries honored their international debt. He showed that he meant business by sending gunboats to Santa Domingo in 1905 and taking over customs revenue collection after the Dominican Republic defaulted on its debts—an action that signaled his determination to protect foreign creditors' interests and sent the prices of Latin American sovereign bonds soaring.[25] The question before the U.S. gunboats appeared was not whether the debts would be collected, but whether it was the Europeans or the Americans who would do it. By preempting the Europeans, Roosevelt intended to leave no doubt that this was an American sphere of influence.

The gold standard and financial globalization were made possible, just as in the case of free trade, by a peculiar combination of domestic politics, belief systems, and third-party enforcement.

When these forces weakened, as a result of mass politics beginning to assert itself, so did international finance. The ultimate collapse of the gold standard during the 1930s provides a revealing window on the fragility of this combination.

The Demise of the Gold Standard

World War I ushered in a period of heavy government controls on foreign exchanges followed by instability during the 1920s. All governments including Britain's suspended gold convertibility during the war and imposed restrictions preventing free exchange of the domestic currency to foreign currencies (exchange controls). Following the conclusion of the war, several European countries experienced hyperinflation during the early 1920s (Germany, Austria, Poland, and Hungary). This was a tumultuous time on foreign exchanges, with currency rates often gyrating wildly. Officials viewed a return to gold as inevitable sometime during the 1920s, to reestablish normalcy in international finance. But questions remained about the timing and about whether the return should take place at the prewar parity (£1 = $4.87) or at a more devalued rate. The argument for devaluing the pound was clear, and in hindsight unassailable: Britain's economic star had dimmed and required a weaker pound to go along with it.

Winston Churchill, for all his subsequent statesmanship during World War II, didn't have much of a head for economics, or much interest in it. So it was particularly unfortunate that he became chancellor of the exchequer in 1924, on the eve of Britain's return to the gold standard. He readily admitted that he was out of his depth when conferring with his Treasury underlings. If they were "soldiers or generals, I would understand what they were talking about," he quipped. "As it is they all talk Persian."[26]

British prices had risen more than threefold during the war, and despite significant deflation (on the order of 50 percent) in the aftermath of the war, they remained higher than in the United States. Britain had also run up large debts against the United States, which now sat on top of a large chunk of the world's gold reserves. The British government had been forced to maintain high interest rates to prevent capital flight, and unemployment remained high at 10 percent. The market value of the pound stood significantly below the prewar $4.87 level for most of this period. Keynes was prominent among those who thought return to the prewar parity would be disaster since it would leave the British economy saddled with an overvalued currency and a serious competitiveness problem in view of where British prices stood. British industrialists and the press magnate Lord Beaverbrook agreed.

Churchill listened to financiers and the Bank of England instead—to his considerable regret later on. The Bank's board and its governor Montagú Norman convinced him that return to the gold standard at anything other than the prewar parity would defeat the purpose of the restoration. They argued that the credibility of the system hinged on the immutability of the parities: change them once, and the markets will think they can be changed again. More than economics, it was a question of ethics. To the purists, return at the old parity was "a moral commitment on the part of the British nation to those around the world who had placed their assets, their confidence, and their trust in Britain and its currency."[27] If British labor and industry ended up uncompetitive, a period of deflation in wages and prices simply would have to be endured. This was neither the first nor the last time in history that bankers have prescribed tough medicine to be swallowed by others. In this instance, as in so many others, they also had the benefit of having what was then considered "sound economics" on their side.

Despite continued price deflation, the British economy never adjusted to the reinstatement of the old parity. Wages and prices remained too high for the British economy to regain its external competitiveness and correct its trade imbalance. Export-oriented industries such as coal, steel, shipbuilding, and textiles were hard hit, and unemployment eventually rose to 20 percent. Labor strife and strikes were rampant. Even though the economy remained in dire straits, the Bank of England was forced to maintain high interest rates to prevent massive outflows of gold—competing in effect with countries like France that had returned to the gold standard in 1926 at a more competitive parity. The United States, despite its early financial support for the pound, did not help much either. When the New York Fed raised its benchmark interest rate in early 1928 to stem what it thought was speculative excess on Wall Street, it also put further pressure on countries with external payments deficits such as Britain. Higher interest rates in the United States forced those countries either to follow suit and raise their own interest rates or to suffer further hemorrhaging of gold and capital. Finally, in September 1931, Britain once again went off gold. Once this standard-bearer of gold was forced out, the regime's days were numbered. Franklin Roosevelt took the United States off gold in 1933 to enable monetary expansion, and France and the so-called "gold-block countries" followed in 1936.

The gold standard had come under pressure in peacetime before, most notably during the deflationary episode of the 1870s spurred by a gold shortage. What was different this time around? First the economics, then the politics, and then the economics once again.

Start with the first-round economic changes. The textbook model of adjustment under the gold standard presumed individualistic, decentralized labor markets with flexible wages. If domestic industries became globally uncompetitive, wages and other costs would fall, helping these industries retain market share. Cheaper labor would also curtail unemployment. This was of course never quite how real economies worked, but it became more of a fantasy over time as labor became organized and trade unions asserted themselves. There was a significant rise in union membership in the two decades before the 1920s, and industrial unrest was on the rise, culminating in the General Strike of 1926. Labor's ability to maintain wages meant that a sustained monetary contraction due to a gold outflow (or the threat thereof), as Britain experienced, would now result in sustained unemployment. The full ramifications for economic policy would not be clear until Keynes published his great work, *The General Theory of Employment, Interest and Money* in 1935–36, explaining why the gold standard fails to operate smoothly in modern economies.

Now the politics kicks in. Regardless of their own instincts, central bankers and their political masters in the 1930s understood that they could no longer remain aloof from the political consequences of economic recession and high unemployment. Workers had become not only unionized; they now also had the vote. The franchise had quadrupled in Britain in the decade after World War I.[28] Newspapers and the radio were well on their way to becoming "mass media"; British national dailies had a combined circulation of 10 million by the 1930s.[29] Economic policy was becoming democratized. There was a growing Socialist movement to contend with. All of this meant that given a choice between suffering the political consequences of mass unemployment and giving up on the gold standard, a democratically elected government would eventually pick the second choice. Democracy was incompatible with absolute priority for the gold standard.

Now to the second-round economics, which provides the coup de grâce. Once financial markets begin to question the credibility of a government's commitment to a fixed parity vis-à-vis gold, they become a force for instability. Governments are now easy prey for speculative attacks. At the slightest hint of things going awry, investors sell the domestic currency, buy foreign currencies, and move capital out of the country. If the parity is maintained, they can simply reverse the transactions and lose nothing. But if the currency is devalued, they will make tons of money as they purchase domestic currency back at a much cheaper price upon repatriating their capital. This is a familiar syndrome in the presence of fixed exchange rates: for financial markets, it is a case of "Heads I win; tails you lose." In the process of selling domestic currency, speculators of course put downward pressure on the value of the currency and end up hastening the collapse of the parity. Their expectations easily become self-fulfilling.

Britain's fate in the interwar period demonstrated that rigid monetary and financial rules such as those of the gold standard don't mix well with a modern economy and modern polity. The gold standard narrative of a smoothly functioning, self-regulating system of global finance ceased to be convincing in the face of the new political reality created by democracy. It is a lesson that would have to be relearned in the 1990s.

Protectionism in the Interwar Period

Domestic politics proved equally powerful during the 1930s on the trade front. The decade saw a massive failure of international cooperation in trade, a free-for-all that aggravated the Great Depression. The United States was among the worst offenders and got the protectionist ball rolling by imposing the highest tariffs in its history in 1930. The infamous Smoot-Hawley Tariff was a response to the fall in commodity prices and economic decline, and aimed to shelter each industry with some voice in Congress behind high protective walls. It has since become synonymous with congressional log-rolling and destructive protectionism. European nations had similar economic reasons to resort to trade barriers, and the U.S. move acted as both excuse and trigger. Even Britain joined the tide, with a 10 percent tariff across a wide range of imports.[30] Particularly damaging was the spread of quantitative limits (quotas) on imports, which had largely been abolished in favor of the more transparent import duties. Once Hitler came to power in 1933, he used trade policies strategically to extract maximum advantage from Germany's neighbors in southeastern

Europe.[31] The protectionist trend also spread to developing areas such as India and Latin America; the British Navy was far too weakened and preoccupied with other matters to enforce free trade in the periphery. Between 1929 and 1937, the volume of world trade was halved.[32]

The proximate cause of this protectionist response was the economic calamity that came to be known as the Great Depression. With farmers defaulting on their loans, businesses closing, and unemployment reaching unprecedented heights, seeking protection against imports was a natural impulse, if ultimately collectively self-defeating for all countries taken together. But the deeper roots of protectionism lay in the changing role of government in society. A politically empowered and active society—the joint result of industrialization, democratization, and World War I—demanded greater economic protection from the government in the face of extreme adversity. Governments did not yet provide extensive safety nets and social insurance to take the edge off international competition and cushion working people from the consequences of trade. Countries that remained on gold for longer (such as France and Switzerland) and therefore had less freedom to stimulate their economies were especially prone to put up high trade barriers.[33] The belief systems and habits of international cooperation that served the world well under reasonably healthy economic conditions collapsed under the joint impact of the changed economic circumstances and the increase in the number of stakeholders to which governments became responsible and accountable.

The world economy had outgrown the classical "liberal" economic order, but there were as yet no palatable alternatives on offer. As the Harvard political scientist Jeffry Frieden notes, "Supporters of the classical order had argued that giving priority to international economic ties required downplaying such concerns as social reform, nation building, and national assertion." Once they lost their argument, the floodgates were open. Communists chose social reform over the global economy and closed themselves off from world markets. Fascists chose nation building, producing a wave of economic nationalism in Europe and in the developing nations.[34]

To avoid such economic and political calamities, any future international economic order would have to strike a better balance between the demands of international economy and those of domestic social groups. Designing that compromise would in turn require a better understanding of how free trade creates social tensions.

Why Doesn't Everyone Get the Case for Free Trade?

Free trade is not the natural order of things. We get free trade—or something approximating it—only when the stars are lined up just right and the interests behind free trade have the upper hand both politically and intellectually. But why should this be so? Doesn't free trade make us all better off—over the long run? If free trade is so difficult to achieve, is that because of narrow self-interest, obscurantism, political failure, or all of these combined?

It would be easy to associate free trade always with economic and political progress and protectionism with backwardness and decline. It would also be misleading, as we saw in the previous chapter. The real case for trade is subtle and therefore depends heavily on context. We need to understand not just the economics of free trade, but also its implications for distributive justice and social norms.

Trade as Technological Progress

There is no better place to begin than in 1701, with a certain Henry Martyn. Martyn, a lawyer and Whig loyalist in early eighteenth-century England, is now all but forgotten. Greatly ahead of his time, he produced, three quarters of a century before Adam Smith and more than a century before David Ricardo, the best argument for free trade known to men.[1]

Martyn thought the mercantilists who dominated thinking on economic policy had it all backwards on trade. The prevailing view held that Britain should import nothing but raw materials so that manufacturing could be reserved for domestic producers. There was great public opposition to the East India Company, which had started to import cotton textiles from India. Martyn thought otherwise. He felt imports of manufactures from India represented a benefit to the English nation rather than a loss.

Martyn wanted to set the mercantilists straight, but there was a problem. He was also interested in public office. He would eventually be appointed in 1715 as Inspector General of Imports and Exports, a post created as a result of the mercantilists' obsession with the volume of trade that required him to tally up England's inbound and outbound trade. Expressing free trade views in public would have damaged his political ambitions; such was the dominance of protectionist sentiment at the time. So when he penned his innocent-sounding but incendiary tract, *Considerations Upon the East-India Trade*, in 1701, he was compelled to do so anonymously.[2] In this remarkable pamphlet, Martyn anticipated many of the arguments that economists who favored free trade would marshal much later. Most impressively, he produced—with greater punch than most textbooks manage even today—the "killer argument" for free trade.

Martyn's argument relies on an analogy between international trade and technological progress. Martyn pointed to instances of technology that would have been familiar to the readers of his day. Take the sawmill, he wrote. The sawmill allows two people to do the work that in its absence would have required thirty people. If we reject the use of the sawmill, we could employ those thirty people, but wouldn't that be twenty-eight more than is really necessary, and hence a waste of the nation's resources? Or consider a barge on a navigable river. Five men on the barge can transport as much freight as one hundred men and as many horses on land. If we neglect the river, we could put that many men and horses to work, but wouldn't that once again be a waste? Martyn assumed his readers would find it self-evident that it would be silly to give up on technological innovations such as the sawmill or the barge. Following the same logic, Martyn offered the clincher. Wouldn't it be a similar waste to employ workers in England if the textiles they produce can be obtained from India by putting fewer people to work?[3]

We can produce textiles at home; or we can obtain the same quantity of textiles from India by producing another commodity which we sell in exchange. If the latter takes less labor than the former, it is the same as if a better technology for supplying textiles has dropped from the sky. We wouldn't think of denying the nation the benefit of sawmills, barges, or any other labor-saving innovations. Isn't it equally silly to reject imports of manufactures from India?

Martyn's argument for free trade captures the essence of what trade accomplishes and it is rhetorically effective—who can seriously be against technological progress? When I confront my students with it, it doesn't take long before one of them will hone in on one of the problems with the argument. It assumes that the labor no longer employed in producing textiles at home will find employment in some other occupation. If the labor remains unemployed instead, the gains are no longer so obvious. But Martyn's analogy is immune to this challenge—at least in the first round. Technological progress is no different, as it too displaces labor and may result in transitional unemployment. If you are in favor of technological progress, you must be in favor of free trade!

There is one loose thread in Martyn's argument: even though it clarifies why trade benefits England, it fails to demonstrate why it should also benefit India. Why would India want to sell textiles to England in return for British manufactures if India's textiles in fact take more labor to produce and would cost India more than what it was buying in exchange? The hole in the argument was not filled until David Ricardo produced his famous example of trade between England and Portugal in cloth and wine in 1817, and conclusively established the principle of comparative advantage. It is unlikely that Indian producers face identical conditions to those that prevail in England. If, compared to England, Indian producers are more productive in textiles than they are in the types of goods that English manufacturers produce, textiles will cost less in India than those English goods. Both countries will end up buying what is cheap abroad and expensive at home, economizing on the use of their labor in the way Martyn suggested. Trade benefits all sides; it is *not* zero-sum.

Significantly, there are mutual gains from trade even if India produces both sets of goods at lower productivity (higher labor costs) than England does. India need only be not as bad in textiles as it is in other manufactures. What creates comparative advantage is differences across nations in *comparative* costs, not in absolute costs.

This is a powerful argument and one that critics of free trade often fail to fully digest before taking it on. As Paul Samuelson once suggested in response to a challenge by a mathematician with little respect for the social sciences, it is probably the only proposition in economics that is at once true and non-trivial. "That it is logically true need not be argued before a mathematician," Samuelson said; "that it is not trivial is attested by the thousands of important and intelligent men who have never been able to grasp the doctrine for themselves or to believe it after it was explained to them."[4] Fallacious reasoning often substitutes for intelligent commentary on trade. In a famous but apocryphal quote attributed to Abraham Lincoln, the Great Emancipator is supposed to have said,

I do not know much about the tariff, but I know this much, when we buy manufactured goods abroad, we get the goods and the foreigner gets the money. When we buy the man-ufactured goods at home, we get both the goods and the money.[5]

Of course this is exactly the kind of mercantilist fallacy that Mar-tyn (and Adam Smith, David Ricardo, and Paul Samuelson after him) wanted to refute. The true cost of consuming a good is the labor and other scarce resources we have to employ to obtain it, not the money that facilitates the transaction.

Public Skepticism on Trade

Such fallacies tend to make economists impatient with objections to free trade and dismissive of those who would want to interfere with it. It is easy to pooh-pooh many anti-trade arguments because they make little sense upon scrutiny. Yet among the general pub-lic, skepticism about trade is too widespread to dismiss so easily. Survey after survey finds that a distinct majority of people support restrictions on imports to "protect" jobs and the economy. The United States is hardly an outlier in this. For example, a global survey undertaken in the late 1990s found overwhelming support for trade protection: nearly 70 percent of the respondents in the global sample favored limiting imports.[6]

Within any given country, highly educated individuals tend to be less protectionist than others. Yet in many countries trade is hardly popular even among those groups. In the United States, for example, anti-trade feelings dominate two-to-one among individuals in the top one third of population with the highest education.[7]

Individuals who are likely to suffer income losses from the

expansion of trade are naturally inclined toward protection. But even though narrowly economic motives play a role, they are only partly responsible for the widespread opposition to trade. People with a strong sense of patriotism and communitarian attachments—to their neighborhoods, region, or nation—also dislike international trade, regardless of the type of jobs they hold or their educational level. Women are systematically less sympathetic to trade than men, even when their economic status and employment are similar. Values, identities, and attachments matter.[8] It is too facile to attribute anti-trade views to naked self-interest or sheer ignorance.

Could it be that ordinary people have a better intuitive sense of the complexity of the case for free trade than we give them credit for? In fact, powerful and elegant as it may be, the argument presented by Henry Martyn, David Ricardo, and others is not the whole story. Life as a trade economist would be pretty boring if it were so. Okay, maybe it's not as much fun as being Mick Jagger, but I can assure you that doing international economics as a living entails a lot more than reaffirming the wonders of comparative advantage day after day. Every advanced student of trade learns that there are a lot of interesting twists and turns to the tale of gains from trade. A long list of requirements needs to be in place before we can reasonably be satisfied that free trade improves a society's overall well-being. Sometimes less trade can be better than more trade. The analogy with technical progress can be misleading, in ways that illuminate why there is such a chasm between economists and common folk in public debate.

The Case for Trade, Qualified

Recall Martyn's point: imports economize on the use of resources. It makes sense to import goods as long as it takes less labor to produce the exports that would pay for those imports than it does to produce those goods ourselves. But how do we actually do the accounting for the labor costs that go into producing different goods—as well as for the other expenses for capital, skilled professionals, land, and so on? What is the appropriate metric?

Early theorists like Henry Martyn and Adam Smith were a bit too glib when they assumed that it was sufficient to look at actual production costs or the number of people employed. The costs that we face as individual consumers and producers are not always the relevant costs from the perspective of the nation as a whole.[9]

The true cost to society of labor (and other resources) used in an activity may be more or less than what the employer directly bears and the consumer pays for. Let's call the first "social" costs and the second "private" costs. Social costs exceed private costs, for example, when production generates harmful effects on the environment. It is the other way around when production generates valuable knowledge and other technological spillovers elsewhere in the economy. These are familiar instances of what economists call "negative" and "positive externalities," which drive a wedge between what is privately profitable and what is socially profitable.

Such wedges also exist when society values equity and other social considerations. When we care about the people at the bottom of the income distribution (and find it hard to increase their incomes directly), the social costs of employing poor or otherwise disadvantaged individuals will be less than the private costs. Consider the antebellum United States mentioned in the previous chapter. It is rather obvious that the expenses Southern slaveholders incurred in their export plantations failed to account for the catastrophic societal costs of slavery as a social and political regime.

In the economist's jargon, the resources used in international exchanges must be valued at their true *social opportunity costs* rather than at prevailing market prices. These two accounting schemes coincide only when markets internalize all social costs, distributional considerations can be shunted aside, and other social and political objectives are not at stake; they don't otherwise. The students who worried that Martyn overlooked unemployment were on to something. There is a wide range of situations, going far beyond transitional unemployment, in which free trade may not look as attractive once its full implications are appropriately evaluated.

Moreover, Martyn was wrong to imply that we always take a hands-off attitude toward technology. We sometimes close off specific avenues to scientific and technological progress— certain kinds of experiments on humans and human cloning, for example—because they conflict with deeply held values. Fields such as nuclear technology and genetic engineering remain tightly circumscribed in most countries. New drugs must go through a stringent and lengthy approval process before they are made available to consumers. Genetically modified crops are subject to detailed restrictions on planting practices when allowed at all. Technologies in many mature industries such as autos, energy, and telecoms are also heavily regulated for reasons of health, safety, and environmental impact, or to ensure widespread access. Legal requirements with respect to emissions, seat belts, and airbags, for example, have been a key force behind technological change in the auto industry.

On the flip side, we subsidize many forms of research and development because we believe they produce positive knowledge spillovers to the economy at large. Governments sanction temporary monopoly in the form of patents to induce innovation. They fund universities and research labs, and they consciously act to influence the direction of technological progress, pushing green technologies over others, for example. Technology is hardly a free-for-all.[10]

Ultimately, the analogy that Henry Martyn and his intellectual descendants employed is a useful one: free trade is indeed just like technical progress. But don't let the rhetoric fool you. The fact that we intervene so heavily in the process of technological change should teach us something. If economics were only about profit maximization, it would be just another name for business administration. It is a *social* discipline, and society has other means of cost accounting besides market prices.

But what exactly does that mean for the conduct of trade policy? What kind of rules should we apply, and how do we prevent ourselves from sliding into unbridled protectionism—from turning into modern-day equivalents of Ned Ludd's followers during the Industrial Revolution, who opposed the spread of new textile technologies and destroyed mechanized looms? To answer these questions, we need to dig a bit deeper into trade's social consequences.

Trade and Income Distribution

College students learn about the gains from trade not from Martyn, Smith, or even Ricardo, but from a diagram which is the staple of every introductory economics textbook. The professor draws a couple of demand and supply curves, points to where the market prices are with and without tariffs, and then asks how much the economy would gain from removing the tariff. He carefully labels areas representing income gain and loss to different groups in society: area A captures the loss to competing producers at home, area B the gain to domestic consumers, and area C the loss in tariff revenue for the government. And the "net" gain to the economy? He adds and subtracts all these areas as appropriate, and voilà! We are left with two triangles that represent the gains from trade to the economy—or equivalently the "deadweight loss" of the tariff. Here is why tariffs are a bad idea, and here is how much we gain by removing them.

It is a handy demonstration, and I must admit that I too take a certain pleasure whenever I go through these motions—the joy of bringing the uninitiated into the fold. No need to confuse the students at this point by pointing out that the supply and demand curves we used to calculate the "net" gains are not necessarily the appropriate ones. The demand and supply schedules represent, respectively, "willingness to pay" and "marginal cost"—of the individual consumers and producers in that specific market. When private and social valuations diverge, neither of these will be a good guide to how much society is willing to pay or the costs society incurs. Even without that complication, however, the blackboard demonstration makes two important points obvious.

First, income redistribution is the other side of the gains from trade. If trade causes some activities to contract and others to expand—as it must if the full gains from trade are to be reaped—those groups whose economic fortunes are tied to shrinking sectors will necessarily take a hit. These losses are not transitory. If I have skills specific to garment production, I will suffer a permanent fall in my earnings even if I manage to avoid unemployment and find a job doing something else. Such income losses are estimated to lie between 8 and 25 percent of pre-displacement earnings in the United States.[11] Any temporary adjustment costs—such as transitional unemployment or a dip in earnings below their long-run level—would be additional to these losses.

Here lies a common misunderstanding in the public debate on trade. Free trade advocates will often grant that some people may get hurt in the short run, but will continue to argue that in the long run everyone (or at least most people) will be better off. In fact there is nothing in economics that guarantees this, and much that suggests otherwise. A famous result due to Wolfgang Stolper and Paul Samuelson states that some groups will *necessarily* suffer long-term losses in income from free trade.[12] In a wealthy country such as the United States, these are likely to be unskilled workers such as high school dropouts.[13] This renders the whole notion of "gains from trade" suspect, since it is not at all clear how we can decide whether a country *as a whole* is better off when some people gain and others lose.

Nor are these ongoing distributional effects specific to the simplified textbook exposition. The trade economist's toolkit encompasses a wide variety of complicated and advanced models of trade, most of which generate sharp distributional conflict from trade.[14] All of these approaches share a fundamental intuition: since economic restructuring generates efficiency gains, and sectors with comparative advantage will expand while others contract, redistribution is often the necessary handmaiden of the gains from trade. Advocates who claim that trade has huge benefits but only modest distributional impacts either do not understand how trade really works, or have to jump through all kinds of hoops to make their arguments halfway coherent. The reality is more simple: no pain, no gain.

The second implication of the classroom exposition is a bit more subtle, and the professor is not likely to dwell on it. But the more attentive among the students will notice that the gains from trade look rather paltry compared to the redistribution of income. It is not just that some win and others lose when tariffs are removed. It is also that the size of the redistribution swamps the "net" gain. This is a generic consequence of trade policy under realistic circumstances.

To drive the point home, I once quantified the ratio of redistribution-to-efficiency gains following the standard assumptions economists make when we present the case for free trade.[15] The numbers I got were huge—so large in fact that I was compelled to redo the calculations several times to make sure I wasn't making a mistake. For example, in an economy like the United States, where average tariffs are below 5 percent, a move to complete free trade would reshuffle more than $50 of income among different groups for each dollar of efficiency or "net" gain created![16] Read the last sentence again in case you went through it quickly: we are talking about $50 of redistribution for every $1 of aggregate gain. It's as if we give $51 to Adam, only to leave David $50 poorer.

A major reason the redistribution-to-efficiency-gains ratio is so high is that tariffs are so low to begin with in today's economy. If tariffs had stood at, say, 40 percent, this ratio would have been around 6 instead.[17] But even in this second case, the redistribution from David to Adam is enormous. It is unlikely that we would countenance so much redistribution in other policy domains without at least some assurance that the process conforms with our conceptions of distributive justice.

When confronted with such situations, most of us would want to know more. Who exactly are David and Adam and what did they do to bring this change about? Is David poorer or richer than Adam, and by how much? How will the proposed move affect them and their families? Does David have access to safety nets and other governmental transfer programs that provide compensation? Some cases will be easy in light of the answers to those questions. If David turns out to be rich, lazy, or otherwise undeserving, and fully responsible for the lousy decisions that result in the loss, we are likely to look kindly on the change. But what if none of these things is true, and Adam has acted in ways that many would consider unethical?

We must ask the same questions when we consider the case of large distributional changes caused by trade. Two questions are of particular importance. Are the gains too small relative to the potential losses to low-income or other disadvantaged groups that may have little recourse to safety nets? And does the trade involve actions that would violate widely shared norms or the social contract if carried out at home—such as employing child labor, repressing labor rights, or using environmentally harmful practices? When the answers to both these questions are yes, the legitimacy of trade will be in question, and appropriately so. There will need to be public debate about the right course of action, which will sometimes result in more rather than less intervention in trade.

These considerations about how we evaluate social changes

with significant distributional effects give us additional insight into why the technical progress analogy fails to provide an airtight argument in favor of free trade. We often assume in the case of new technology that it is generated by innovators and firms that play under a common set of rules. If firm X beats firm Y to a new product or process, it is because X has spent more on R&D, has employed a better business strategy, or has just been lucky—not because Y has been burdened by a different and more costly set of rules. This presumption contributes to our bias in favor of technical progress because it reduces, if not eliminates altogether, the concern that the playing field was tilted against the loser.

Free trade is different. Firms abroad can obtain a competitive advantage not only because they are more productive or labor is more abundant (and hence cheaper), but also because they prevent their workers from engaging in collective bargaining, they have to comply with lower health and safety standards, or they are subsidized by their governments. This is another important way in which differences in institutional arrangements across nations generate opposition and create frictions in international trade.

A second difference is that the adverse effects of new technologies hit different groups over time, so that one can plausibly argue that most, if not all people are made better off over the long run. The candlemaker gets displaced by electric bulbs and the carriagemaker by the auto industry. But each gains from the other innovation. Add these and all other innovations together, let them accumulate over time, and the chance is that everyone comes out better off. Trade, by contrast, often affects the same people time and again. If you are of low skill, have little education, and are not very mobile, international trade has been bad news for you pretty much throughout your entire life. It is much harder in this instance to argue that things will even out in the end.

Finally, low levels of trade barriers bring another issue into play. Even when technological change generates redistribution, it isn't self-limiting. Technology has been the fountain of human economic progress since the Industrial Revolution, and there is no reason to suspect that it won't be in the future. By contrast, the gains from removing restrictions on trade run into diminishing returns as trade becomes freer and freer, with the consequence that the distributional effects begin to loom larger and larger. Most recent estimates put the "overall" gains to the United States from a global move to free trade in tenths of 1 percent of U.S. gross domestic product.[18] No doubt certain export interests would benefit considerably more; but the losses to others would be commensurately large as well. The more open an economy is, the worse the redistribution-to-efficiency ratio gets. The political and social-cost-benefit ratio of trade liberalization looks very different when tariffs are 5 percent instead of 50 percent. It is inherent in the economics of trade that going the last few steps to free trade will be particularly difficult because it generates lots of dislocation but little overall gain. There is nothing similarly self-exhausting in the case of technical progress.

So the economist's triangles and technical progress analogy are conversation starters, not conversation enders. Considerations of justice and procedural fairness may complicate the simple (simplistic?) case for gains from trade, but they help us understand why trade is often so contentious. Resistance to free trade is not just a matter of narrow self-interest or ignorance—at least not always.

Importantly, this broader perspective also helps us distinguish pure protectionism from legitimate and well-grounded opposition to free trade. A deserving argument against free trade must overcome at least one of the two hurdles mentioned above: the economic gains from freer trade must remain small compared to the distributional "costs"; and trade must entail practices that violate prevailing norms and social contracts at home. Redistributions that provide large net gains and do not infringe on accepted ways of doing business may be okay; redistributions that fail these tests are open to greater scrutiny. Remember these principles, as we will use them as building blocks for the reform of the global economic system.

What Economists Will Not Tell You

Here is an interesting experiment I wish a news reporter would undertake. Let him call an economist on the phone, identifying himself as a reporter, and ask the economist whether she thinks free trade with country X or Y is a good idea. We can be fairly certain about the kind of response he will get: "Oh yes, free trade is a great idea," the economist will immediately say, possibly adding: "And those who are opposed to it either do not understand the principle of comparative advantage, or they represent the selfish interests of certain lobbies (such as labor unions)."

Now let the reporter dress in the casual and rumpled clothes of the typical graduate student in economics and walk into an advanced seminar on international trade theory in any one of the leading universities of the nation. Let him pose the same question to the instructor: Is free trade good? I doubt that the question will be answered as quickly and succinctly this time around. The professor is in fact likely to be stymied and confused by the question. "What do you mean by 'good'?" she may ask. "Good for whom?" If the reporter/student looks puzzled, she will add: "As we will see later in this course, in most of our models free trade makes some groups better off and others worse off." If this gets disappointed looks, she will then expand: "But under certain conditions, and assuming we can tax the beneficiaries and compensate the losers, freer trade has the *potential* to increase everyone's well-being."

Now the economist has begun to warm up to the subject. She will continue: "Notice how I said, 'under some conditions.' Asking you to list those conditions would make a good exam question, so pay attention as I run through them." Unless your lifelong dream was to become a PhD economist, it is unlikely that you will derive any pleasure from what is about to come (or any illumination, for that matter). But I must provide a full account of the economics professor's answer, so I will put it all into really small font. Here is what her list of preconditions will look like:

The import liberalization must be complete, covering all goods and trade partners, or else the reduction in import restrictions must take into account the potentially quite complicated structure of substitutability and complementarity across restricted commodities. (So in fact a preferential trade agreement with one or a few trade partners is unlikely to satisfy the requirement.) There must be no microeconomic market imperfections other than the trade restrictions in question, or if there are some, the second-best interactions that are entailed must not be too adverse. The home economy must be "small" in world markets, or else the liberalization must not put the economy on the wrong side of the "optimum tariff." The economy must be in reasonably full employment, or if not, the monetary and fiscal authorities must have effective tools of demand management at their disposal. The income redistributive effects of the liberalization should not be judged undesirable by society at large, or if they are, there must be compensatory tax-transfer schemes with low enough excess burden. There must be no adverse effects on the fiscal balance, or if there are, there must be alternative and expedient ways of making up for the lost fiscal revenues. The liberalization must be politically sustainable and hence credible so that economic agents do not fear or anticipate a reversal.

By now the professor is looking really smug, because she has just shown her students not only how complicated even seemingly simple economics questions are, but also how economic science can shed light (if that is what this jargon can be called!) on the answers.

The journalist/graduate student will not have understood much of this, but at least he has gotten an answer. "So, provided these conditions are satisfied, we can be sure that freer trade will improve our economy's performance and raise its rate of growth?" he may ask hopefully. "Oh, no!" the professor will reply. "Who said anything about growth? These were only the requirements for an increase in the *level* of aggregate real income. Saying something definite about growth is much, much harder." With a self-satisfied smile on her face, she may then provide the following explanation:

> In our standard models with exogenous technological change and diminishing returns to reproducible factors of production (e.g., the neoclassical model of growth), a trade restriction has no effect on the long-run (steady-state) rate of growth of output. This is true regardless of the existence of market imperfections. However, there may be growth effects during the transition to the steady state. (These transitional effects could be positive or negative depending on how the long-run level of output is affected by the trade restriction.) In models of endogenous growth generated by non-diminishing returns to reproducible factors of production or by learning-by-doing and other forms of endogenous technological change, the presumption is that lower trade restrictions boost output growth in the world economy as a whole. But a subset of countries may experience diminished growth depending on their initial factor endowments and levels of technological development. It all depends on whether the forces of comparative advantage pull resources into growth-generating sectors and activities, or away from them.

Noticing the student's expression, the professor may helpfully add, "I think you really have to come to me during office hours for all this."

You don't have to read the fine print above, but if you have deduced that the answer in the seminar room differs greatly from the answer on the phone, you are quite correct. A direct, unqualified assertion about the unquestionable benefits of trade has now been transformed into a statement adorned by all kinds of ifs and buts. Yet somehow the knowledge that the professor willingly imparts with great pride to her advanced students is deemed to be too dangerous for the general public. The qualifications of the seminar room are forgotten lest they lead the public "astray."

This disconnect has always bothered me. In my own research career, I have never—well, almost never—felt censored or pressured to stand for the party line. Academic economists are rewarded for divergent thinking and being innovative. That includes identifying different ways in which markets fail and crafting new arguments for how government intervention in the economy can make things better.[19] Yet unless you are a PhD economist yourself, you are unlikely to have experienced anything of this richness and diversity. In public, economists can always be counted upon to utter the same tired words of praise on behalf of free trade.

Confronted by the gap between what they teach and what they preach, economists will take refuge in a number of arm-waving arguments. Here is a fairly complete list of what you might hear:

1. In practice free trade will make most people better off in the long run, just as technological progress does.
2. Even if trade creates complications, the best way to deal with those is through other policies and not trade restrictions.
3. Even if some people lose out, it should be possible to compensate them and still have everyone come out ahead.
4. The case for free trade goes beyond economics: it is a moral one that has to do with people's freedom to choose who they do business with.
5. Anti-trade views are prevalent enough; our job is to present the other side.
6. The caveats will be hijacked by protectionists who will use them for their own purposes.
7. And besides, the nuances will simply confuse people.

Yet none of these arguments is thought through with anything approaching the level of rigor that goes into demonstrating the standard theorems of trade. None is particularly convincing.

Robert Driskill, a Vanderbilt University economist, has taken the economics profession to task over these failings in a fascinating piece titled "Deconstructing the Argument for Free Trade." He provides a litany of examples from leading textbooks and popular essays in which economists glibly conclude that free trade is "good for the nation" without fully addressing the ethical and philosophical difficulties in making such a statement. As he remarks wryly, these writings suggest that economists somehow "have solved the problematic nature of knowing what is good for society even when some members of that society are hurt."[20] "[T]he profession has stopped thinking critically about the question," he writes, "and, as a consequence, makes poor-quality arguments justifying their consensus." Most writing by economists on the gains from trade is not a "balanced weighting of the evidence or a critical evaluation of the pros and cons." It is instead akin to "a zealous prosecutor's advocacy." It aims to persuade rather than provide the information with which the reader can form an educated judgment.[21] As Driskill argues, economists should be in the business of presenting the trade-offs rather than passing off their value judgments as the conclusion of scientific research.

Why do economists' analytical minds turn into mush when they talk about trade policy in the real world? Some of it has to do with the idea of comparative advantage being the crown jewel of the profession. It is too painful to let go of. Some boils down to what I call the "barbarians at the gate" syndrome. Economists worry that any doubts they express in public on the benefits of free trade will serve to empower those "barbarians" who are interested not in nuanced views but in pushing for their *dirigiste* agendas. No doubt some has to do with ideology. Even if many economists don't think of themselves as politically conservative, their views tend to be aligned with free market enthusiasts rather than interventionists.

The unanimity that economists exhibit over free trade does not apply to other areas of economic policy. Economists speak with many voices when it comes to important areas of domestic policy such as health, education, or taxes. But on globalization one would have had to look really hard until recently to locate a scholar in any of the top universities who would depart from the boilerplate response. When Driskill submitted his paper for publication to professional journals, he was met by a string of rejections. The editors felt Driskill's arguments didn't add much of significance to the economics literature or to research. They were right, of course. His points (and mine) about the ambiguities of the case for trade are well known within the professional economics community. The problem is that economists guard them like state secrets and look on those who would share them with ordinary folk as apostates.

When economists oversell globalization by presenting an incomplete case for it, they not only lose an opportunity to educate the public, they also lose credibility. They become viewed as advocates or as hired guns for the "stateless elites" whose only interest is to remove impediments to their international operations. This wouldn't be all that bad if economics didn't have a lot to offer. Applied with a good dose of common sense, economics would have prepared us for the flaws we have experienced in globalization. And used appropriately, economic analysis can point us in the right direction for the fixes. Designing a better balance between states and markets—a better globalization—does not mean that we jettison conventional economics. It requires that we actually pay more attention to it. The economics we need is of the "seminar room" variety, not the "rule-of-thumb" kind. It is an economics that recognizes its limitations and caveats and knows that the right message depends on the context. The fine print *is* what economists have to contribute. I hope the reader will agree that such an economics is possible and think better of economics (even if not of economists) by the end of this book.

4

Bretton Woods, GATT, and the WTO

Trade in a Politicized World

Trade policy is politically contentious because it has important domestic distributional consequences and because it generates clashes between values and institutions in different nations. None of this would matter much if trade policy could be insulated from national politics and remain the province of a technocracy—the free trade economist's fantasy. That has never been the world we live in; nor are we likely to find ourselves in such a world in the near future. Under mercantilism, trade policy and statecraft were one and the same, as we have seen. Even at the height of economic liberalism during the nineteenth century, political insulation of trade policy remained limited and protection made a quick reappearance when agricultural prices fell. The politicization of trade policy increased further during the interwar period. The inability of governments to respond to the grievances of domestic businesses, workers, and farmers in the context of an open economy contributed to the Great Depression.

As World War II drew to a close, John Maynard Keynes and Harry Dexter White were looking for ways to square the circle. How could an open global economy be restored in a world where domestic politics reigned supreme? Keynes, the English don, had already made his mark as the preeminent economist of his generation and as an acute commentator on contemporary politics and politicians. White was a much-admired U.S. Treasury official who would be later discovered to have passed classified U.S. information to the Soviets during and before World War II. Both men were determined to avoid the mistakes of the interwar period. In a reflection of American economic supremacy, White, in particular, was keen to unchain the world economy from the extensive restrictions and controls imposed during the interwar period and then tightened even further during the war. But these two remarkable men were also realists and understood that the rules for international trade (and international money, to which we shall turn in the next chapter) needed to change. It would no longer work— if it ever did—to prescribe economic openness and then expect domestic politics to adjust one way or another.

Keynes had written a remarkable piece at the height of the Great Depression in 1933 describing his change of heart on free trade and his newfound preference for a certain amount of "national self-sufficiency." Like most Englishmen, Keynes wrote, he had an almost moral attachment to the doctrine of free trade. "I regarded ordinary departures from [free trade] as being at the same time an imbecility and an outrage." Yet when he looked upon his advocacy of free trade of the 1920s, he did not feel the same self-assurance. His orientation had changed, and he now shared the more skeptical views on trade expressed by many of those writing during the 1930s. Unqualified commitment to free trade was feasible only when societies were ruled by narrow technocracies with faith in a uniform type of capitalism. It ceased to be practical, or even desirable, in a world where nations were experimenting with alternative visions of political economy.[1]

Historical experience showed that when domestic needs clash with the requirements of the global economy, domestic needs ultimately emerge victorious. Keynes and White realized that it was better to accept this and build the safety valves into the system than to ignore it and risk total collapse.

The Bretton Woods Model

The system they crafted came to be called the Bretton Woods regime, after the New Hampshire resort town at which Keynes, White, and other officials from forty-four nations met in July 1944 at a conference to draft the new rules. The Bretton Woods agreement was an amazing piece of institutional engineering. In about three weeks, Keynes and White supplied the world economy with a new economic philosophy and created two new international organizations: the International Monetary Fund and the World Bank. The deal struck at Bretton Woods would govern the world economy for the first three decades following World War II. Long after the regime became undone during the 1970s and 1980s, the term "Bretton Woods" would remain a wistful reminder of the possibilities of collective deliberation at the global level.

Neither Keynes nor White was motivated purely by cosmopolitan considerations; domestic political motives loomed large in both of their minds. Keynes was aware of Britain's economic decline and dependence on the United States and did his utmost to further Britain's interests within those constraints. White advanced the cause of American commerce and investment and worked to strengthen America's power in the new international organizations. At one point, White unilaterally decided the voting shares of the leading powers (the United States, Britain, Soviet Union, and China) and sent off a staff economist to work out overnight the economic formula and justification that would produce these shares.[2] Yet the agreement that emerged from Bretton Woods transcended narrow national interests and did much more than buttress American economic hegemony.

A delicate compromise animated the new regime: allow enough international discipline and progress toward trade liberalization to ensure vibrant world commerce, but give plenty of space for governments to respond to social and economic needs at home.[3]

International economic policy would have to be subservient to domestic policy objectives—full employment, economic growth, equity, social insurance, and the welfare state—and not the other way around. The goal would be moderate globalization, not hyperglobalization.

The most notable American contribution to the postwar international economic system was *multilateralism*—rule-setting through international organizations, based on the cornerstone principle of non-discrimination. This reflected in part America's preference for legalism over ad hoc relationships, an external projection of the New Deal regulatory state and FDR's desire to counter domestic isolationists by tying America and its interests to international organizations.[4] Equally important, White's push for multilateralism and non-discrimination targeted Great Britain's preferential arrangements with colonies that hampered American commercial expansion. Predictably, Keynes resisted dismantling these preferences, but in the end the United States had the upper hand.

Multilateralism meant that rule enforcement and belief systems would work henceforth through international institutions—the International Monetary Fund, the World Bank, and the General Agreement on Tariffs and Trade (GATT)—rather than through naked power politics or imperial rule. This was a very important innovation. Even though the influence of the United States was undeniable, multilateralism endowed these institutions with a certain degree of legitimacy independent of the American power that backed them up. They never became truly autonomous from the United States or other major economic powers, but neither were they purely an extension of these powers. They played important rulemaking, rule-enforcing, and legitimating roles. Multilateralism gave smaller and poorer nations a voice and protected their interests in an unprecedented way. Hence the Americans, unlike the British before them, ended up creating an institutional infrastructure for the international economy that would outlast their uncontested hegemony.

The institutional embodiment of multilateralism in trade during the fifty years subsequent to the Bretton Woods Conference was the GATT. The GATT was only part of what was originally meant to be a more ambitious organization, the International Trade Organization (ITO). The proposed ITO included agreements on commodity price stabilization, international antitrust, and fair labor standards, but it floundered in domestic U.S. politics. The Congress worried that it encroached too much on domestic prerogatives. Even though the GATT was not constituted formally as a full-fledged organization like the IMF or the World Bank, it was managed by a small secretariat in Geneva. This allowed it to become de facto the multilateral forum overseeing global trade liberalization.

And what a roaring success it was! Despite a slow start, successive rounds of multilateral trade negotiations (eight in all between 1947 and 1995) managed to eliminate a substantial part of the import restrictions in place since the 1930s and reduce tariffs from their postwar heights.[5] The most-favored nation (MFN) principle ensured that all signatories to GATT benefited from this relaxation in restrictions, regardless of how actively they participated in the negotiations. Domestic trade politics remained contentious, of course, but of low salience in national politics. The numbers tell the story best. The volume of world trade grew at an average annual rate of almost 7 percent between 1948 and 1990, considerably faster than anything experienced to date. Output also expanded at a higher rate than ever before in rich and poor nations alike—both a cause and effect of the rapid rise in trade. In terms of the breadth and depth of economic progress, the Bretton Woods regime eclipsed all previous periods, including the gold standard and era of free trade during the nineteenth century. If there ever was a golden era of globalization, this was it.

Except for one odd thing: GATT policies did not directly take aim at globalization all that much. As we have seen, globalization requires a significant reduction in transaction costs in cross-border trade and finance. This did occur in certain areas. Trade in most manufactured products among industrial countries was progressively and substantially liberalized, within certain important limits (see below). Transport costs continued to decline. And yet, policy makers displayed a decided lack of ambition in pushing for liberalization under Bretton Woods. Large parts of world trade remained either completely outside multilateral agreements or protected by generous exceptions to the existing agreements. The goal was freer trade in some areas, not free trade in all.

What pushed globalization along instead was the background of economic growth, equity, security, and stability that the Bretton Woods compromise helped prop up. Broad-based growth facilitated globalization because it helped take the sharp edge off the distributional impacts of trade. The choppiness of the waters becomes less noticeable when a rapidly rising tide of economic opportunities lifts all boats. Thus national policies promoted globalization mostly as a byproduct of widely shared economic growth along with some modest opening up. The success of the Bretton Woods era suggests that healthy national economies make for a bustling world economy, even in the presence of trade controls.[6]

Consider the long list of areas liberalization barely touched. Agriculture was kept out of GATT negotiations and remained riddled with tariff and non-tariff barriers—most infamously in the form of variable import quotas aimed at stabilizing domestic prices at levels much higher than in exporting countries. Most services (insurance, banking, construction, utilities, and the like) escaped liberalization as well. Manufacturing sectors that were liberalized but began to face significant competitive threat from lower-cost/higher-productivity exporters soon received protection rather than meet their fate. So the textile and clothing industries of the developed countries were sheltered from 1974 on by the Multi-Fibre Arrangement (MFA), a set of bilaterally negotiated quotas on exports from developing nations. The 1980s witnessed the spread of voluntary export restrictions (VERs), arrangements whereby (typically) Japanese exporters of autos, steel, and some other industrial products undertook to keep their exports within specific quotas.

Meanwhile, developing nations themselves were pretty much free to do as they pleased with their trade policies. They typically were not required to offer tariff "concessions" during GATT negotiations, even while they benefited from others' tariff reductions under the MFA rule. They had recourse to various GATT clauses that allowed them to resort to limitations on imports virtually on a permanent basis.

Even for the industrial countries, the rules contained loopholes wide enough for an elephant to pass. Any business with a good law firm on its payroll could buy itself protection through the GATT's Anti-Dumping (AD) or Safeguard clauses. The AD arrangement in particular was an abomination from the standpoint of free trade. The importing country could impose duties as long as it determined that an exporter had sold its products at "less than normal value" and caused "injury" to the competing industry at home. Domestic authorities could easily manipulate the notion of "less than normal value." And punitive tariffs could be imposed even if the behavior in question constituted normal commercial practice, such as selling below full cost at the bottom of a business cycle, or if the offender had no ability to monopolize the home market. These rules were widely—and predictably—exploited by domestic firms to obtain custom-made protection.

Finally, the enforcement powers of the GATT were a joke. If a government thought another one had violated the rules, it could ask a GATT panel to adjudicate. If the panel ruled for the plaintiff and the panel's report was approved by GATT's membership, the guilty party had to change the offending policy or else the plaintiff was entitled to compensation. The only catch was that approval of the panel report required a unanimous decision. Every single member of GATT, including the government that had been found in violation of the rules, had to sign off on it. If a jury includes the defendant, it is a safe bet that it will not often rule against him.

So the GATT rules left whole segments of world trade uncovered; they were weak where they existed; and they were patently unenforceable. These features made the institution obviously deficient—and made the ensuing World Trade Organization, which took over in 1995, much more attractive from the perspective of free trade. But to find fault with the GATT regime because it fell considerably short of free trade would be to judge GATT from an inappropriate perspective. The GATT may not have been aimed at "minimizing economic entanglements among nations," the objective for which the interwar Keynes had expressed some sympathy. But it certainly was designed to leave each trading nation room to pursue its social and economic objectives relatively unencumbered by external constraints, albeit within a loose framework of international cooperation. When trade threatened domestic distributional bargains, trade would give way. John Ruggie, the preeminent analyst of the Bretton Woods era, has called this mechanism "the compromise of embedded liberalism." "Unlike the economic nationalism of the thirties," Ruggie writes, the regime "would be multilateral in character; unlike the liberalism of the gold standard and free trade, its multilateralism would be predicated upon domestic interventionism."[7]

The considerable maneuvering room afforded by these trade rules allowed advanced nations to build customized versions of capitalism around distinct approaches to corporate governance, labor markets, tax regimes, business-government relations, and welfare state arrangements. What emerged, in a phrase coined by the political scientists Peter Hall and David Soskice, were "varieties of capitalism."[8] The United States, Britain, France, Germany, or Sweden were each market-based economies, but the institutions that underpinned their markets differed substantially and bore unmistakably national characteristics. In Continental Europe alone, there were at least three different types of capitalism: the German model of social market economy; the Scandinavian welfare state; and the French system based on "indicative planning" and extensive regulations. Japan also went its own way, erecting a hypercompetitive export sector alongside a highly regulated and protected traditional economy. The United States stood as the leading exemplar of the liberal market economy, even though its economic liberalism lacked the ambition it would acquire in the 1980s.

It was much the same in the developing world where national efforts were directed at fostering industrialization and economic growth. In the absence of external discipline, developing nations—both of the inward- and outward-looking type—were free to deploy a vast range of industrial policies to transform their economies and reduce their dependence on natural resources and commodities. Many among them were thus able to embark on high growth on the back of production of manufactures.

GATT's purpose was never to maximize free trade. It was to achieve the maximum amount of trade compatible with different nations doing their own thing. In that respect the institution proved spectacularly successful.

Viewed this way, we begin to appreciate a key point about Bretton Woods: what purists increasingly viewed as "derogations" from the principles of free trade were in fact instances of regime maintenance. Anti-dumping duties, the MFA, and VERs were hardly consistent with economic liberalism. Then again neither were so many other features of GATT. The wholesale exclusion of agriculture and services from trade negotiations or, even more curiously from the free trade standpoint, the prevailing principle that a country's reduction of import barriers was a "concession" to its trade partners made no sense in light of standard economic doctrine. In reality, trade became (and remained) free only where it posed little challenge to domestic institutions, distributional preferences, or values. Much of the trade in manufactures carried out among advanced countries at similar levels of income raised few of the questions of distributional justice we confronted earlier. Other kinds of trade—in agriculture, say, or with developing countries—were different because they pitted domestic groups starkly against each other. They threatened farming groups, garment producers, or low-skilled workers with sharp income losses. So these types of trade were heavily circumscribed. Under the GATT priorities rested solidly in the domestic policy agenda, and this produced both its success and its endless departures from the logic of free trade.

The WTO Regime: Striving for Deep Integration

The creation of the World Trade Organization (WTO) in 1995, after nearly eight years of negotiations and as the culmination of the so-called "Uruguay Round" (the last under the GATT), ushered quite a different understanding. Along with the onset of financial globalization around 1990, the WTO marks the pursuit of a new kind of globalization that reversed the Bretton Woods priorities: hyperglobalization. Domestic economic management was to become subservient to international trade and finance rather than the other way around. Economic globalization, the international integration of markets for goods and capital (but not labor), became an end in itself, overshadowing domestic agendas.

The thrust of policy discussions increasingly reflected this change. From the 1980s on, if you wanted to argue for or against something, you couldn't do better than adorn your case with the words "our country's international competitiveness requires it." Globalization became an imperative, apparently requiring all nations to pursue a common strategy of low corporate taxation, tight fiscal policy, deregulation, and reduction of the power of unions.[9]

What lay behind the transition? In part, the GATT became a victim of its own success. Trade policy elites and technocrats ascribed postwar prosperity to multilateral trade liberalization. The WTO represented their desire to do it "even better," by removing many of the impurities and shortcomings discussed in the previous section. Multinational companies demanded more extensive global rules that would facilitate their international operations. Developing nations sought to become export platforms and became increasingly willing to submit themselves to such rules in their drive to attract foreign investment.

Entangled with these changes was an important ideological transformation. The 1980s were the decade of the Reagan-Thatcher revolutions. Free market economics was in the ascendancy, producing what has been variously called the Washington Consensus, market fundamentalism, or neoliberalism. Whatever the appellation, this belief system combined excessive optimism about what markets could achieve on their own with a very bleak view of the capacity of governments to act in socially desirable ways. Governments stood in the way of markets instead of being indispensable to their functioning, and accordingly had to be cut down to size. This new vision elevated the simplistic case for trade—the one that economics professors dole out to journalists—over the appropriately qualified version. It regarded any obstacle to free trade as an abomination to be removed; caveats be damned.

Correspondingly, the WTO envisaged both a significant ramping up of ambitions with respect to economic globalization and a dramatic rebalancing of nation states' domestic and international responsibilities. Once completed, the Uruguay Round of trade negotiations resulted in an impressive agreement with much broader coverage than anything else accomplished under the GATT. Agriculture and certain services, two areas which had eluded trade negotiators in the past, were now firmly brought into the liberalizing fold. In services, countries were required to specify areas they were willing to open up, and the extent of liberalization varied across countries and sectors such as banking and telecoms. In agriculture, import quotas were to be phased out and converted into tariffs and subsidies. The push for removal of agricultural quotas, tariffs, and subsides would henceforth gain center stage. The quota regime of the Multi-Fibre Arrangement, which governed trade in textiles and clothing, would also be phased out within a decade. While the initial liberalization in all these areas remained limited, an important threshold had been crossed.

In addition, there were new rules on patents and copyrights, requiring developing countries to bring their laws into conformity with those in the rich countries. Domestic health and safety regulations became subject to WTO scrutiny if they were not harmonized internationally, and could be ruled illegal if they did not have "scientific justification" or were applied in ways that did not have the least adverse affect on trade possible. Tighter restrictions were put in place on the use of government subsidies. And there were prohibitions on government rules requiring firms to use local content or limit their imports in relation to their exports. For the first time, developing nations, except for the poorest among them which remained exempt, had to comply with rules that tightly circumscribed certain important areas of industrial policy.

Perhaps the signal achievement of the Uruguay Round, and the defining feature of the WTO, was a new procedure for settling disputes. A new appellate court gave recourse to countries on the losing side of a panel decision. But the appellate body's decision—whether in favor of the plaintiff or the defendant—would become final unless it was reversed collectively by *every single member* of the organization. Evading the trade regime's judicial verdict had been child's play under the GATT; now it became virtually impossible. As subsequent practice showed, the process could be lengthy and was open to delaying tactics. But the significance of the new dispute settlement system cannot be underestimated. It takes multilateralism to new heights. As the legal scholars Susan Esserman and Robert Howse put it,

Nowhere else has international conflict resolution by judges emerged more forcefully or developed more rapidly. As in a domestic court—but unlike in most international bodies— WTO dispute settlement is both compulsory and binding. Member states have no choice but to submit to it and must accept the consequences of the WTO's ruling.[10]

Countries that lose their cases have to remove the offending policies or provide compensation to the plaintiff. This is as true of big, powerful counties as small ones. The WTO is the only international body that has ever managed to force the United States to change its policies, as it did in cases involving U.S. tax and environmental policies.

What have WTO cases been about? Under GATT trade policies, cases were largely about tariffs and quotas. As quotas were phased out and tariffs came down, the WTO became an instrument for attacking the full range of transaction costs that impeded international commerce, including differences in national regulations and standards. Under WTO, trade disputes began to reach into domestic areas that were previously immune from external pressures. Tax systems, food safety rules, environmental regulations, and industrial promotion policies were open to challenge from trade partners.

One of the most contested cases that came before the WTO was the European ban on hormone-treated beef, which nicely illustrates the ratcheting up of international discipline in trade. The European Union (EU) directive, which went into effect in 1989 following years of intense pressure from consumer groups, effectively shut out U.S. beef exports to Europe. The United States had sought support from international institutions to block the European move, but none had been willing or able to do so. The United States first went to the World Organization for Animal Health, which declined to look at hormones. An American complaint in the GATT—these were pre-WTO days—was easily blocked by the Europeans. The Codex Alimentarius Commission (a joint arm of the UN Food and Agriculture Organization and the World Health Organization) proved ineffective as well: the United States lost a vote there in 1991 to establish a global standard on the safety of four of the hormones used in beef production. The big change came with the negotiation of the Agreement on Sanitary and Phytosanitary (SPS) Measures as part of the WTO. There was finally a set of global rules and an international forum with adequate reach over domestic regulations. In one of its best-known decisions, the WTO Appellate Body ruled in 1998 that the European Union's prohibition of hormone-treated beef violated international trade rules because it was not adequately based on scientific risk assessment.[11] The political fallout was immediate. The case remains a cause célèbre among anti-WTO advocates for its apparent lack of sympathy to the European Union's cautious approach to food safety. To date the European Union has failed to comply with WTO's ruling, risking retaliation from the United States.

Other examples of the WTO's reach abound. In one of the earliest complaints filed under the WTO, U.S. fuel emission standards were found to discriminate against imported gasoline. Japan's tax regime was found at fault because the distilled liquor *shochu* was taxed at a lower rate than imported vodka, whiskey, or brandy. An EU moratorium on genetically modified products was successfully challenged on grounds similar to the hormone beef case. In another well-known case, a U.S. ban on shrimp caught without using turtle-excluder devices was judged "arbitrary and unjustifiable" discrimination against Asian exporters. Automotive industry promotion programs in India, Indonesia, and China, patent rules on pharmaceuticals and agricultural chemical products in India, and credit subsidies for the aircraft industry in Brazil were all found inconsistent with WTO rules. (All these cases led to the policies in question being modified, except for the hormone beef case, which is yet to be resolved.)

Such rulings have raised the ire of anti-globalization advocates and made the WTO a dirty word in many circles. Is the trade regime subverting democracy by allowing judges in Geneva to override domestic legislation, as these critics charge? Or is it helping nations achieve better outcomes by preventing protectionist groups from hijacking the domestic political process for their narrow interests? The reality is a bit of both. The appellate body rulings are not nearly as crude as many of the critics suggest. The rulings recognize the need to respect national differences in values and standards. On the other hand, the absence of a clear and bright line between where domestic prerogatives end and external obligations begin creates substantial friction. In fact, the trade regime's growing legitimacy crisis can be traced back to this fundamental ambiguity.

The WTO's difficulties hit a high public note in November 1999 during the trade body's meeting in Seattle—the so-called "teargas ministerial." A motley assortment of demonstrators—ranging from labor and consumer advocates to students to anarchists— created havoc outside the conference venue as the ministers inside tried to launch, unsuccessfully, the first new round of trade negotiations since the Uruguay Round. The collapse of the talks had as much to do with the intransigence of the governments as with the demonstrations. There were two main axes of conflict. First, developing countries felt cheated by the results of the Uruguay Round; they sought redress and resisted opening negotiations in additional areas such as investment, environment, labor standards, competition policy, and transparency in government procurement as the rich countries wanted. Second, the United States locked horns with the European Union (and Japan) over the dismantling of agricultural subsidies and barriers.

Two years later, trade ministers had better luck when they met in Doha, Qatar—an emirate in the Middle East. They were now able to launch a new round of negotiations, christened the "Development Round." Aside from the fact that Doha was a considerably less hospitable environment for potential demonstrators, a remarkable piece of marketing spurred the new attitude. A few large developing agricultural exporters, such as Brazil, Argentina, and Thailand, had significant interests in agricultural liberalization. This enabled Mike Moore, then director-general of the WTO, to sell an agriculture-centered round as one that focused on the needs of developing countries, and helped isolate the European Union. "By *making* agriculture a development issue," Moore subsequently wrote, perhaps revealing more than he intended, "we brought Africa, most of Asia and Latin America together on a common agenda"[12] (emphasis added). Europe could not walk away without appearing to turn its back on the cause of development and developing nations had a declaration that seemed to put their interests front and center. Americans were happy too as they now had a stick with which to beat Europe on agricultural subsidies, not fully aware yet of how much the agriculture agenda would come back to haunt them.

As subsequent events demonstrated, the opening of talks was a Pyrrhic victory. The negotiations have stalled several times since 2001 and have yet to be concluded. As time went on, it became clear that agricultural liberalization was a mixed blessing for developing countries. Academic studies underscored what should have been obvious at the outset, namely, that the removal of European subsidies would actually harm food-importing developing nations such as Egypt or Ethiopia by raising the prices they would have to pay. Cotton was one of the few instances of clear-cut gains to the world's poor. An increase in world prices for cotton, a non-food crop, would benefit growers in West Africa without hurting poor people elsewhere. This is why cotton became such a poster child for NGOs and other advocates for developing nations. But serious agricultural liberalization was too painful in the rich nations and the demonstrable gains to others too meager and nar-rowly based for agreement to be reached.[13] The last serious push for concluding the round collapsed in the summer of 2008 when the United States refused to accept India and China's request for a special safeguard mechanism that would have protected poor farmers against a sudden surge of agricultural imports.[14]

These tensions are inherent in the aggressive push for hyper-globalization that replaced the Bretton Woods consensus and shat-tered Ruggie's "embedded liberalism compromise." Trade officials and technocrats become tone-deaf to other economic and social objectives when the pursuit of globalization develops a life of its own. My Harvard colleague Robert Lawrence makes a useful dis-tinction between "shallow" and "deep" versions of global integra-tion.[15] Under shallow integration, as in Bretton Woods, the trade regime requires relatively little of domestic policy. Under deep integration, by contrast, the distinction between domestic policy and trade policy disappears; any discretionary use of domestic regulations can be construed as posing an impediment to—a transaction cost on—international trade. Global rules in effect become the domestic rules.

Previous instances of deep integration relied on institutions that would be unthinkable today. Recall how trade was fostered under mercantilism or the imperialism of the nineteenth century. What kept transaction costs in check then were the rules imposed by a powerful external enforcer—the trading company or the metro-politan power. The modern-day equivalent would be a multilateral regime centered on the WTO. This is no doubt much preferable, but it still leaves us with difficult questions. Where do the rules of the WTO come from? How can we ensure that they are designed to benefit all rather than the few? What happens when different nations desire or need different rules? Can *any* model of deep integration prove sustainable when democratic politics remains organized along national lines?

Trade and Wages in the Real World

Economists do not change their minds often, let alone feel bad about it. Keynes was an exception, as he was in so many other ways. "When the facts change, I change my mind—what do you do, sir?" he is supposed to have replied when a critic accused him of inconsistency. We have seen how Keynes did an about-face on free trade in the 1930s. Similarly, Paul Krugman, who like most contemporary economists is not much prone to admitting mistakes, started a 2008 talk on trade with a startling statement: "This paper is the manifestation of a guilty conscience."[16] This was a few months before he would receive the Nobel memorial prize in Economics, which gave his words even greater currency.

What was Krugman feeling guilty about? He had changed his mind about the effects of globalization on income inequality, and he worried that his earlier nonchalance might have contributed to the neglect of important tensions engendered by trade. Krugman had been at the forefront of a wave of academic studies during the nineties that downplayed the impact of globalization on domestic income distribution. Yes, the increase in inequality in the United States was undeniable; but the evidence at the time seemed to point to other instigating factors. In particular, most economists thought the real culprit was "skill-biased technological change"—information and communication technologies that raised the demand for educated and highly skilled workers while reducing the demand for less educated workers. Income gaps were the result of technological advances, not increased globalization.[17] Krugman's conversion showed that globalization's negative effects on domestic equity could not be written off so easily.

Why was Krugman having second thoughts in 2008? Krugman cited two changes since the mid-1990s which he felt intensified the role of trade as a force behind widening inequality. First, U.S. imports from developing nations had doubled since the 1990s in relation to the size of the American economy. Second, the developing nations against which U.S. producers now compete have much lower wages compared to the developing country exporters of earlier decades. China, in other words, has made all the difference. China has penetrated a large share of the American market and wages in China are a tiny fraction of those in the United States (Krugman cites a ratio of 3 percent). These facts suggest that trade does exert a significant downward pressure on U.S. wages, in addition to the contribution of technological change, particularly for workers at the low end of the income distribution.

These conclusions are controversial among economists, and even Krugman has had to admit that the evidence is not all there. A more detailed look at trends in distribution and in trade exposes some puzzles. By some measures, wage inequality in the United States has stopped growing (or has even come down since the late 1990s), despite the rapid pace of outsourcing.[18] Much of China's exports are in technologically sophisticated and skill-intensive sectors such as computers, where they do not pose a particular threat to the wages of low-skill workers. Then there are ways in which China's exports may have improved matters by reducing poor households' cost of living: China tends to exports goods that make up a large share of what poor households consume.[19] For these reasons, many economists continue to think that globalization accounts for just a small part—10 or 15 percent at most—of the rise in U.S. inequality since the 1970s.[20]

Even if the economywide consequences are small, however, they provide small comfort to the individual worker who gets displaced by imports and has to take on another job at a substantial pay cut. Consider a shoe machine operator in the United States. Between 1983 and 2002, the import competition faced by this worker roughly doubled.[21] It is inconceivable that this change would not have had a substantial impact on his or her wages. Indeed, according to one estimate, trade produced an 11 percent reduction in the average shoe machine operator's earnings over this period.

Similar effects hold for many other occupations in the textile and clothing industries.[22]

Krugman is not the only prominent economist who has been having second thoughts. Before he joined the Obama administration as director of the National Economic Council, Larry Summers, a staunch free trade advocate until recently, wrote a couple of remarkable opinion pieces in which he expressed concern that globalization was no longer a good deal for working people.[23] The opposition to globalization, he said, reflects a "growing recognition by workers that what is good for the global economy and its business champions [is] not necessarily good for them." He agreed that there were "reasonable grounds" for this view. Greater global integration "places more competitive pressure on an individual economy [and] workers are likely disproportionately to bear the brunt of this pressure." Sounding like a populist, he complained about "stateless elites whose allegiance is to global economic success and their own prosperity rather than the interests of the nation where they are headquartered." These companies have little stake in the "quality of the workforce and infrastructure in their home country" and "can use the threat of relocating as a lever to extract concessions." He added:

> Even as globalization increases inequality and insecurity, it is constantly and often legitimately invoked as an argument against the viability of progressive taxation, support for labor unions, strong regulation and substantial production of public goods that mitigate its adverse impacts.[24]

These issues gain salience as international outsourcing extends to services that have been traditionally homebound, exposing a significantly larger part of the economy to international competition. In a much-discussed essay, Alan Blinder, a Princeton professor and former vice chairman of the Federal Reserve Board, warned of the "disruptive effect" of what he called "the next

Industrial Revolution."[25] Thanks to new information and communication technologies, jobs that were previously considered "safe"—certain medical and education services, and financial services, for example—are now increasingly moved offshore to other countries where the services can be performed more cheaply. "Thus, coping with foreign competition, currently a concern for only a minority of workers in rich countries, will become a major concern for many more."[26] Blinder estimates that the number of potentially offshorable service-sector jobs is two to three times the current number of manufacturing jobs. As he takes care to point out, the problem here is not unemployment; displaced workers will eventually find jobs, just as in previous industrial revolutions. The problem is the sheer magnitude of the dislocation and income losses that affected workers will experience.

Blinder's argument recalls the point I made earlier about redistribution being the flip side of the gains from trade. The new industrial revolution that Blinder talks about promises to bring huge economic rewards as larger and larger parts of the economy reorganize along the lines of comparative advantage. It is a necessary consequence of this restructuring that workers will experience economic insecurity. Many will see their wages permanently reduced. Once again: no pain, no gain. These stresses will only be magnified by Summers's stateless elites and footloose corporations, who are in a position to bargain wages and standards down as the price of keeping jobs at home. Broad-based economic growth could help diminish the tensions, but that objective would require locally tailored strategies and the requisite domestic maneuvering room, as under Bretton Woods. As Blinder indicates, we cannot take it for granted that the potential economic benefits of this new wave of globalization will accrue to the many rather than the few.

To free trade fundamentalists, none of these arguments weakens the case for trade liberalization. Take Jagdish Bhagwati, the Columbia University economist and prominent free trade advocate. Bhagwati argues that Krugman, Summers, Blinder, and other skeptics exaggerate the inequalities and dislocations that trade with low-income countries generates. But more fundamentally, he thinks that these authors draw the wrong policy lessons. If trade makes some people worse off and exacerbates inequality, the correct response is to enhance social safety nets and adjustment assistance. The problems that trade creates should be solved not by protectionism but through domestic policies that compensate the losers.[27] Fine, in principle. But these losers have every right to ask what happens when promises of adjustment assistance and compensation fall short, as they have repeatedly done in recent decades.[28] Reassuring workers by telling them that they would have been better off had the appropriate compensation taken place is a weird way of selling free trade.

The reality is that we lack the domestic and global strategies needed to manage globalization's disruptions. As a result, we run the risk that the social costs of trade will outweigh the narrow economic gains and spark an even worse globalization backlash.

5

Financial Globalization Follies

The annual meetings of the International Monetary Fund are a premier social occasion for the world's top economic policy makers and bankers. It's not quite the World Economic Forum at Davos, the meeting place of the world's business and policy elite: what gets you in is a government connection rather than corporate sponsorship, skiing is not an option, the topics discussed rarely stray beyond the economic and financial, and a tie is obligatory. But it is a time for top officials from the United States and Europe to revel in the limelight cast by each other and by the media. Meanwhile finance ministers and central bankers from developing countries can easily fool themselves into thinking that the rest of the world is paying them some attention.[1] There are boring official speeches, panels on topics of global interest, and of course plenty of parties. As is typical of such official occasions, the real work of reaching decisions and drafting communiqués has been accomplished earlier, and any remaining negotiations usually take place on the sidelines.

The Push to Free Up Global Capital

The Hong Kong IMF meeting in September 1997, however, had some real business to attend to. The IMF's managing director Michel Camdessus hoped to crown his tenure by obtaining formal approval from his board to extend the institution's jurisdiction over the liberalization of capital flows. Since the late 1980s, the IMF had become a strong supporter of freeing up capital markets. The advice that it gave to countries that came under its influence increasingly reflected that preference. Many developing countries had begun to dismantle the controls they maintained over cross-border lending and borrowing, as the advanced countries themselves did following the dissolution of the Bretton Woods regime.

Traditionally, domestic residents in these countries had legally not been permitted to take their money out of the country to invest in foreign stock markets or purchase financial assets abroad. Similarly, domestic banks or firms had faced strict limits on their ability to borrow from abroad. Governments typically imposed intricate regulations—taxes, licensing requirements, outright prohibitions—that made moving money in and out of the country a nightmare. Most countries did welcome multinational enterprises and long-term foreign investors, but short-term lending and borrowing or portfolio flows (so-called "hot money") were viewed differently, as a source of financial instability rather than economic growth.

Even though countries were now moving in the right direction from the perspective of the IMF, there was still a problem. Unlike restrictions on payments for current account (that is, trade) purposes, IMF rules did not cover policies that regulated payments for international financial or capital transactions. Effectively, the IMF had no legal authority over capital flows; countries were free to do as they pleased. If the IMF was truly to preside over the emancipation of global capital markets, it needed to amend the institution's original Articles of Agreement.

Camdessus made an impassioned plea in favor of the proposed amendment. "Freedom has its risks," he exclaimed, "[but] is there any more fertile field for development and prosperity?"[2] All the indications were that he was winning his argument. Despite resistance from many developing countries, an IMF interim committee declared that it "is time to add a new chapter to the Bretton Woods agreement." Private capital flows had become much more important to the global economy, and the committee expressed its view that "an increasingly open and liberal system has proved to be highly beneficial to the world economy." Capital movements would increase investment, growth, and prosperity by enabling global savings to flow to their most productive uses. Of course, governments would need to proceed "in an orderly manner," and policies at the national and international level would need to ensure that things went as planned. In the committee's view there was no doubt as to the right path forward: "the liberalization of capital flows is an essential element of an efficient international monetary system in this age of globalization," they declared.[3]

Camdessus's deputy Stanley Fischer, a prominent academic economist who had joined the IMF in 1994, was also busy making the intellectual case for free capital mobility. He too acknowledged that there were risks, but he emphatically rejected the argument that countries should refuse to liberalize their capital accounts. The benefits of free capital flows clearly outweighed the costs. Capital mobility would allow global savings to be allocated more efficiently, channel resources to their most productive uses, and raise economic growth. Besides, it was an "inevitable step on the path of development, which cannot be avoided." To underscore the inevitability, all advanced countries had already freed up their capital markets.[4] Fischer would later acknowledge there was scant evidence that the presumed benefits of openness to capital movements would be realized in practice. Nonetheless, so strong were the theoretical expectations that he felt confident evidence in favor of capital mobility would emerge over time, just as the evidence on the benefits of trade liberalization had surfaced in earlier decades.[5]

Perhaps nothing better illustrates the shift in belief systems around the time of the Hong Kong meetings than the about-face by the late Rudi Dornbusch, another prominent economist and colleague of Fischer's from MIT. In 1996, Dornbusch had published an article called "It's Time for a Financial Transactions Tax," which remains one of the most eloquent and convincing briefs on the desirability of placing roadblocks on cross-border financial flows. Two years later, in 1998, Dornbusch would declare capital controls "an idea whose time is past." He wrote: "The correct answer to the question of capital mobility is that it ought to be unrestricted."[6]

What is astonishing, and not just with hindsight, is that this discussion was going on at the same time that a stupendous failure of global financial markets was unfolding in front of everyone's eyes. Some of the most successful economies of East and Southeast Asia, long the darlings of financial markets and of multilateral institutions, were suddenly hit by a financial tsunami that no one had anticipated. In 1996, five of these economies (Indonesia, Malaysia, the Philippines, South Korea, and Thailand) had received net private capital inflows of $93 billion. In 1997, they experienced an outflow of $12 billion, a turnaround of $105 billion in a single year, which amounted to more than 10 percent of their combined GDP.[7] A shock of this magnitude would cause havoc in the strongest of economies, so it came as no surprise that these countries found themselves in the throes of the most severe economic crisis they had experienced in decades. The crisis eventually spilled over to countries in other regions as well. Having borrowed significant amounts on global financial markets, Russia (in 1998) and Argentina (in 1999–2000) were particularly badly hit.

Governments that grossly mismanage their economies by running huge fiscal and current account deficits and engaging in inflationary finance have no right to complain if financial markets lose confidence in them. When investors punish such misbehaving countries by fleeing in droves, we ought to applaud financial markets for doing their job right. The Asian financial crisis did not fit this mold. It was hard to explain what these economies had done to deserve the fate that financial markets had in store for them. The IMF had touted their "sound fundamentals" and their prospects for "sustained growth" just a few months earlier.[8]

At the time, many observers argued that corrupt relationships between government and big business—Asian-style political cronyism, for short—had led to excessive borrowing and inefficient investments. Yet there were several problems with this account. How had these countries registered such miraculous rates of economic growth if corruption was rampant? And why had foreign creditors apparently not noticed these failures until 1997, at which point they all seem to have converged simultaneously on the view that these countries' debts were as good as junk? The quick recovery of South Korea, Thailand, and Malaysia after 1998 once financial conditions stabilized suggests that there was fundamentally little that was wrong with their economies. Just a few years back, in 1992, Sweden had experienced a financial crisis of similar proportions. Yet the terms "corruption" and "cronyism" don't quite roll off the tongue when one thinks of that country.[9] Clearly the crises indicated something endemic to financial markets, not any egregious sins committed by the Asian governments themselves.

Indeed, a much more plausible explanation was that Thailand, South Korea, Indonesia, and the others had succumbed to one of the chronic pathologies of financial markets: an old-fashioned run on the bank. The "banks" in question were whole countries, of course, but otherwise there was little difference.

Consider how a commercial bank operates. It borrows short term from its depositors to provide financing for long-term investments. If all the depositors showed up at the door and demanded to withdraw their deposits, the bank would run out of cash pretty quickly. That possibility makes these depositors very anxious: they want to be first in line at the slightest hint of trouble. And the stampede ensues. A bank may face a run for no good reason other than public fear that it will face a run. Modern economies have invented powerful tools against this pathology. Their central banks act as lenders-of-last-resort, providing the liquidity needed to stabilize troubled banks and stem potential panic. In addition, bank deposits are insured up to certain limits in most countries. Thanks to these governmental safeguards, conventional bank runs have become a thing of the past.

Except in international finance. The countries of East Asia had been doing just what traditional commercial banks do. They borrowed short term in international financial markets to finance domestic investments. (Short-term debt was preferred both because it was cheaper and because prevailing capital-adequacy standards required lenders to set aside less capital when they were extending short-term loans.) But there was no international lender-of-last-resort and no international authority to guarantee short-term debt. When a few lenders began to think twice about rolling over their credit lines, it was rational for *all* lenders to withhold credit. As the prominent economist Jeffrey Sachs (then at Harvard and now at Columbia) forcefully and correctly argued, against the views of the IMF and the U.S. Treasury, the crisis was a financial panic largely unrelated to economic fundamentals and internal weaknesses.[10] Asia was going through the bust stage of a boom-and-bust cycle. Banks had overlent in the run-up to the crisis and now they were overreacting in pulling back. It wasn't the first time financial markets misbehaved, and it certainly wouldn't be the last.

The IMF's pursuit of new authority to free up capital movements would eventually be doomed by the scale of the Asian financial crisis and its spillovers (the Russian crisis of 1998 in particular).

But the quest reflected a remarkable new consensus among officialdom in advanced countries. Clearly, the case for removing government controls on international financial markets had become widely accepted. And despite the failure to have the amendment ratified, the IMF and the U.S. Treasury remained champions of capital account liberalization until the subprime crisis struck in 2008. The IMF continued to goad countries it dealt with to remove domestic impediments on international finance, and the United States pushed its partners in trade agreements to renounce capital controls. This signaled a momentous transformation in policy beliefs. We need to return to the original Bretton Woods agreement to appreciate its full significance.

The Bretton Woods Consensus on Capital Controls

It would be difficult to overstate the strength of the consensus in favor of capital controls in the immediate aftermath of World War II. As one American economist put it in 1946: "It is now highly respectable doctrine, in academic and banking circles alike, that a substantial measure of direct control over private capital movements, especially of the so-called 'hot money' varieties, will be desirable for most countries not only in the years immediately ahead but also in the long run as well."[11] The Bretton Woods arrangements fully reflected this consensus. As Keynes himself would make clear, the agreement gave every government the "explicit right to control all capital movements" on a permanent basis. "What used to be heresy," he said, "is now endorsed as orthodoxy."[12]

There was almost complete convergence of views among the economists and policy makers of the day on the need for capital controls. That this consensus was a significant departure from the gold standard–era narrative on the benefits of free finance was well recognized. Moreover, capital controls were not viewed as simply a temporary expedient, to be removed once financial markets stabilized and returned to normal. As Keynes and others underscored, they were meant to be a "permanent arrangement."

This about-face had its roots in the turbulence of global finance during the interwar period. As we saw in chapter Two, private capital flows had played a destabilizing role during the 1920s and 1930s. Countries that had not gone back to gold found their currencies fluctuating wildly and moving in directions not always consistent with underlying economic developments. Countries on gold faced rapid capital outflows at the slightest hint of trouble, which required high interest rates and endangered their governments' ability to maintain fixed parities. Stability on the foreign exchanges clashed with the goal of full employment. These financial market pressures ultimately condemned Britain's return to the gold standard to failure. Once markets' dynamics became intertwined with domestic politics, there was no hope that a world of smoothly functioning, self-equilibrating finance would lie within reach.

Keynes identified another, more fundamental problem. Unfettered capital flows undermined not only financial stability but also macroeconomic equilibrium—full employment and price stability. The idea that the macroeconomy would self-adjust, without help from domestic fiscal and monetary policies, had been buried by the experience of the Great Depression and the chaos of the 1930s. Even in periods of relative calm, the combination of fixed exchange rates with capital mobility enslaved a country's economic management to other countries' monetary policies. If others had tight money and high interest rates, you had no choice but to follow suit. If you tried to reduce your interest rates, you would experience a massive outflow of private capital. If, on the other hand, you wanted tighter credit than in other countries, higher interest rates at home would trigger a massive inflow of foreign money, leaving your economy flush with credit and undoing the effects of your own policies. Keynes argued that there was no reason for different countries to have identical monetary policies. Some countries facing rising unemployment may want to expand domestic demand while others may see inflation as the bigger threat. Gold standard rules would leave no room for such differences and would force domestic economic management in every country to reflect some average of the policies pursued elsewhere. This global leveling of policy was unacceptable in view of Keynes's desire (widely shared by other architects of the Bretton Woods regime) to put domestic economic and social goals ahead of the global economy.

There was an alternative to capital controls. Countries might opt for floating currencies instead, letting their exchange rates move in response to private capital flows while domestic monetary policy remained autonomous and insulated. You could, for example, have lower interest rates than elsewhere if you were willing to allow your currency to depreciate in value. That in any case was the theory of how floating currencies would work. This theory eventually became the dominant paradigm among advanced countries from the 1970s on, but Keynes and his contemporaries rejected this option for two reasons. First, they worried, as noted above, that financial markets would create excessively volatile currencies driven by successive bouts of euphoria and pessimism. Second, they were concerned about the effects of currency instability and uncertainty on international trade. Their narrative made a clear distinction between the world of employment and production and the world of finance. They considered the world of finance a casino instead of a driver of economic well-being. Trade, not short-term finance, needed promotion. Hence the paradox: reduced transaction costs in trade required higher transaction costs in international finance—in other words, capital controls. Free capital mobility was out and capital controls were in.

The Bretton Woods regime championed the principle that national economies needed management to ensure full employment and adequate growth. This in turn required that they have

sufficient "policy space" to conduct their monetary and fiscal policies. In addition to capital controls, there were two features of
the new system geared toward providing that space. The first of
these was the provision of short-term financing from the IMF to
help countries weather temporary shortages of foreign currency
and difficulties in external payments. Previously, such financing
had been arranged in an ad hoc manner and depended on the
availability of private creditors willing to cough up the money.
The lending capacity of the IMF would not be as large as Keynes
wanted, but it established an important principle: short-term
balance-of-payments financing had become an official intergovernmental responsibility. This was a central element in multilater-
alizing the international financial system.

Second, even though countries were expected to maintain their
currencies at fixed parities, these parities could be changed in the
event of "fundamental disequilibrium." The IMF agreement did
not define what constituted fundamental disequilibrium, but the
addition of this safety valve established another important prec-
edent. If a country's growth and employment prospects came into
conflict with its external payments, even after resort to capital controls and IMF financing, the incompatibility would be removed by
adjusting the exchange rate rather than letting the domestic economy suffer. "Fixed but adjustable" was a new concept in exchange
rate policy. It was a compromise designed to provide for stability in
international commerce, but not at the cost of damage to domestic
employment and growth.

As in the case of the trade system, the international financial
regime was built around the belief that domestic economic needs
would (and should) trump the requirements of the global economy. If this priority resulted in high international transaction
costs, so be it. Domestic and international policies fully reflected
this consensus for the next quarter century. Even though European countries removed most foreign currency payment restrictions for international trade in the late 1950s, they maintained

those restrictions for financial transactions. As Professor Rawi Abdelal of the Harvard Business School notes, the Treaty of Rome, which established the European Economic Community in 1957, treated capital flows as a distinctly second-class citizen.[13] Most countries in Europe maintained capital controls well into the 1980s. Even though Germany favored greater openness to capital flows, opposition from France and others frustrated any move in that direction. The United States did not employ capital controls until the early 1960s, but neither did it pressure other countries to remove theirs. In 1963, faced with a capital outflow, the United States imposed a special tax on interest earnings on foreign deposits, a measure it maintained until 1974. In developing countries, of course, capital controls were very much the norm, with very rare exceptions. Capital controls were effective through the 1960s, and they worked as the architects of the Bretton Woods regime imagined they would, opening up space for domestic macroeconomic management.[14]

The Achilles' heel of the Bretton Woods regime was that it did not address a fundamental conundrum for the international economy: What will play the role of international money in the system? Sustaining a global economy requires a global medium of transaction and store of value—a "money"—that is made available in ample quantities when needed and can be reliably redeemed in exchange for real goods or assets. Gold played this role under the gold standard; we saw the problems that this gave rise to in the 1870s (when a global shortage of gold forced price deflation) and, fatally, in the 1930s. Under Bretton Woods, the U.S. dollar became effectively the "global currency," serving as the reserve asset of choice for central banks around the world. Confidence in the dollar was underpinned by the dollar's peg to gold, at a fixed value of $35 per ounce. Even though all other countries could in principle devalue their currencies, the system relied on the United States never doing so itself. The Bretton Woods regime depended on what came to be called the "dollar-exchange standard."

What if the United States faced a conflict between its domestic requirements and its external balances? The balance of payments on foreign transactions had been largely irrelevant for U.S. policy makers until the late 1950s. The United States was the predominant economy in the world and the most important source of international lending. However, when the United States began to run deficits during the 1960s due to the Vietnam War and rapid economic growth in Europe and Asia, its external payments became a major preoccupation.[15] As long as the rest of the world was happy absorbing U.S. dollars as part of their global money supply, there was no problem. But continued U.S. balance-of-payments deficits would ultimately cast doubt on the U.S. guarantee to redeem dollars at a fixed parity against gold. In a domestic context, confidence in the national currency depends on the ability and willingness of the government to raise revenues from its own citizens to back up the value of its currency. The equivalent internationally was for the U.S. government to stand ready to raise taxes or cut expenditures at home in order to pay *foreigners*. The gold standard rules were back, except that everyone understood the United States was unlikely to play along.

In 1971, confronted with growing demands from foreign countries to convert their dollar holdings to gold, President Richard Nixon and his Treasury secretary John Connolly faced a choice: either tighten domestic economic policies or suspend the convertibility of dollars to gold at a fixed rate. They naturally chose the second option.[16] Nixon and Connolly threw in a 10 percent surcharge on imports for good measure to signal that they would not idly stand by and allow other countries to take advantage of their competitive currencies and run large trade surpluses with the United States. This fateful decision, taken on August 15, 1971, sealed the fate of the global regime of fixed exchange rates, the monetary cornerstone of the Bretton Woods regime. Once again, the domestic economy had triumphed over the needs of the global economy. In subsequent years there were various attempts to estab-

lish new currency parities, but none proved durable. The move to
floating currencies was officially sanctioned in 1973.

The Dissolution of the Bretton Woods Consensus

The success of the Bretton Woods regime contained the seeds of
its undermining. As world trade and finance expanded, the "policy space" that the existing controls afforded shrank and external
constraints began to play a larger role. The IMF and its resources
proved inadequate, despite the creation of an artificial reserve
asset designed to augment its lending capacity (the Special Drawing Right or SDR). When the country at the center of the system,
the United States, came under attack in the late 1960s, the regime
of fixed exchange rates could no longer be sustained. Moreover,
the belief system that supported capital controls began to dissolve
over the 1970s and was replaced in subsequent decades by an alternative narrative emphasizing the inevitability of liberalization and
the benefits of capital mobility. Just as in trade, an agenda of deep
integration centered on free capital mobility would replace the
Bretton Woods compromise.

The 1960s were the heyday of Keynesian ideas on economic management. The oil shocks and the stagflation of the 1970s—which
confronted advanced economies with unemployment and inflation together—pushed attention away from Keynes's focus on
demand management to the supply side of the economy. In the
traditional Keynesian model, unemployment was the result of too
little demand for domestic products; but the simultaneous increase
in inflation belied that explanation. Discretionary monetary and
fiscal policies à la Keynes began to be seen by economists and
technocrats as a force for instability rather than stability. Interventionist philosophies lost ground, in tandem with the spread
of market-oriented ideas among the economics profession. The
growth of trade paradoxically made it harder for governments to

administer capital controls since capital flows could be disguised by manipulating trade flows.[17] Keynes had correctly predicted that capital controls would require extensive oversight over all international transactions, but governments were increasingly hesitant to deploy the required controls in view of the changing zeitgeist.

National economic interests also played a role. The United States and Britain were major financial centers and stood to gain from global financial liberalization. The removal of capital controls would increase demand for the services of Wall Street and the City of London.[18] Britain actively promoted the growth of the Eurodollar market—U.S. dollar-denominated deposits held, typically, in London—to which the United States turned a blind eye even though the official American policy was to discourage capital outflows. American attitudes toward financial liberalization were also shaped by the expectation that a more open international financial system would help finance U.S. deficits.[19] (It would for a while, but it would also facilitate the eventual flight from the dollar.) As memories of interwar instability faded, financial interests began to carry even greater weight in the shaping of economic policy. The Europeans and Japanese were willing to contemplate cooperative capital controls to bring some stability to foreign currency markets after 1973, but their demands were blocked by the United States.[20] Policy makers in the United States and Britain increasingly advocated global financial deregulation, and they eventually gained an unlikely and crucial ally in France.

The impetus behind the French change of heart was the failure of a reflation program the Socialist president François Mitterrand had embarked on in 1981—the so-called "experiment of socialism in one country."[21] Financial markets had responded to Mitterrand by fleeing in droves, putting upward pressure on French interest rates. Mitterrand's government responded at first by tightening capital controls, to the point that French travelers were required to carry a little booklet—the *carnet de change*—as they traveled across national frontiers, keeping track of their foreign currency purchases. The inconvenience they suffered didn't increase Mitterrand's popularity. In any case, capital flight continued unabated, aided by the strong network of European trade. Eventually, Mitterrand and his advisers came to the conclusion that capital controls had backfired: their costs were borne mostly by ordinary Frenchmen while the rich retained ready access to bank accounts in Switzerland and other financial havens.

The Socialist government changed course in the spring of 1983, dropping the reflation program, relaxing capital controls, and adopting an agenda of domestic financial liberalization. "What a conservative government had feared to do," an observer noted, "a Socialist government accomplished."[22] More important for our purposes, France became an ardent advocate of new international rules in favor of capital mobility. Jacques Delors, a minister of finance under Mitterrand, became president of the European Commission in 1985 and pushed for capital liberalization as part of a drive toward a "Single Europe." Even though the Delors commission originally envisaged limiting liberalization to flows within Europe, Germany succeeded in extending coverage to non-member countries. By the late 1980s, capital controls had been removed in all of the major European countries, making the region the most financially open in the world. Free capital flows subsequently became a European norm—an integral part of the European legal rules, the *acquis communitaire*—to which all prospective EU members had to adhere. The Maastricht Treaty, signed in 1992, codified the new norm and made Europe's capital controls history.

The French conversion also enabled the new norm to migrate to another important international forum, the Organization of Economic Cooperation and Development (OECD). The OECD is a rich-country club established in 1961 that has enormous agenda-setting and legitimizing powers even though it exercises no formal sanctions.[23] By the end of the 1980s, the OECD had dropped previous distinctions between short-term capital ("hot money") and long-term investments. It also adopted the objective of full capital mobility as part of its amended Code of Liberalization of Capital Movements, effectively making removal of capital controls a condition for membership in the OECD. Between 1994 and 2000, six developing and transitional countries became members, and all of them had to undertake commitments to liberalize their capital accounts in short order. Two of these countries, Mexico and South Korea, would undergo severe financial crises shortly after joining the club.[24]

By the time Michel Camdessus addressed the IMF Board in 1997 to make the case for an amendment that would allow the organization to push for freedom in capital movements globally, his argument was largely accepted by economists and policy makers in the advanced nations. Capital controls had become a no-no. What was heresy and then became orthodoxy had become heresy once again.

When Financial Markets Misbehave

With fixed exchange rates and capital controls gone, two key planks of the original Bretton Woods consensus had been shelved. In the years that followed, international financial markets would exert significant influence on the conduct of economic policy. At the time, many economists and policy makers were prone to gloss over this transformation with a story that went something like this: First, the liberalization of capital movements was both inevitable and desirable. Free capital flows, just like free trade, would help improve the global allocation of resources and encourage governments to pursue better fiscal and monetary polices. Second, market-determined exchange rates were a double blessing. They would prevent currency misalignments while allowing countries to conduct their monetary policies independently. If a government wanted to follow more expansionary policies than its partners, it could still do so by letting its currency depreciate. There would be no gold standard–type stranglehold on domestic policies.

This story line betrayed remarkable—and remarkably misplaced—confidence in the ability of financial markets to send the correct signals. Theories that asserted financial market efficiency had become the dominant intellectual doctrine of the day. These theories were based on implausible assumptions about how speculators and investors behaved: how rational and forward-looking they were and how much their activities contributed to economic progress. Moreover, the new consensus showed little appreciation for the differences between domestic and international finance. The institutional underpinnings that global finance required—global regulations, standards, supervision, enforcement, lenders-of-last-resort—were as absent in this narrative as they were in the real world. The pitfalls of finance operating across jurisdictional and regulatory boundaries and evading supervision remained unexplored. Markets were presumed to need very few things other than willing participants. When financial opening produced one disappointment after another, no one should have been surprised. Alas, they were. The missing ingredients would be brought into the picture much later as the problems of free finance became more apparent. The painful lessons of the interwar period would have to be relearned.

Currency floating, in particular, worked very differently from what most economists expected at the time. By the 1980s, "excessive volatility" and "misalignment" had become bywords for floating exchange rates. As these pieces of economist's jargon suggest, there were two problems: currency values fluctuated too much on a day-to-day basis; and there were prolonged periods of currency under- or overvaluation that created difficulties at home and for trade partners.

Consider the travails of the British pound. We have historical data on the value of the pound against the U.S. dollar back to 1791 that provide us with a long historical perspective on currency instability. Few periods during this 200-year stretch display greater instability than the years since the transition to floating in 1973. In fact, the only other eras with similar turbulence include certain military conflicts and the interwar era, with its ill-fated attempt to return the pound to the gold standard. The pound experienced some wild movements during the Napoleonic Wars and the U.S. Civil War in particular. Outside of these periods, however, the pound has tended to remain stable. Britain had two major devaluations between 1945 and 1973 (in 1949 and 1967), but these were aimed at removing what in the Bretton Woods regime were called "fundamental disequilibria," and were followed by periods of stability in foreign currency markets. The post-1973 floating experience looks like something else altogether, with yearly changes in the value of the pound of 10–15 percent not uncommon—a see-saw ride that follows little apparent rhyme or reason.

Much of the instability was driven by the dollar's own wild gyrations. There were three major cycles of dollar depreciation, followed by appreciation, after 1973. Then there were ups and downs specific to the pound, which were superimposed. To someone without much knowledge of history, it would appear that the world was shaken by a series of cataclysmic political and military events after 1973. Floating currencies became a source of instability for the international economic system rather than a safety valve.

Economists and policy makers would endlessly debate during the eighties and nineties whether currency values reflected fundamental economic conditions or simply distortions in foreign currency markets: bubbles, irrationality, myopic expectations, or short-term trading strategies. What do all these men in their twenties and thirties—they are mostly men—sitting in front of huge computer screens, who move hundreds of millions of dollars across the globe at a keystroke and determine the fate of nations' currencies, really do? Do they serve to eliminate inefficiencies in the market and bring currency values closer to their true underlying economic worth? Or do they magnify the ups and downs in the market by acting like a herd and chasing phantom profits.

This debate did little for those who had to suffer the consequences of currency swings. When the dollar appreciated by 40 percent during the first half of the 1980s, it was as if each manufacturer in the United States had been hit by a tax of equal proportion on its exports and all of its foreign competitors in the American market subsidized by that same amount. The moderate increase in protectionism that took place during this period is hardly surprising; what's astonishing is that it didn't go much further. Whatever the source of the problem in financial markets, it wasn't lack of competition or market liquidity. By 2007, the *daily* volume of foreign currency transactions had risen to $3.2 trillion, orders of magnitude larger than the volume of trade (with a daily average of $38 billion in the same year).[25] Finance had swamped the real economy.

Floating also taught us an important lesson. Once capital was freed, it made little difference whether currencies were pegged or allowed to float. Already by 1978, James Tobin, a Keynesian economist at Yale and a future Nobel laureate, had put his finger on the central problem. "Debate on the [exchange rate] regime evades and obscures the essential problem," he wrote. The fundamental problem is the "excessive" mobility of private financial capital. "National economies and national governments are not capable of adjusting to massive movements of funds across the foreign exchanges, without real hardship and without significant sacrifice of the objectives of national economic policy with respect to employment, output, and inflation." His argument was essentially the same as Keynes's, but it now applied also to a world with floating currencies. Capital mobility, he noted, prevents nations from pursuing monetary and fiscal policies that differ from those in other economies and therefore undermines the conduct of policies appropriate to the domestic economy. Regardless of whether trading in international financial markets leads to vast shifts in funds across nations or large movements in exchange rates, Tobin complained, they have "serious and frequently painful real internal economic consequences."

Tobin pointed out that the world economy could go one of two ways. We could adopt a single world currency and emulate globally what was true domestically. This would eliminate all the difficulties and distortions created by differences in national currencies, at the price, of course, of subjecting all nations to a single monetary policy. Judging this scenario a political impossibility, he advanced an alternative solution. What we need, he famously argued, was "to throw some sand in the wheels of our excessively efficient international money markets."[26] His specific recommendation was a tax on international currency transactions, a "Tobin tax," as it has come to be called.

Tobin was in a distinct minority, however, and his plea fell on deaf ears against the background of the post–Bretton Woods zeitgeist. Belief in the efficiency and inevitability of global capital mobility remained strong. The world economy would have to suffer more damage before Tobin's views would receive a sympathetic hearing from leading economists and regulators.[27]

The waves of financial crises that buffeted countries who left themselves at the mercy of international capital markets produced severe damage indeed. First it was the Latin American debt crisis of the 1980s, which, aggravated by poor economic management, engulfed the countries of the region and produced a "lost decade" of economic stagnation. It was Europe's turn in the early 1990s, when currency traders successfully speculated against the central banks of several European countries (such as England, Italy, and Sweden). These countries had tried to limit currency movement by tying their currencies closely to the deutschmark, but financial markets forced devaluations on them. The mid-1990s saw another round of financial crises, the most severe of which was the "tequila crisis" in Mexico (1994) brought on by a sudden reversal in capital flows. The Asian financial crisis followed in 1997–98, which would then spill over to Russia (1998), Brazil (1999), Argentina (2000), and eventually Turkey (2001). These are only the better-known cases. One review identified 124 banking crises, 208 currency crises, and 63 sovereign debt crises between 1970 and 2008.[28] After a lull in the early years of the new millennium, the subprime mortgage crisis centered in the United States triggered another powerful set of tremors, confronting financially open economies with a sudden dearth of foreign finance and bankrupting a few among them (Iceland, Latvia).

Most of these cases follow the same boom-and-bust pattern. First, there is a phase of relative euphoria during which a country receives significant amounts of foreign lending. This stage is fueled by stories in financial markets that emphasize the bright prospects ahead. The country has reformed its policies and stands at the cusp of a productivity explosion. There is no need to worry about the debt buildup because future incomes will be high and there will be ample capacity to repay the loans. The borrowers can be the government, private banks, or corporate entities. In the end, it doesn't seem to make much of a difference. Then a bit of bad news, either domestic or external, sets off what Guillermo Calvo, the preeminent analyst of financial crises, has called a "sudden stop."[29] The country's story in financial markets changes completely: the country has overborrowed, its government is acting irresponsibly, and the economy looks risky. Foreign finance dries up and in short order the economy has to go through painful contortions to adjust. Interest rates shoot up, the currency collapses, firms face a credit crunch, and domestic demand contracts, typically aggravated by tight fiscal policies aimed at restoring "market confidence." By the time it's all over, the economy will have forfeited, on average, around 20 percent of its GDP.[30]

None of this should have come as a real surprise. Whenever capital has been free to move around the world, it has produced what the economic historian Charles Kindleberger has memorably called "manias, panics and crashes."[31] Recent research by Carmen Reinhart and Ken Rogoff has quantified what had long been obvious to economic historians. These two economists painstakingly sifted through the historical record to identify every single important instance of banking crisis since 1800. When they superimposed their results on the historic trajectory of capital mobility, they discovered that the two series lined up almost perfectly. As they put it, "Periods of high international capital mobility have repeatedly produced international banking crises, not only famously as they did in the 1990s, but historically."[32]

Perhaps increased volatility and crises are the price that the world economy paid for improved financial discipline. Many defenders would point out that the world has profited from capital mobility despite these disappointments. The argument that free finance improves the global allocation of resources is not quite dead yet. There is still an ongoing academic debate on whether countries that remove impediments to foreign capital grow more rapidly than others. This is academic hairsplitting. The historical record of capital mobility is quite clear.

A cursory look at this record yields three important discoveries. First, the world economy has achieved unprecedented levels of growth since World War II. Nothing in history comes even close— not the Industrial Revolution and not the nineteenth-century era of globalization. Second, the growth rates attained during the first quarter century following the end of World War II have yet to be matched. The world economy grew at roughly 3 percent per year on a per capita basis between 1950 and 1973, nearly triple the rate prior to the 1930s and double the rate since the late 1970s. Post-1990 economic performance looks very good in historical perspective, but it still falls short of the Bretton Woods standard. The world economy simply has not performed as well during the era of financial globalization as it did under Bretton Woods.

And third, the growth champions of the last three decades, just as those of the immediate postwar decades, were countries such as China that played the globalization game by Bretton-Woods rules rather than deep integration rules. They maintained capital controls, kept foreign finance at bay, and used their policy space for domestic economic management (as we shall see in chapter Seven). The inevitable conclusion is that financial globalization has failed us. Countries that have opened themselves up to international capital markets have faced greater risks, without compensating benefits in the form of higher economic growth.[33]

The Foxes and Hedgehogs of Finance

T he conclusion we reached at the end of the previous chapter should be puzzling. Shouldn't an economy perform better when individuals and firms are able to borrow and lend freely across national borders? Why would openness to finance be anything but an advantage?

Capital flows *can* be a boon to an economy under the right circumstances. In countries with plentiful investment opportunities and a shortage of savings, they allow firms to undertake projects that they would otherwise be unable to. Especially when it comes bundled with technology, market knowledge, and other skills, long-term foreign direct investment is an essential component of economic growth. But why do other kinds of international financial so often produce perverse results?

Recall one of the points I made when we discussed the gains from trade. A profitable exchange between a buyer and a seller is only desirable for society as a whole when prices reflect the full social (opportunity) costs involved in the exchange. This principle applies equally well to financial markets. When I invest in a piece of paper issued by an entity on the other side of the world—a debt obligation, a bond, or a derivative—do I have an accurate understanding of the risks I am taking? Does the promised yield reflect those risks? When I borrow money, does the interest rate reflect the costs that others will face, or the fiscal expenses required to bail me out when I find myself unable to service my debts? When I engineer a newfangled security, do I take into account the possible effects on the company's bottom line over the long term (beyond the effects on my compensation package)? If the answer is not an unqualified yes to these and a multitude of other similar questions, financial markets will fail. Unfortunately, such failings are legion, which is why we have become so accustomed to the financial market pathologies they produce.

Economists are not unaware of these problems. The economics literature is chockful of analyses of these failings, which go by names such as asymmetric information, limited liability, moral hazard, agency costs, multiple equilibria, systemic risk, implicit guarantees, information cascades, and so on. Each one of these phenomena has been studied to death with intricate mathematical reasoning and empirical illustrations. By now most economists also understand that these problems have not been adequately addressed in the global economy. Domestic finance is underpinned by common standards, deposit insurance, bankruptcy rules, court-enforced contracts, a lender-of-last-resort, a fiscal backstop, and an alphabet soup of regulatory and supervisory agencies. None of these exists globally. So global regulations and standards are an ineffective patchwork and crisis response remains ad hoc.

Given what we know, why are global markets so poorly managed? The problem derives from a tendency among economists and policy makers to downplay the consequences of these failures for the actual conduct of policy, sheltering the case for financial liberalization from their ominous implications. It's not that financial markets don't fail; it's that we can carry on as if they don't. To understand how this particular professional deformation plays out, we need to recognize the difference between foxes and hedgehogs in the economics forest.

The Fox and the Hedgehog

In a famous essay on Tolstoy, the liberal philosopher Sir Isaiah Berlin distinguished between two kinds of thinkers by harking back to an ancient saying attributed to the Greek lyric poet Archilochus (seventh century BC): "The fox knows many things, but the hedgehog knows one big thing." Hedgehogs have one central idea and see the world exclusively through the prism of that idea. They overlook complications and exceptions, or mold them to fit into their worldview. There is one true answer that fits at all times and all circumstances. Foxes, for whom Berlin had greater sympathy, have a variegated take on the world, which prevents them from articulating one big slogan. They are skeptical of grand theories as they feel the world's complexity prevents generalizations. Berlin thought Dante was a hedgehog while Shakespeare was a fox.[1]

The distinction captures neatly the divide within economics between the hedgehogs who think freeing up markets is always the right solution (the "big idea") and the foxes who believe the devil is in the details.[2] Foxes believe in markets, too—they are economists, after all—but they believe real world complications require a much more cautious approach that is sensitive to context. To the extent that they take these complications into account, the hedgehogs see them as strengthening the case for market liberalization rather than as standing in the way.

You can tell what kind of an economist someone is by the nature of their response when confronted with a policy issue. On gut instinct, a hedgehog economist will apply the simplest textbook analysis to the question at hand. Markets maximize efficiency, and the freer the market, the better. In this world, every tax has an efficiency cost; every restriction on individual behavior reduces the size of the economic pie. Questions of equity and efficiency can be neatly separated. Market failures are presumed nonexistent unless proved otherwise and, if present, are to be addressed only by the most directly targeted remedies. People are rational and forward-looking. Demand curves always slope down (and supply curves up). Economywide interactions do not overturn the logic of partial analyses. Adam Smith and his subsequent followers have proved that unfettered markets work best. No matter how technical, complex, and full of surprises these economists' own research might be, their takes on the issues of the day are driven by a straightforward, almost knee-jerk logic: remove a government intervention or barrier and economic performance will get better.

The foxes among economists have a healthy respect for the power of markets, but they are inclined to see all kinds of complications that make the textbook answers incomplete. In their world, the economy is full of market imperfections, equity and efficiency cannot be neatly separated, people do not always behave rationally, some otherwise undesirable policy interventions can generate positive outcomes, and complications that arise from economywide interactions render doctrinaire analyses suspect. Adam Smith's followers have demonstrated a long list of exceptions to the principle that unfettered markets enhance social welfare. Government intervention can improve market outcomes in many ways. Foxes see the economy as inherently "second-best"—too impure for the hedgehogs' ideal policies to be always the right ones.

Some of the differences stem from how each group perceives the prevalence of market failures. Hedgehogs are less likely to think these failures are as common as the foxes make them out to be. But the more significant difference between these two groups lies in their *response* to market failures.

A hedgehog will argue that when markets break down, the solution is not to restrict them or to look to government for help, but to simply make them work better. The complications that worry the fox must be addressed directly, by removing the distortions that give rise to them. If the fox is concerned about excessive risk taking within banks, the right approach is to fix incentives to rein in risky behavior. If too much government debt creates financial fragility, it is the government's fiscal policy that needs adjustment. Each problem requires its own specific remedy; they are no reason to delay or give up on liberalization as a whole. This is called the "principle of policy targeting"—aiming the policy intervention at the source of the problem. It is sensible as far as it goes. But in the hands of hedgehog economists who presume that all relevant complications should and can be addressed through the most appropriate means, the principle cycles back as a powerful tool for liberalizing everything in sight without worries about adverse effects. After all, those adverse effects can be handled directly and separately. In effect, it allows these economists to expect that the world will adjust to their recommendation, rather than the other way around.

In reality, we often have just a hazy idea about the root source of a given problem. And even when we have a good fix on it, administrative and political difficulties may stand in the way of addressing it directly. Attempts at liberalization backfire because not all the necessary safeguards are in place. A similar fate befalls the hedgehogs' recommendation to remove trade restrictions and deal with any adverse distributional consequences through compensatory measures. The liberalization takes place and the economist walks away happy. Meanwhile it turns out that arranging the compensation is not as easy as it seems. By the time the backlash (or the financial crisis) sets in, the economist is busy advocating liberalization elsewhere.

The hedgehog economist will buttress his (or her) case by arguing that market solutions are the lesser evil when compared to government interventions. This is where the battle gets explicitly ideological. Even if markets are prone to fail, the hedgehog will say, governments will make things even worse. Bureaucrats do not have the necessary information to do the right things; they are captured by the interests they are supposed to regulate; and they are prone to corruption. For one or more of these reasons, the argument goes, government restrictions on international finance will prove a remedy worse than the disease. Notice how this is almost the complete opposite of the argument for policy targeting, insofar as it assumes governments have virtually zero capacity to get the simplest things right—let alone undertake finely tuned interventions targeted at the very source of market failures. Fortunately, this argument cannot be entirely right since, as we saw in chapter One, modern market economies require a wide range of supporting institutions, many of which are provided by the state. If the hedgehogs were right, modern market economies would not have prospered; they would be dysfunctional.

These arguments have been widely deployed in support of free capital flows. When Stanley Fischer made the case for capital mobility during the 1997 meetings of the IMF, he devoted a major part of his presentation to the adjustments required for countries to "prepare well" for capital mobility. As he put it, "economic policies and institutions, particularly the financial system, need to be adapted to operate in a world of liberalized capital markets." Some of what needs to be done was well known, he said. Macroeconomic policies need to be "sound"; the domestic financial system needs to be "strengthened"; and the removal of capital controls should be phased in "appropriately." But there were also issues about which there was less knowledge or consensus. How much information about their conduct of policy should central banks and other government authorities share with financial markets? How can the IMF and other multilateral agencies improve "surveillance"—their monitoring of financial market trends and risks? How can they increase financial support to countries in crisis without providing a blanket guarantee to creditors and borrowers?[3] For Fischer, neither the scale of the required adjustments nor the presence of open-ended questions were a convincing argument for delaying liberalization. Reforms would ensure that the gains from capital mobility were reaped while the risks were contained.

Frederic Mishkin, a distinguished monetary economist at

Columbia who has also served as a member of the Board of Governors of the Federal Reserve, provides a more recent example of the hedgehog mind-set. His book *The Next Globalization: How Disadvantaged Nations Can Harness Their Financial Systems to Get Rich*,[4] published in 2006 just as the global financial crisis was about to strike, is one of the most upbeat books on globalization in recent years. Even though many globalization advocates are ambivalent about *financial* globalization for the reasons outlined earlier, Mishkin remains an unabashed booster.[5] He is also under no illusion as to what will make financial globalization work. Emerging market economies need "good institutions" that promote property rights "such as the rule of law, constraints on government expropriation, and absence of corruption." They also need institutions that promote an efficient financial system, such as "financial regulation to encourage transparency, good corporate governance, prudential supervision to limit excessive risk taking, and good enforcement of financial contracts." These reforms in turn require extensive legal and political transformations to relax the grip of incumbents in the system and open it to competition.[6]

What is striking in arguments such as these is how extensive and imprecise—simultaneously—the list of prerequisites can be. Many economists describe the institutional requirements for successful opening to finance as if they were simply a matter of turning certain policy switches on and off. Fix institutions. Establish the rule of law. Eliminate corruption. Get rid of excessive financial risk taking. And don't forget political reform. Done? Good. Now stand ready for the economic boom that financial globalization has in store for you.

A laundry list of reforms of this kind assumes that developing countries have some magic tools at their disposal to accomplish changes that have taken today's developed countries centuries to achieve. Even worse, as the subprime crisis has demonstrated, not even the most sophisticated regulators in the world have a good fix on how to police excessive risk taking or foster adequate levels of transparency. But no matter. We can be sure that the list of pre-requisites will only grow in length. And when countries run into trouble with financial markets, there will be always something on that list which they haven't gotten quite right and on which the crisis can be blamed. There is something self-serving in this type of advocacy; the hedgehog economist can never be wrong, no matter how badly things end up.

Consider Argentina during the 1990s. This country enthusiastically embraced capital mobility in the early part of the decade alongside wide-ranging reforms in finance, trade, fiscal policy, and governance. Its rules on financial regulation and supervision were first rate and considered to be better than those in many advanced countries. The reforms turned Argentina into one of the IMF's brightest stars. On a visit to Argentina in 1996, IMF managing director Michel Camdessus expressed his admiration thus: "when I come to Argentina, I no longer see the dramatic symptoms of crisis, but rather what is in many respects a blueprint for success."[7] Three years later, Argentina was the massive casualty of a sudden stop in capital inflows, triggered by the Brazilian devaluation of 1999.

In his book, Mishkin grants that Argentina did much to improve its financial markets and regulation. But as he ruefully puts it, "Unfortunately, these efforts were not enough to ensure success." The financial crisis, he writes, was the result of "[s]tructural problems in the Argentine economy, a failure to deal with fiscal problems, and some bad luck."[8] In other words, no matter how much a country does, it is rarely enough. Financial markets demand more.

Michael Lewis, one of our greatest raconteurs of financial she-nanigans, reports a conversation with a friend who created the first mortgage derivative in 1986. This friend says: "The problem isn't the tools. It's who is using the tools. Derivatives are like guns."[9] The analogy is revealing. In effect, hedgehog advocates of financial liberalization are like proponents of relaxing restrictions on guns. The battle cry of these proponents is: "It's not guns that kill people, it's people that kill people." The implication is that we should let firearms circulate freely while preventing them from falling into the hands of criminals and enforcing tough sanctions for misuse. This is a pretty good argument if you believe several things: that we can identify future criminals; that we can do a good job of catching those who commit crimes; and that punishment tomorrow strongly deters crime today. Otherwise, the cost to society from individual freedom is too high. A blunter but more effective instrument is needed: restricting access to guns.

The fox's perspective on financial liberalization runs along similar lines. In a perfect world, we would minimize the adverse side effects of free capital mobility through appropriate regulations without having to resort to direct controls on capital flows. We do not live in a perfect world, and caution dictates that we not let financial markets run wild.

Let us return to James Tobin, one of the earliest post–Bretton Woods advocates of capital controls within the economics establishment. Before he floated his proposal to tax international currency transactions, Tobin carefully considered the hedgehogs' ideal solution. "[L]et us pay our respects to the 'one world' ideal," he wrote. What would it take to construct a world financial market as integrated and unified as that which exists within a nation, say the United States?

Capital flows freely within the United States and this clearly produces important economic benefits. "With nationwide product and labor markets," Tobin explained, "goods and labor . . . flow readily to areas of high demand, and this mobility is the essential solution to the problems of regional depression and obsolescence that inevitably occur." Under these conditions, macroeconomic policies on a regional level are superfluous, and in any case could not be conducted. A common currency, fully integrated national financial and capital markets, and a nationwide monetary policy ensure that speculative capital movements aimed at exploiting differences in interest rates or changes in exchange rates cannot exert a destabilizing force.

A hedgehog approach would entail building the same kind of economy globally as exists nationally. But to describe how U.S. markets work, Tobin pointed out, "is to remind us how difficult it would be to replicate [their] prerequisites on a worldwide basis." In reality, "private financial markets have become internationalized much more rapidly and completely than other economic and political institutions." In light of this, Tobin felt compelled to propose a foxlike remedy: a tax to segment international currency markets.[10] Such a tax on international financial transactions, even if set at a very low rate, would deter traders from engaging in excessive buying and selling of currencies and other financial assets in search of very short run profits.[11]

Keynes would have approved, of course. He too might have preferred addressing the root causes of speculative excesses, which he would identify as human foibles and herd effects in addition to regulatory weaknesses and political fragmentation. But Keynes was a fox with a keen sense of the practical limits of what can be achieved in the real world. That is why he envisaged capital controls as an integral part of any stable system of international finance.

Perhaps the most consummate fox among today's economists is Joe Stiglitz, whose research constitutes a nearly endless catalogue of the ways in which markets can fail. Stiglitz won a Nobel Prize in 2001 (along with George Akerlof and Mike Spence) for theoretical work showing how "asymmetric information" distorts incentives in a wide range of markets. If you know more than I do about the value of what you are selling me—whether it is your used car, your labor, or your debt—then we're in for a troubled relationship. Prices in such transactions tend to provide the wrong signals. Many trades that should not happen do, while others that should happen don't. Many of the pathologies of financial markets— boom-and-bust cycles, financial panics, lack of access to credit by otherwise creditworthy borrowers—can be explained by information asymmetries of this type (often interacting with other market distortions). Unlike many others who have done work on market failures, Stiglitz actually takes the results of this research seriously. He has been a vocal opponent of freeing up capital flows and an ardent critic of the IMF.[12]

The oddest member of the group of capital market skeptics is Jagdish Bhagwati, the Columbia University economist. Bhagwati created quite a stir during the Asian financial crisis when he published an article in 1998 called "The Capital Myth: The Difference Between Trade in Widgets and Dollars."[13] Bhagwati is one of the world's most passionate advocates of free trade. So when he wrote that advocates of free capital markets were motivated by ideology and narrow self-interest (what he called the "Wall Street–Treasury complex") rather than economics, ears perked up. Bhagwati pointed to the familiar problems with international capital markets: short-term speculation, the propensity to panics, and the costly adjustments caused by reversals in flows. In view of these risks, he argued, there was no good reason to push countries to remove their controls on capital flows.

What makes Bhagwati's stand peculiar is not that he is against free capital flows while he favors free trade in goods. After all, one can reasonably claim that market failures are much more rampant in the market for "dollars" than they are in the market for "widgets." A difference of another kind stands out. Bhagwati is a hedgehog in trade, but a fox when it comes to finance. Having established his academic reputation by showing how market imperfections—divergences between private and social valuations—may lead to unexpected results in trade, Bhagwati would never deny the possibility that such imperfections exist in the real world. His case for free trade relies instead on the hedgehog's principle of policy targeting. He accepts free trade's "downsides," but proposes that we deal with them through "a complex set of new policies and institutions," such as domestic and international compensation mechanisms and other interventions targeted at the source of the problem.[14] This is of course exactly the kind of argument made by Fischer, Mishkin, and other defenders of free capital mobility. Don't restrict capital mobility; deal with the underlying problems directly. Bhagwati rejects this approach in the case of finance, presumably because he finds it impractical. He is quite right to do so.

Collateral Benefits or Collateral Damage?

The latest generation of arguments in favor of unrestricted capital mobility takes a different tack, emphasizing the indirect and catalytic role of financial globalization. The writings of Ken Rogoff, the Harvard economist who served as IMF's chief economist, best represent this line of thought.

Rogoff and his collaborators grant that the existing evidence has not been very kind to those who expected to see significant benefits from free capital flows in the form of higher investment and faster growth. But if there has been disappointment, they argue, it is only because people have been looking in the wrong places. The real benefits lie elsewhere. In their view, financial globalization promotes better domestic financial sectors, imposes discipline on the conduct of macroeconomic policies, exposes domestic firms to foreign competition, and creates pressures for better governance, both public and corporate. In other words, financial globalization generates significant "collateral" benefits.[15]

Rogoff's argument has a certain appeal. Many developing countries could use better macroeconomic discipline and institutional improvement, regardless of how these come about. But we can just as easily argue the other way, suggesting that financial globalization weakens (rather then strengthens) macroeconomic discipline and undermines (rather than promotes) institutional development.

Clearly, access to international finance often enables profligate governments to run larger deficits for longer than would be the case if they relied on domestic creditors alone. Take the case of Turkey, a country that went through a wrenching financial crisis in 2001. After it removed controls on capital flows in the late 1980s, the Turkish government found a ready source of cheap finance despite poor macroeconomic management. Public debt was on an explosive path and inflation remained high. Nevertheless, domestic commercial banks would borrow abroad and use the money to buy government bonds, profiting from the interest margin. When the eventual correction came, precipitated by a "sudden stop" in capital inflows, the economy experienced its worst decline in decades. Without financial globalization, Turkey would have been forced to put its fiscal house in order a lot sooner than in 2001, and it would have cost the country much less.

Or consider Greece, the European Union's profligate problem child. This country flouted for years Brussels' ceilings on government deficits by manipulating its budget statistics. The Greek government had handy accomplices in carrying out this statistical legerdemain. In return for hundreds of millions of dollars in fees, Wall Street firms such as Goldman Sachs engineered the financial derivatives that helped hide the scale of Greece's budget woes.[16] When the full scale of the government's bankruptcy came to light in early 2010, it threw not only Greece but the entire Eurozone into crisis. Germany and France were confronted by a cruel choice: either bail out Greece, thereby rewarding misbehavior and flouting EU rules, or let Greece (and possibly other weaker nations as well) drop out of the euro, dealing a potentially fatal flow to the currency union.

External finance is a fair-weather friend: there when it is least needed, and absent when it could do some good. This is not news. It was a running joke during the 1930s that foreign finance is like an umbrella which a man is allowed to borrow, but must return as soon as it starts to rain.[17] Financial globalization aggravates rather than moderates economic cycles in emerging market economies—the upswings and downswings in economic activity.[18] It is difficult to see how this contributes to fiscal discipline.

The argument about governance improvements proves suspect as well. Financial globalization does force governments to pay more attention to what bankers want, but finance and banking is one industry among many, with its own special interests. Why should its demands line up always, or even most of the time, with what a country needs?

Consider a typical conflict in a developing economy: foreign bankers prefer high interest rates and an appreciated currency while domestic exporters prefer low interest rates and a cheaper currency. Which of these two outcomes should monetary and fiscal institutions be designed to deliver? More often than not, exporters' preferences will do the most good for the economy as a whole, and hence the economies where finance does not have the upper hand politically will prosper.

More generally, banking interests tend to have a preference for very light regulation regardless of the implications for the rest of the economy. Their influence can have quite a corrupting effect on politics and institutions when it goes unchallenged by others. Indeed, the mortal blow to the "collateral benefits" argument was struck by the subprime mortgage meltdown, which demonstrated finance's remarkable ability to undermine governance—and to do so in the richest and oldest democracy in the world. In its wake, it would be very difficult to argue that banking interests contribute to better institutions.

The Seductions of Financial Innovation

In the aftermath of the subprime mortgage meltdown no one has to break a sweat to be a finance skeptic. But we should give hedgehog economists their due. To most of us, their narrative on the financial innovation that led to the crisis seemed quite compelling when we first heard it.

Everyone wanted credit markets to serve the cause of home ownership, so we started by introducing real competition into the mortgage lending business. We allowed non-banks to make home loans and let them offer creative, more affordable mortgages to prospective homeowners who were not well served by conventional lenders. Then we enabled these loans to be pooled and packaged into securities that could be sold to investors, which should have reduced risk in the process. We then divvied up the stream of payments on these home loans into bond tranches of varying risk, compensating holders of the riskier tranches with higher interest rates. We then asked credit rating agencies to certify that the less risky of these mortgage-backed securities were safe enough for pension funds and insurance companies to invest in. And just in case anyone was still nervous, we created derivatives that allowed investors to purchase insurance against default by issuers of those securities.

If we had wanted to showcase the benefits of financial innovation, we could not have devised a better set of arrangements. Thanks to them, millions of poorer and hitherto excluded families were made homeowners, investors made high returns, and financial intermediaries pocketed the fees and commissions. It might have worked like a dream—and until the crisis struck, many financiers, economists, and policy makers thought that it did. The narrative they all relied on was appealing. Financial innovation can allow people to access credit in ways they could not before by pooling risk and passing it on to those in the best position to bear it. If some people and institutions make mistakes and get overstretched in the process, they will pay the price for it. Financial markets will police and discipline themselves. Who can be against all this?

The crisis that engulfed financial markets in 2007 buried Wall Street and humbled the United States. The gigantic multi-trillion-dollar bailout of troubled financial institutions which the U.S. Treasury and Federal Reserve had to mount makes emerging market crises look like footnotes by comparison. And the benefits of financial innovation? They were hard to see amidst the rubble. As Paul Volcker would say afterwards in all seriousness, the automated teller machine had brought far more gains to most people than any asset-backed bond.[19] Or as Ben Bernanke put it, much more diplomatically, "One would be forgiven for concluding that the assumed benefits of financial innovation are not all they were cracked up to be."[20]

Where exactly did it all go wrong? The subprime mortgage crisis demonstrated once again how difficult it is to tame finance, an industry which is both the lifeline of all modern economies and the gravest threat to their stability. This is not news to emerging market economies. But in advanced economies, the challenge was obscured by a half century lull of financial stability. Before the Great Depression, the United States had been hit by major banking crises every fifteen or twenty years or so. Nothing comparable took place in the subsequent fifty years until the savings and loan crisis of the 1980s.[21]

This era of financial stability owed its existence to an uneasy accommodation between Main Street and Wall Street—between the real and financial sectors—following long centuries of experimentation. The quid pro quo took a simple form: regulation in exchange for freedom to operate. Governments brought commercial banks under a heavy dose of prudential regulation in return for providing public deposit insurance and lender-of-last-resort functions. And equity markets were encumbered with extensive disclosure and transparency requirements before they could develop.

The financial deregulation of the 1980s upended the bargain and ushered us into new, uncharted territory. Advocates of liberalization argued that supervision and regulation would hinder financial innovation, and in any case government agencies could not possibly keep up with the technological changes. Self-regulation was the way to go. A multitude of new financial instruments emerged, with strange acronyms and risk characteristics about which even the most sophisticated market players were ultimately clueless.

Financial globalization greatly intensified the fragility of the newly deregulated system. It enabled banks, firms, and governments to greatly boost their short-term borrowings, increasing leverage throughout the system. It also created much stronger contagion across national borders, as financial difficulties in one country would now quickly contaminate the balance sheets of banks in others. Prior to the late 1980s, the United States had been practically self-sufficient in credit. U.S. banks borrowed from other countries, but this was offset by long-term lending abroad in the form of direct investment, and the two sides of the ledger balanced. Later on, foreign borrowing would finance more than half of credit expansion at home.[22] An increase in Asian saving rates in the late 1990s—itself a response to Asia's own financial crisis a decade earlier—made a particular contribution. It drove down real interest rates in the United States and Europe and sparked a credit boom, inducing banks to go on a wild goose chase for yield and inflate their balance sheets.

Free capital mobility ensured that investors in Europe and elsewhere ended up sitting on a pile of toxic mortgage assets exported from the United States. Whole countries such as Iceland turned into hedge funds, leveraging themselves to the hilt in international financial markets in order to exploit small differentials in margins. Calls for increased regulation of finance were rebuffed by pointing out that banks would simply get up and move to less regulated jurisdictions.[23]

The immediate causes of the financial crisis of 2008 are easy to identify in hindsight: mortgage lenders (and borrowers) who assumed housing prices would keep rising, a housing bubble stoked by a global saving glut and the reluctance of Alan Greenspan's Federal Reserve to deflate it, financial institutions addicted to excessive leverage, credit rating agencies that fell asleep on the job, and of course policy makers who failed to get their act together in time as the first signs of the crisis began to appear. Without these regulatory failings, the glut in global finance would not have proved dangerous; after all, low interest rates are a *good* thing insofar as they enable higher investment. And without the global commingling of banks' balance sheets, the consequences of inadequate regulation would not have been as damaging; bank failures would have remained local and their effects contained.

A deeper problem will need to be addressed in the long term: deregulation and the pursuit of hyperglobalization have allowed a huge chasm to develop between the reach of financial markets and the scope of their governance. Domestically, large reservoirs of systemic risk untouched by regulation and supervision have been created. Internationally, the result has been fickle, volatile, and crisis-prone capital flows: abundant when they are least needed and nowhere to be seen where they could be doing some good. Almost all observers agree that the entire regulatory system needs to be rethought, both domestically and internationally.

But the very idea that we could erect a perfect system of global regulation for international financial flows is itself a fairy tale. A fox understands that markets and regulations are both condemned to remain imperfect. The systems we devise must anticipate both sets of weaknesses. It will take lots of practice and experimentation to get the balance right. It may be hard to say, "Thanks, but no thanks," to the siren song of financial liberalization and innovation, but in a world of imperfect regulation and divided sovereignty, that will often be the only safe option.

Our international financial architecture will have to accommodate countries that want tighter controls on finance as well as those with more relaxed attitudes toward financial innovation. That means leaving room for capital controls and financial transaction taxes—imposed by national policy makers—in addition to improved international regulatory standards designed, among other things, to penalize excessive leverage. We cannot return to the Bretton Woods regime, but we can still learn a lot from that experience. The compromise that energized the world economy in the aftermath of World War II will need to be refashioned for a world that has changed much in the interim.

It's the Economists, Stupid!

Ask populists why the finance industry went unchecked and was allowed to wreak such havoc, and you will likely hear a story about political power. The industry has become so powerful in the United States, the argument will go, that it has turned the country into a banana republic where politicians are beholden to Wall Street's interests. In the aftermath of the subprime crisis an unlikely group of allies joined these populists: mainstream economists. The most powerful salvo was fired by Simon Johnson, an economist with solid establishment credentials, in a strongly worded piece in the May 2009 issue of *The Atlantic*. Johnson had been the chief economist of the IMF in the run-up to the crisis, which gave his words added credibility.

Johnson laid the blame for the crisis squarely on Russian- and Asian-style cronyism in the United States. Wall Street had become so powerful that it got whatever it wanted out of Washington. Lax regulation, the promotion of imprudent levels of home ownership, low interest rates, the fragile U.S.-China financial relationship—everything that had precipitated the crisis had been promoted by the financial industry. Banks may not have guns and armies at their disposal, Johnson argued, but they had other means that were equally effective: campaign contributions, the revolving door between Wall Street and Washington, and an ability to foster a belief system supportive of their interests. "A whole generation of policy makers has been mesmerized by Wall Street," he wrote.

The result was "a river of deregulatory policies that is, in hindsight, astonishing." Johnson listed among these the free movement of capital across borders, the repeal of regulations separating commercial and investment banking, the major increases in the leverage allowed to investment banks, and many others.[24]

It was hard to disagree with the view that the banking industry had exerted a generally malign influence on the direction of economic policy, but I thought Johnson's article paid too little attention to the role of economists and their ideas in erecting the belief system that had produced the "river of deregulatory policies" Johnson complained about. By placing the blame on the power of the finance industry, his article seemed to exonerate economists. Most perplexing of all, Johnson himself had been an active supporter of financial liberalization in the global economy and had remained ambivalent about the value of tightening regulations until late in 2007.[25] Nothing that capital market skeptics were recommending prior to the crisis was as radical as the solution that Johnson would eventually adopt in his *Atlantic* piece, which consisted of deep surgery to cut banks down to size.

In a subsequent interview, Johnson would clarify when and how his change of heart took place. He recalled how during his early IMF days he would happily sign off on reports recommending financial liberalization to developing countries. "If you have strong institutions and a well-run regulatory structure, you can and should move towards capital market liberalization," he thought at the time. His epiphany came apparently one evening in September 2008 at the height of the financial crisis. Now, he said, he would no longer condone financial liberalization so easily. "We should go back and look at everything," he added, "and wonder about if anybody has the regulatory structures able to withstand what happens when you liberalize."[26] Mugged by reality, Johnson had turned into a fox.

Johnson should be admired for being so upfront about his conversion. In his new role, he has become one of our most clearsighted voices on the dangers of financial excess. At the same time, he is himself a strong reason to believe that his *Atlantic* argument was incomplete. No one can doubt that banks became politically powerful in the United States, but in getting policy makers to do their bidding they received immense help from economists. The economists' narrative gave intellectual cover to freeing up finance and convinced politicians that what was good for Wall Street was also good for Main Street. Beyond the United States, economists sparked a *global* push for financial liberalization, as we have seen. The French Socialists embraced financial deregulation not because of Wall Street's influence but because their own technocrats had no other alternatives to offer. The IMF's push for free capital flows was supported by the economics profession's best minds.

Simon Johnson and other economists who had influence and held policy positions actively encouraged the process. I find it difficult to believe that they were the hired guns of the banking industry. If the IMF's chief economist was complacent about the risks of financial liberalization, it wasn't because he was in the pocket of the industry. I'd rather believe Johnson's own story; his views changed because his understanding of the facts changed. Economists converged on a particular (and misleading) story about how financial markets worked and they oversold it to policy makers. The ideas of economists and the interests of Wall Street complemented each other.[27]

Why Economists Get It Wrong

A common complaint against economists is that they have a single, uniform model of the economy that relies on narrow and unrealistic assumptions. This misses the true source of the problem. As we have seen, Keynes, Tobin, and other economists who preferred restraints on global finance had models in mind that were quite different from those that animated finance enthusiasts. When an economist like Simon Johnson changes his model, it doesn't make him less of an economist. Professional training as an economist requires acquiring familiarity with an entire repertory of diverse models, each of which produces different results. Economists recognize the complexity of the world, which is why they have so many models of it. The true motto of an economist is, "Tell me your assumptions, and I will tell you how markets will work."

How then do economists make policy recommendations? The applied economist's *craft* hinges on striking the right balance between realism and tractability: picking assumptions so as to do the least amount of damage to the underlying reality while still being able to say something meaningful about the consequences of different policies. Models become useful when applied judiciously and in the relevant context. It is in practicing this craft that economists have frequently gone wrong. The hedgehogs among them have fallen into the trap of putting too much emphasis on a single model, at the expense of the rest. By displaying excessive confidence and downplaying the risks of misdiagnosis ("What if we have the wrong model?"), they have often led themselves and policy makers astray.

There are good sociological reasons why academic economics follows fashion and fads. New models and ideas naturally take economics departments by storm and drive scholarly research in one direction and then another. But the "science" of economic policy is not like physics, where each generation of ideas successively displaces the previous generation's. At best, we learn how to tackle the complexities of the world a bit better with each new wave of research.

The new thinking that developed after the 1970s and that underlay financial deregulation did not make the insights of Keynes and Tobin any less relevant. The "rational expectations" revolution, which took as its premise that individuals do not make systematic prediction errors about the future course of the economy, gave us a better appreciation of the role that anticipatory, forward-looking behavior by firms, workers, and consumers plays in shaping economic outcomes. The "efficient market hypothesis," built on the joint supposition of rational expectations *and* frictionless markets, taught us about the good that financial markets can do in the absence of transaction costs. These ideas made useful contributions to economics and to economic policy. But they did not upend everything we already knew. They simply gave us additional tools with which we could anticipate the economic consequences of different circumstances.

An honest practitioner of academic economics should respond with a blank stare when asked what the implications of his work are for policy. "That depends on so many other things," would be the appropriate answer. Frustrating perhaps for the student or the journalist, but correct nevertheless. When economists mistake academic fashions for the real thing, they do considerable damage. When the hedgehogs' highly stylized models become the basis for one grand narrative, the world needs to run for cover.

The antidote to these tendencies requires us to maintain a healthy skepticism toward the reigning economic fad of the day, to keep history's lessons alive, and to rely on local and experiential knowledge in addition to economic theory. The world is better served by syncretic economists and policy makers who can hold multiple ideas in their heads than by "one-handed" economists who promote one big idea regardless of context.[28]

Poor Countries in a Rich World

I n the first lecture I give them, I confront my economic development students at Harvard with the following teaser: Would you rather be rich in a poor country or poor in a rich country?

The question typically leads at first to a lot of nervous shuffling in the seats and puzzled looks. So I clarify the question. I ask them to consider only their own consumption and not worry about the well-being of others in the society they choose. I then spell out what I mean by "rich" and "poor." I tell them that they should think of a rich person as someone in the top 10 percent of a country's income distribution while a poor person is in the bottom 10 percent. Similarly, a rich country is in the top decile of all countries ranked by average income per person while a poor country is in the bottom decile of that list. Now, I say, you are ready to answer the question. Which would you choose?

The students are graduate students and have been to developing countries, so they have all seen the flashy cars the wealthy drive and the mansions where they live. Most have little hesitation in responding that they'd rather be rich in a poor country.

That is the wrong answer. The correct answer is "Poor in a rich country"—and it's not even close. The average poor person in a rich country, according to my parameters, earns *three times more* than the average rich person in the poor country ($9,400 versus $3,000, adjusted for differences in purchasing power across countries).[1] Disparities in other aspects of well-being, such as infant mortality, go the same way too. The poor in a rich country have it much, much better than the rich in the poor country.

Students get it wrong because they don't realize what a minute share of society those BMW-driving superrich represent—no larger perhaps than one hundredth of 1 percent of the total population. When we expand the numbers to cover the full top 10 percent of a typical poor country, we have come down to income levels that are a fraction of what most poor people in rich countries make. It is an easy mistake to make. I once had one of the world's foremost experts on economic development in the audience when I asked the question, and he gave the wrong answer too!

That it is far better to be poor in a rich country than rich in a poor country tells us something fundamental about today's global economy. Disparities in income (as well as health and other indicators of well-being) are much larger across nations than they are within nations. The country you are born in largely determines your life possibilities.

It wasn't always so. At the onset of the Industrial Revolution, the gap between the richest and poorest regions of the world was of the order of 2:1. Today, the same ratio stands at 20:1.[2] The gap between the richest and poorest *country* has risen to about 80:1. Over time, some parts of the world—Western Europe, America, and later East Asia—took off while the rest grew very slowly, when at all, and often lost ground after bursts of expansion. In the words of my Harvard colleague, Lant Pritchett, the global economy experienced "divergence, big time."[3]

By the middle of the twentieth century the world was divided between a small group of wealthy countries and a large number of others struggling under varying degrees of poverty. The next six decades witnessed extraordinary growth on a global scale. But except for a handful of countries, mostly in Asia, few poor countries were able to close the gap between them and the advanced countries in a sustained manner. Luckily, the successful countries (notably China) were home to hundreds of millions of very poor people, so the development record of the last few decades is in fact quite impressive. Other countries were unable to match this performance, ensuring that the chasm between rich and poor nations would widen to unprecedented depths.

Why so much poverty amidst plenty? What role did globalization play in the "great divergence"? What can countries do to redress poverty? These are the questions that this and the next chapter address.

Globalization and the Great Divergence

The proximate cause of poverty is low productivity. Poor people are poor because their labor enables them to produce too little to adequately feed and house themselves, let alone provide for other needs such as health and education. Low productivity in turn has diverse and multiple causes. It may be the result of lack of credit, which prevents producers from making the investments that would increase their output and hence incomes. It may be result of lack of access to new and better technologies. It may be due to lack of skills, knowledge, or job opportunities. It may be the consequence of small market size, which depresses the profitability of acquiring new equipment and technologies. Or it may be due to exploitative elites, typically in cahoots with the government, who block any improvement in economic conditions that would threaten their power. The ultimate reasons for poverty can be traced to one or more of these causes.

Globalization promises to give everyone access to markets, capital, and technology, and foster good governance. In other words, globalization has the potential to remove all of the deficiencies that create and sustain poverty. As such, globalization ought to be a powerful engine for economic catch-up in the lagging regions of the world. And yet the last two centuries of globalization have witnessed massive economic divergence on a global scale. How is that possible?

This question has preoccupied economists and policy makers for a very long time. The answers they have produced coalesce around two opposing narratives. One says the problem is "too little globalization," while the other blames "too much globalization." At different times in history, each of these narratives has found favor and they have experienced varying appeal in different parts of the world. But the debate on globalization and development ultimately always comes back to the conundrum framed by these competing narratives: If we want to increase our economic growth, should we throw ourselves open to the forces emanating from the world economy, or protect ourselves from them?

Unfortunately, neither of these two narratives offers much help in explaining why some countries have done better than others, and therefore neither is a very good guide for policy. The truth lies in an uncomfortable place, the middle. Globalization does greatly enhance the potential for economic growth, but the best way to take advantage of it is not to remove the transaction costs that block full integration to the maximum extent possible. A "thin" version of globalization, à la Bretton Woods, seems to work best. Consider a metaphor I once heard from a student from China (appropriately enough): keep the windows open, but don't forget the mosquito screen. This way you get the fresh air but you also keep the bugs away.

Globalization's Uneven Impact During the Nineteenth Century

The Industrial Revolution spread from England to the European Continent and to some of the lands of recent settlement (North America, Australia, and New Zealand), but did not go much further. The world economy soon split between an increasingly industrial core and a largely raw materials–producing periphery. Globalization played the parts of both Dr. Jekyll and Mr. Hyde in this. It enabled new technologies to disseminate in areas with the requisite preconditions, but also entrenched and accentuated a long-term division between the core and the periphery.

Those parts of the world which proved receptive to the forces of the Industrial Revolution shared two advantages. They had a large enough stock of relatively educated and skilled workers that could fill up and run the new factories. They also had sufficiently good institutions—well-functioning legal systems, stable politics, and restraints on expropriations by the state—to generate incentives for private investment and market expansion. With these pre-conditions, much of Continental Europe was ready to absorb the new production techniques developed and applied in Britain. Chalk up one for globalization.

Elsewhere, industrialization depended on "importing" skills and institutions. Intercontinental labor mobility was a tremendous advantage here. Where Europeans settled en masse, they brought with them both the skills and the drive for more representative, market-friendly institutions that would promote economic activity alongside their interests. The consequences were disastrous for the native populations, who perished in large numbers courtesy of European aggression and germs. But the regions of the world that the economic historian Angus Maddison has called "Western offshoots"[4]—the United States, Canada, Australia, and New Zealand—were able to acquire the necessary prerequisites thanks to large immigrations. Supported also by sizable capital flows from Europe, these economies would eventually become part of the industrial "core." Chalk up two for globalization.

Colonization's impact on other parts of the world was quite different. When Europeans encountered inhospitable conditions that precluded their settlement in large numbers or began to exploit natural resources that required armies of manual workers, they set up institutions that were quite different from those in the Western offshoots. These purely "extractive" institutions were designed to get the raw materials to the core as cheaply as possible. They entailed vast inequalities in wealth and power, with a narrow elite, typically white and European, dominating a vast number of natives or slaves. Colonies built on the extractive model did little to protect general property rights, support market development, or stimulate other kinds of economic activity. The plantation-based economies in the Caribbean and the mineral economies of Africa were typical examples. Studies by economists and economic historians have established that this early experience with institutional development—or lack thereof—has produced a debilitating effect on economies in Africa and Latin America that is still felt today.[5] Chalk up one *against* globalization.

Those regions of the world that avoided European colonization weren't exactly shielded from the adverse effects of globalization. The free trade treaties that European powers imposed on peripheral regions froze their initial comparative advantage in raw materials. Low tariffs combined with the decline in shipping costs exposed their textile and other nascent industrial activities to competition from Britain and decimated them. In the Ottoman Empire, for example, textile imports shot up to capture nearly 75 percent of the home market by the 1870s, up from a mere 3 percent in the 1820s.[6]

Once the lines were clearly drawn between industrializing and commodity-producing countries, there were strong economic dynamics that reinforced the demarcation. Globalization played a crucial role here by deepening the international division of labor. Commodity-based economies faced little incentive or opportunity to diversify. As transport costs fell during the nineteenth century and growth in the industrial core fed demand, these economies experienced commodity booms. This was very good for the small number of people who reaped the windfall from the mines and plantations that produced such commodities, but not very good for manufacturing industries that were squeezed as a result.[7] International trade worked just as in textbook models: profits rose in economic activities in which countries had comparative advantage, but fell elsewhere.

International trade induced industrial countries to keep investing in skills, technology, and other drivers of economic growth. It also encouraged families to have fewer, better-educated children, in light of the high returns to skills that modern manufacturing industries brought. These effects were reversed in the developing countries of the periphery. Specialization in primary commodities did not encourage skill accumulation and delayed the reduction in fertility and population growth. Birth rates remained high in the developing world well into the twentieth century, unlike the industrialized countries, which experienced sharp declines in fertility toward the end of the nineteenth century. In the words of the economists Oded Galor and Andrew Mountford, commodity-exporting countries gave up productivity in exchange for population.[8]

The countries of the periphery not only failed to industrialize, they actually lost whatever industry they had. They *deindustrialized*. At the dawn of the Industrial Revolution, Asia and Latin America had levels of industrial activity roughly similar to Europe's. Europe experienced a nearly sixfold increase in these levels between 1750 and 1913. Asia and Latin America meanwhile witnessed a decline to less than a third of their initial level.[9] In 1900, developing nations produced only about half the quantity of manufactured goods that they did in 1830. As the economic historian Paul Bairoch, the source of these estimates, writes: "There cannot be any question but that the cause of de-industrialization in the Third World lay in the massive influx of European manufactured goods, especially textiles, on the markets of these countries."[10] Chalk up two against globalization.

The pre-1914 international division of labor did produce wealth in commodity-exporting countries. But just as in today's oil-rich economies, the wealth was highly concentrated and ended up sti-fling institutional and productive development. Where independence had not yet arrived, it accrued to the metropolitan powers. Where it had, it went to a narrow group of domestic elites.

Argentina, to take the leading example, became one of the world's richest economies on the back of the produce of its fertile lowlands, its *pampas*. With its chic boulevards, polo clubs, grand opera house, Eton-educated children, and refined aristocracy, Buenos Aires could outdo any of the major European capitals. This wealth came at the expense of crippling future economic development. Exports of grains and livestock along with large infusions of British capital mainly benefited large landowners who had little interest in diversifying the economy or building better market-supporting institutions. The contrast with the United States is instructive. There Northern industrialists and Western farmers gained the upper hand over Southern plantation owners and fostered broader-based institutions and industrialization, on the back of high import tariffs.[11]

The Japanese Exception

So geography and natural endowments largely determined nations' economic fates under the first era of globalization. One major exception to this rule would ultimately become an inspiration to all commodity-dependent countries intent on breaking the curse. The exception was Japan, the only non-Western society to industrialize before 1914.

Japan had many of the features of the economies of the periphery. It exported primarily raw materials—raw silk, yarn, tea, fish—in exchange for manufactures, and this trade had boomed in the aftermath of the opening to free trade imposed by Commodore Perry in 1854. Left to its own devices, the economy would have likely followed the same path as so many others in the periphery. But Japan had an indigenous group of well-educated and patriotic businessmen and merchants, and even more important, a government, following the Meiji Restoration of 1868, that was single-mindedly focused on economic (and political) modernization. The government was little moved with the laissez-faire ideas prevailing among Western policy elites at the time. In a document that could be called the world's first development plan, Japanese officials made clear that the state had a significant role to play in developing the economy, even though its actions "might interfere with individual freedom and with the gains of speculators."[12]

Many of the reforms introduced by the Meiji bureaucrats were aimed at creating the infrastructure of a modern national economy: a unified currency, railroads, public education, banking laws, and other legislation. Considerable effort also went into what today would be called "industrial policy"—state initiatives targeted at promoting new industries. The Japanese government built and ran state-owned plants in a wide range of industries, including cotton textiles and shipbuilding. Even though many of these enterprises ended as failures, they produced important demonstration effects and trained many skilled artisans and managers who would subsequently ply their trade in private establishments. These enterprises were eventually privatized, enabling the private sector to build on the foundations established by the state. The government also paid to employ foreign technicians and technology in manufacturing industries and it financed training abroad for Japanese students. In addition, as Japan regained tariff autonomy from international treaties, the government raised import tariffs on many industrial products to encourage domestic production. These efforts paid off most remarkably in cotton textiles, where Japan established by 1914 a world-class industry that was able to displace British exports not just from the Japanese markets but from neighboring Asian markets as well.[13]

Japan's militarist and expansionist policies in the run-up to World War II tarred these accomplishments, but its achievements on the economic front demonstrated that an alternative path was available. It was possible to steer an economy away from its natural specialization in raw materials. Economic growth was achievable—even if a country started at the wrong end of the international division of labor—if you combined the efforts of a determined government with the energies of a vibrant private sector. The key was not more or less globalization, but just the right kind of globalization.

These lessons would be relearned in the decades that followed World War II.

The East Asian "Miracle"

One hundred years after the Meiji bureaucrats produced their first development plan, Japan was a major economic power with significant say in global institutions.[14] It had become the second largest shareholder in the World Bank, forcing the institution's management to pay more attention to its views. Masaki Shiratori, Japan's executive director at the World Bank, one of twenty-four country representatives who oversee the institution's operations, was growing increasingly uncomfortable with the policy advice the Bank gave to developing nations. He and his colleagues in Japan's powerful Ministry of Finance felt that this advice relied too much on the American preference for a free market model and underplayed the role of the state in promoting industrialization and development. In their view, the World Bank did not pay enough attention to the lessons of Japan's own development experience.[15]

The Japanese government pushed the Bank to prepare a study of the "Asian miracle," agreeing also to pay for the bulk of it. The miracle in question referred not only to Japan's experience but also to that of seven other East and Southeast Asian economies that had grown very rapidly since the early 1960s—South Korea,

Taiwan, Hong Kong, Singapore, Malaysia, Thailand, and Indonesia. All of these countries had benefited enormously from exports, and hence from globalization. But none, with the exception of the British colony of Hong Kong, came even close to being free market economies. The state had played an important guiding and coordinating role in all of them.

The World Bank's report was eventually released in 1993 with the title *The East Asian Miracle: Economic Growth and Public Policy.* Produced by a large team of economists and consultants, and encompassing nearly 400 pages of text, charts, and statistical analysis along with more than 40 background studies, it could lay claim to being the most authoritative analysis of the subject. But more than anything else, the report demonstrated the World Bank's inability to fashion a coherent account of how Asian nations had managed to grow so rapidly. There was too much state intervention in Asia for it not to have had some beneficial effect, yet the Bank did not want to suggest that state intervention works. Fixated on an absolute distinction between markets and state intervention, the Bank could not see how the two could mutually reinforce each other. The resulting report proceeded in a schizophrenic manner and presented a deeply contradictory argument.

The analysis of financial markets—drafted by Joe Stiglitz, well known for his skeptical views on financial liberalization—painted a positive picture of the Japanese and South Korean governments' controls: ceilings on interest rates, credit subsidies targeted at new industries, and restrictions on international capital flows. This part of the report accepted the Japanese argument that government-supported loans to industry had played a positive role in accelerating industrialization and growth. Yet in other chapters the line was that industrial policies—the promotion of specific industries through government inducements—had not worked and should not be advocated for other developing nations. Depending on which chapters you read, you would have come away with a very different view as to whether Asian countries had succeeded because of their governments' efforts to promote new industries or despite these efforts.[16]

Asia's economic experience violates stereotypes and yet offers something for everyone. In effect, it acts as a reflecting pool for the biases of the observer. If you think unleashing markets is the best way to foster economic development, you will find plenty of evidence for that. If you think markets need the firm commanding hand of the government, well, there is much evidence for that, too. Globalization as an engine for growth? East Asian countries are a case in point. Globalization needs to be tamed? Ditto. However, if you leave aside these stale arguments and listen to the real message that emanates from the success of the region, you find that what works is a combination of states and markets. Globalization is a tremendously positive force, but only if you are able to domesticate it to work for you rather than against you.

Consider two of the most successful countries of the region: South Korea and Taiwan. In the late 1950s, neither of these economies was much richer than the countries of sub-Saharan Africa. South Korea was mired in political instability and had virtually no industry, having lost whatever it had to the more developed North Korea. Taiwan too was a predominantly agricultural economy, with sugar and rice as its main exports. The transformation that the two economies began to experience in the early 1960s placed them on a path that would turn them into major industrial powers.

Their strategies in many ways mirrored Japan's. They required first a government that was single-mindedly focused on economic growth. Prior land reform in both countries had established some space for governments to act independently from landed elites. Both countries also possessed an overarching geopolitical motive. South Korea needed to grow so it could counter any possible threats from North Korea. Taiwan, having given up on the idea of reconquest of mainland China, wanted to forestall any possible challenge from the Communists. In many parts of the world, regional hostilities become an excuse for building a strong state at the expense of the economy; think, for example, of the Middle East. But the governments in South Korea and Taiwan understood that achieving their political and military goals required rapid economic growth as well. In particular, developing industrial capabilities and a strong manufactured exports base became the predominant objective of both governments' policies.

This objective was accomplished by unleashing the energies of private business. Even though both governments invested heavily in public enterprises during the 1960s, this investment was designed to facilitate private enterprise—by providing cheap inputs, for example—and not to supplant it. One plank of the strategy called for removing the obstacles to private investment that stifled many other low-income countries: excessive taxation, red tape and bureaucratic corruption, inadequate infrastructure, high inflation. These were improvements in what today would be called "investment climate."

Equally important were interventionist policies—government incentives designed to stimulate investments in modern manufactures. Both governments designated such industries as "priority sectors" and provided businesses with generous subsidies. In South Korea, these took the form largely of subsidized loans administered through the banking sector. In Taiwan, they came in the form of tax incentives for investments in designated sectors. In both countries, bureaucrats often played the role of midwife to new industries: they coordinated private firms' investments, supplied the inputs, twisted arms when needed, and provided sweeteners when necessary. Even though they removed some of the most egregious import restrictions, neither country exposed its nascent industries to much import competition until well into the 1980s. The domestic market was protected to enable the "infant" industries to make sufficient profits. South Korea also discouraged multinational enterprises from coming in, which allowed maximum room for domestic firms to engage in technological learning.

While they enjoyed protection from international competition, these infant industries were goaded to export from day one. This was achieved by a combination of explicit export subsidies and intense pressure from bureaucrats to ensure export targets were met. In effect, private businesses were offered a quid pro quo: they would be the beneficiary of state largesse, but only so long as they exported, and did so in increasing amounts. If gaining a beach-head in international markets required loss-making prices early on, these could be recouped by the subsidies and profits on the home market. But, importantly, these policies gave private firms a strong incentive to improve their productivity so they could hold their own against established competitors abroad.[17]

We can see how this growth strategy offered something to sat-isfy all tastes. A macroeconomist could walk away with the conclu-sion that macroeconomic stability in the form of low inflation held the key. A labor economist could point to the importance of a rela-tively well educated labor force. A trade economist would note the high rates of protection, but take comfort from the fact that their trade-inhibiting effects were nullified by export subsidies that pushed the other way. A political economist would emphasize the role of the strong state and its "autonomy" from elites. The World Bank could emphasize the leading role that private investment and exports played. An interventionist could emphasize the heavy hand of the state in guiding private investment.

They would all be missing the big picture. Economic growth requires a pragmatic government willing to do whatever it takes to energize the private sector. It requires using markets and global-ization strategically to diversify the domestic economy away from natural resources. The specific tools and instruments needed to achieve this can vary and will depend heavily on the context. Specific recipes for success do not travel well. It is the broad vision behind them that needs emulation.

These lessons were put to good use in the most astounding development success the world has ever known.

Marching to Its Own Drum: China and Globalization

The feat that China's economy pulled off would have been difficult to imagine had it not happened in front of our eyes. Since 1978, income per capita in China has grown at an average rate of 8.3 percent per annum—a rate that implies a doubling of incomes every nine years. Thanks to this rapid economic growth, half a billion people were lifted out of extreme poverty.[18] During the same period China transformed itself from near autarky to the most feared competitor on world markets. That this happened in a country with a complete lack of private property rights (until recently) and run by the Communist Party only deepens the mystery.

China's experience offers compelling evidence that globalization can be a great boon for poor nations. Yet it also presents the strongest argument against the reigning orthodoxy in globalization—emphasizing financial globalization and deep integration through the WTO. China's ability to shield itself from the global economy proved critical to its efforts to build a modern industrial base, which would be leveraged in turn through world markets.

China's big break came when Deng Xiaoping and other post-Mao leaders decided to trust markets instead of central planning. But their real genius lay in their recognition that the market-supporting institutions they built, most of which were sorely lacking at the time, would have to possess distinctly Chinese characteristics. Western economists would propose European- or American-style regulations to enforce contracts, protect property rights, liberalize markets, and free up trade. These ideas faced huge practical difficulties and moreover violated, in many cases, official Party doctrine (as in the case of private property). Instead, the Chinese leaders pragmatically experimented with alternative institutional arrangements. No fewer than half of all national regulations in China in the early to mid-1980s had explicitly experimental status.[19] Through experimentation, China's policy makers sought to discover solutions that would overcome their constraints and be more suited to local conditions. China's institutional innovations proved remarkably successful. They effectively turned institutional weakness into an advantage.

China's economy was predominantly rural in 1978. A key problem Deng faced early on was how to energize farmers in an environment where prices and quantities were still determined by central planning. The state fixed all the prices and demanded that peasants deliver mandated quantities of grains to the government in accordance with the plan. Farmers were organized into communes and prohibited from selling any of their produce in private markets. The food that the state extracted from the countryside in this fashion was then rationed to workers in urban areas. The system ensured that workers would be fed at no cost to the government budget. The downside was that farmers had little incentive to increase production or make more efficient use of the land.

A Western-trained economist would have recommended abolishing the plan and removing all price controls. Yet without the quotas, urban workers would be deprived of their cheap rations and the government of an important source of revenue. There would be masses of disgruntled workers in the cities and the government would have to resort to printing money, risking hyperinflation. The Chinese solution to this conundrum was to graft a market system *on top* of the plan. Communes were abolished and family farming restored; but land remained state property. Obligatory grain deliveries at controlled prices were also kept in place; but once farmers had fulfilled their state quota, they were now free to sell their surplus at market-determined prices. This dual-track regime gave farmers market-based incentives and yet did not dispossess the state from its revenue or the urban workers from their cheap food.[20] Agricultural productivity rose sharply, setting off the first phase of China's post-1978 growth.

Another problem was how to provide a semblance of property rights when the state remained the ultimate owner of all property. Privatization would have been the conventional route, but it was ruled out by the Chinese Communist Party's ideology. Once again, it was an innovation that came to the rescue. Township and village enterprises (TVEs) proved remarkably adept at stimulating domestic private investment. They were owned not by private entities or the central government, but by local governments (townships or villages). TVEs produced virtually the full gamut of products, everything from consumer goods to capital goods, and spearheaded Chinese economic growth from the mid-1980s until the mid-1990s.

The key to their success was that local governments were keen to ensure the prosperity of TVEs as their equity stake generated substantial income for them. Local authorities gave private entrepreneurs considerable freedom and also protected them from challenge—most critically from the local Party bosses themselves. This offered a better deal to the entrepreneurs than having formal private ownership rights and then hoping that local courts—weak and corruptible as they were—would enforce those rights in the face of disputes. Many a former Socialist economy has painfully discovered that property rights reform often flounders because domestic courts are too fragile to enforce the new rules. As the Berkeley economist Yingyi Qian emphasizes, property rights were effectively more secure when backed up by partnerships with the local government than they would have been under a standard regime of private property rights.[21]

China's strategy to open its economy to the world also diverged from received theory. The standard list of recommendations for countries pursuing this goal includes: dismantling quantitative restrictions on imports; reducing import tariffs and their dispersion; and making the currency convertible for trade transactions. Measured by these guidelines, China's policies suggest a country that messed up big time, not one that became a formidable competitive threat in world markets. In brief, China opened up very gradually, and significant reforms lagged behind growth (in exports and overall incomes) by at least a decade or more. While state trading monopolies were dismantled relatively early (starting in the late 1970s), what took their place was a complex and highly restrictive set of tariffs, non-tariff barriers, and licenses restricting imports. These were not substantially relaxed until the early 1990s.

The Chinese leadership resisted the conventional advice in opening their economy because removing barriers to trade would have forced many state enterprises to close without doing much to stimulate new investments in industrial activities. Employment and economic growth would have suffered, threatening social stability. The Chinese decided to experiment with alternative mechanisms that would not create too much pressure on existing industrial structures. In particular, they relied on Special Economic Zones (SEZs) to generate exports and attract foreign investment. Enterprises in these zones operated under different rules than those that applied in the rest of the country; they had access to better infrastructure and could import inputs duty-free. The SEZs generated incentives for export-oriented investments without pulling the rug from under state enterprises.

What fueled China's growth, along with these institutional innovations, was a dramatic productive transformation. The Chinese economy latched on to advanced, high-productivity products that no one would expect a poor, labor-abundant country like China to produce, let alone export. By the end of the 1990s, China's export portfolio resembled that of a country with an income-per-capita level at least *three times higher* than China's.[22]

This was the result not of natural, market-led processes but of a determined push by the Chinese government. Low labor costs did help China's export drive, but they don't tell the whole story. In areas such as consumer electronics and auto parts China made stupendous productivity gains, catching up with countries at much higher levels of income. Furthermore, China steadily moved away from being simply an assembler of components. Increasingly, production became integrated backwards and the supply chain moved from richer countries to China where the assembly was undertaken.

Foreign investors played a key role in the evolution of China's industries. They were the most productive among the firms, they were the source of technology, and they dominated exports. The SEZs where foreign producers could operate with good infrastructure and a minimum of hassles deserve considerable credit. But if China welcomed foreign companies, it always did so with the objective of fostering domestic capabilities.

The Chinese government used a number of policies to ensure that technology transfer would take place and strong domestic players would emerge. Early on, it relied predominantly on state-owned national champions. Later, the government used a variety of incentives and disincentives. In mobile phone and computer production, foreign investors were required to undertake joint ventures with domestic firms. In autos, the government required foreign car companies investing in the domestic market to achieve a relatively high level of Chinese content within a short period of time (typically 70 percent within three years).[23] This forced these companies to work closely with local suppliers to ensure that their technology and quality were up to par. Domestic markets were protected to attract investors seeking a large consumer base, in addition to those that looked for cost savings. Weak enforcement of intellectual protection laws enabled domestic producers to reverse engineer and imitate foreign technologies with little fear of prosecution. Cities and provinces were given substantial freedoms to fashion their own policies of stimulation and support, which led to the creation of industrial clusters in Shanghai, Shenzhen, Hangzhou, and elsewhere.[24]

Many of the Chinese companies created through government efforts failed. Accounts of industrial policy in China point to the low productivity and low-technology absorption of many state enterprises and to the lack of coordination (across national ministries as well as across different levels of government) that characterizes Chinese policies.[25] But as in Japan a century earlier, state-led efforts played an important role in training workers and managers and in creating demonstration effects. Would China have been able to produce a company like Lenovo, which became large and profitable enough to purchase IBM's PC unit in 2004, without state support and financial assistance?

Moreover, as in other areas of policy, government attitudes were pragmatic and open to trying new approaches when old ones failed. A well-known case involves the early development of the color TV industry, which consisted in the 1980s of more than one hundred companies operating at short production runs and high cost. By the early 1990s, the industry had been consolidated thanks to the efforts of local governments and national leadership, which forced mergers and joint ventures with foreign firms. This policy reversal led to the emergence in quick order of a profitable, export-oriented industry.[26]

Many of these early policies would have run afoul of WTO rules that ban export subsidies and prohibit discrimination in favor of domestic firms—if China had been a member of the organization. Chinese policy makers were not constrained by any external rules in their conduct of trade and industrial policies and could act freely to promote industrialization. By the time China did join the WTO in 2001, it had created a strong industrial base, much of which did not need protection or nurturing. China substantially reduced its tariffs in preparation for WTO membership, bringing them down from the high levels of the early 1990s (an average of around 40 percent) to single digits in 2001. Many other industrial policies were also phased out.

However, China was not yet ready to let the push and pull of global markets determine the fate of its industries. It began to rely increasingly on a competitive exchange rate to effectively subsidize these industries. By intervening in currency markets and keeping short-term capital flows out, the government prevented its currency (the renminbi) from appreciating, which would have been the natural consequence of China's rapid economic growth. Explicit industrial policies gave way to an implicit industrial policy conducted by way of currency policy. The renminbi has been undervalued by around 25 percent in recent years, implying an effective subsidy to export-oriented industries (and import-competing firms) of an equal magnitude.[27] Once again, China bent globalization's rules to its own requirements. Since floating currencies and free capital mobility would not have helped its economic development, China simply did without them. Its flouting of these "rules" would eventually become a serious source of conflict in its relationship with the United States. I will return to this conflict in chapter Twelve, as the growing role of China in the world economy renders its foreign economic policy one of the thorniest issues that the world will have to confront in years ahead.

In sum, Chinese policy makers maintained their maneuvering space and they exploited it skillfully. They gave markets and private incentives a much greater role, but did so in ways that were adapted to domestic economic realities and respected political and ideological constraints. The international rulebook was not suited to their needs, so their reforms necessarily took on unorthodox characteristics. They resisted international disciplines, and submitted to them only once their economy had become sufficiently strong. They would have found it very difficult to diversify out of agriculture and other traditional products otherwise. China (like

South Korea and Taiwan before it) played the globalization game by Bretton Woods rules rather than the post-1990 rules of deep integration.

The Diversification Imperative

You become what you produce. That is the inevitable fate of nations. Specialize in commodities and raw materials, and you will get stuck in the periphery of the world economy. You will remain hostage to fluctuations in world prices and suffer under the rule of a small group of domestic elites. If you can push your way into manufactures and other modern tradable products, you may pave a path toward convergence with the world's rich countries. You will have greater ability to withstand swings in world markets, and you will acquire the broad-based, representative institutions that a growing middle class demands instead of the repressive ones that elites need to hide behind.

Globalization accentuates the dilemma because it makes it easier for countries to fall into the commodities trap. The international division of labor makes it possible for you to produce little else besides commodities, if that is what you choose to do. You can always import the other stuff from the rich countries. At the same time, globalization also greatly increases the rewards of the alternative strategy, as the experiences of Japan, South Korea, Taiwan, and China amply show. A government committed to economic diversification and capable of energizing its private sector can spur growth rates that would have been unthinkable in a world untouched by globalization.

In principle, well-functioning markets—both domestic and global—should help countries move up the ladder from commodities to new industries without a push from the government. Many economists believe the transition doesn't need a helping hand beyond ensuring that markets do their job. But in practice there are too many things that can go wrong. Learning new technologies and investing in new products is a difficult process that has many built-in obstacles if a country is not already predisposed toward it.

In particular, industrialization requires the development of social capabilities that are subject to significant economic spillovers—adapting foreign technologies to local conditions, acquiring skills, producing specialized inputs for production, coordinating complementary investments in diverse areas. In all of these cases, social benefits exceed the gains captured by the relevant private actors alone, producing what economists call "positive externalities." Markets are not very good at providing signals beyond short-term private profitability. Left to their own devices, they undersupply the incentives needed for productive upgrading. That is why, in the words of the Harvard Business School innovation expert Josh Lerner, "virtually every hub of cutting-edge entrepreneurial activity in the world today had its origins in proactive government intervention."[28]

The benefits of globalization come to those who invest in domestic social capabilities. Those investments in turn require some degree of support for domestic firms—protective tariffs, subsidies, undervalued currencies, cheap funding, and other kinds of government assistance that increase the rewards for entering new lines of business without closing the economy to the outside world. If the rest of the world does not create high-productivity jobs for your workers, you have no choice but to create those jobs yourself. The deep integration model of globalization overlooks this imperative. By restricting in the name of freer trade the scope for industrial policies needed to restructure and diversify national economies, it undercuts globalization as a positive force for development.

It may seem like the ultimate paradox that reaping globalization's gains may require an increase rather than a decrease in international transaction costs, but the paradox is more apparent than real. A complicated world requires foxlike policies. There is no more contradiction here than there is when we mount a screen on an open window; in a perfect world there would be no mosquitoes and no need for a screen.

Why have not more countries followed the East Asian examples? Why has it proved so difficult to emulate their strategies? Why do scores of countries in Africa and elsewhere remain mired in poverty, unable to make the transition to modern industries and services? Unfortunately, many of these countries have governments with little interest in real development. These governments are unlikely to unleash economic changes that threaten their hold on power.

Politics is only part of the answer. We cannot understand the disappointments of the rest of the world without giving economists their due. Economists have been responsible for the narratives that interpret developmental success and failure, narratives which in turn have guided policy in many parts of the world. Economists have been the ultimate arbiters of how those narratives would be shaped, which would survive, and how they would spread. As we shall see in the next chapter, they have not always got it right.

8

Trade Fundamentalism in the Tropics

n March 1960, James Meade, a Cambridge don and future Nobel Prize winner for his research in international economics, traveled to the British colony of Mauritius with a small team of economists. The island was getting ready for independence, which it would acquire in 1968. The British fretted about the country's prospects under self-rule, shorn of support from London. Meade, a left-leaning economist and admirer of Keynes, had been invited by the island's British governor to survey the economy and make proposals for its future development.

Meade stood for a practical, commonsense brand of economics, and his eventual recommendations would reflect this pragmatism. However, three decades after his trip to Mauritius, development economics was transformed beyond recognition and became dominated by a vision that elevated free markets and free trade above all else. The central insights of Meade and his contemporaries— the need to tailor reforms to local circumstances and for proactive government policies to stimulate structural transformation—were shunted aside. It is only recently that these older insights have been resuscitated and are being reincorporated into thinking on development strategy. This chapter recounts this strange tale of the loss and (partial) recovery of common sense.

The Unmaking of a Malthusian Nightmare

An island off the coast of Africa, Mauritius lies about 560 miles east of Madagascar. Its people are a mix of descendants from Africa (Creoles), India (Indo-Mauritians), France (Franco-Mauritians), and China (Sino-Mauritians)—a combination of ethnicities, languages, and religions that could be described as either "lively" or "explosive" depending on which side of the bed one got up in the morning. At the time of Meade's visit, the country was exceedingly poor. The economy wholly depended on sugar cultivation, which employed more than a third of the labor force and generated the country's sole export.

Moreover, the island confronted the threat of a population explosion. Thanks largely to the elimination of malaria under colonial public health policies, the population growth rate had risen from around 0.5 percent per annum in the immediate aftermath of World War II to closer to 3 percent by the time of Meade's visit. The island's population was projected to rise from 600,000 to 3 million by the end of the twentieth century. "This," Meade wrote at the time, "is a truly terrifying prospect."[1]

The problem, as Meade saw, was that a growing population would put pressure on the limited arable land that was available and drive living standards down. Sugar and other agricultural products would never be able to absorb the growing workforce. Emigration was at best a partial solution, and domestic investment was limited by the small scale of domestic saving. The island's ethnic and social divisions made an already difficult problem almost insoluble. "It would be difficult with present attitudes in Mauritius," noted Meade, "to conceive of a man with business acumen (who happened to be Chinese) managing a firm for which a wealthy person (who happened to be Indian) had provided the capital to exploit an imaginative idea of an engineer (who happened to be of European extraction)."[2]

Though pessimistic, Meade did not give up. The solution was to create a large number of employment opportunities in labor-intensive light industries. One plank of his proposed strategy called for restraining wage increases, to ensure there was no disincentive to the establishment of such industries. The other advocated a concerted government effort to stimulate the creation of new industries. Since the island had few industries, they would need to be started from scratch, and that required an active government.

Meade recommended the formation of an Industrial Development Board which, in consultation with the private sector, would seek new investment opportunities and grant tax holidays and other incentives to firms with the greatest prospect for job creation. He advocated the creation of industrial estates with adequate infrastructure that would lease factories and workshops to manufacturers at low cost. Meade understood that Mauritian producers could overcome the limitations of the small home market by exporting to the world—just as the East Asian Tigers were beginning to do. But he thought that these "infant industries" would need to be nurtured until they could compete on their own. He recommended moderately high import tariffs that would protect nascent industries from foreign competition.

For Meade, the key to Mauritius' future lay in economic diversification and the growth of new industries. The island did not have to remain a mono-crop economy: it could move into manufactures, relieving the population pressure on land and setting the stage for future growth. He also knew that this transformation would not be automatic; it required the helping hand of the government. Market forces would need to be supplemented by government programs aimed at stimulating the new industries. Industrial policy had to be part of the development strategy.

Despite its inauspicious beginnings, Mauritius would turn out to be one of Africa's few success stories. In time, textiles and clothing replaced sugar as the island's main exports. A vibrant political democracy was able to contain the ethnic tensions simmering just

below the surface. And the nightmare of population explosion
never came to pass. Rapid economic growth not only created jobs,
it also fed into fertility declines. The island's population stood at
1.2 million by the year 2000, a fraction of the 3 million that Meade
had projected. The island became an upper-middle-income country, with an income level similar to that of Southeastern Europe.

The strategy that Meade devised had a lot to do with this success, although not all his recommendations were followed. In
particular, successive Mauritian governments found it difficult to
keep a lid on wages and instead chose to buy social peace through
generous social programs and nationwide wage bargains that
gave organized labor a strong voice at the negotiating table. But
Meade's proposals on industrial promotion effectively became
government policy over the subsequent decade. Domestic industry received significant incentives and trade protection, and by the
end of the 1960s a substantial group of light-manufacturing producers oriented toward the home market had been created. Starting in 1970, the government began to promote export-oriented
firms too, mainly in garments, under a very successful export-
processing zone (EPZ) scheme, using tax incentives, import-duty
exemptions, and weaker labor rules. Industrial activity was further
stimulated through currency devaluations in the 1980s.

These two segments of industry—one oriented toward the
home market and the other oriented toward export—co-existed
for quite some time. As late as the early 1990s, Mauritius remained
one of the world's most protected economies, despite a thriving
EPZ and rapid export growth.[3] The protected sector did not perform as well as the EPZ; but, just as Meade had anticipated, it was
an important incubator for entrepreneurship in modern industry.
Indeed, the growth of the EPZ was fueled not simply by foreign
investors and technology but also by domestic capital and entrepreneurship. Unlike similar zones in other countries, domestic
investors and entrepreneurs participated substantially in the Mau-

ritian EPZ.[4] That helps explain why it was so much more successful than copycats in other countries.

Today, Mauritius has an open economy with a strong manufacturing base, but it faces the challenges of the next stages of diversification. The garment sector can no longer propel the economy forward in view of rising domestic wages and competitive pressure from low-cost producers on the world market. Boosting growth requires a new strategy.

What would a modern-day James Meade recommend?

The Revisionists Take Over

Economists' views on development policy took a strange turn in the decades following Meade's report. During the 1950s and 1960s, most economists who studied the underdeveloped countries of the world, as they were then called, took it for granted that their infant industries needed nurturing and that government leadership played an important role. There was much, indeed excessive, skepticism about markets and the influence of the global economy. The leading development economists of the day, such as W. Arthur Lewis, Raul Prebisch, Paul Rosenstein-Rodan, and Albert Hirschman, had their debates, of course. But none would have endorsed the view that free trade and small government are the best way to promote economic growth and development.[5] The lessons of the Great Divergence during the nineteenth century— the division of the world between a rich industrial core and a poor commodity-producing periphery—were clear to all.

By the 1980s, the dominant view among North American development experts and their followers had changed dramatically. The state went from being a handmaiden of economic growth to the principal obstacle blocking it. The international division of labor was transformed from a threat to a savior. During the 1990s, enthusiasm for free capital mobility was added to the package too, as we saw in an earlier chapter. This narrative infused development agencies such as the World Bank with a new sense of mission and reshaped the policy advice they dished out.

An early version of the revisionist package was codified in the so-called "Washington Consensus." Coined in 1989 by the economist John Williamson, the term originally referred to some of the common elements in the reforms that Latin American countries had embarked on at the time. Williamson's original list contained ten distinct reforms, with a heavy emphasis on deregulation, trade and financial liberalization, privatization, avoidance of currency overvaluation, and fiscal discipline. Over time, the "Washington Consensus" was transformed into a more doctrinaire approach, a mantra for the über-liberalizers. Even though Williamson was a skeptic on financial globalization, to his great chagrin capital market liberalization was soon folded into the package as well.[6]

By the mid-1990s, few people remembered specific items on Williamson's original list, but everyone knew the moniker referred to an agenda that could be summarized in three words: stabilize, liberalize, and privatize. Williamson himself, a moderate economist, would become the target of much abuse as the originator of this "neoliberal dogma." In my own travels in developing countries during the 1990s, I was struck by the ideological fervor with which policy makers, especially those in Latin America, had embraced this agenda as the only path to economic salvation. What in East Asia remained a pragmatic respect for the power of price incentives and of world markets had been transmogrified into a religion of sorts.

The Big Fix

Ultimately, the Washington Consensus derived its appeal from a simple narrative about the power of globalization to lift developing nations out of poverty. But rather than promote the mixed, pragmatic strategies that China and others had employed in order to develop domestic industrial capabilities, advocates of this narrative stressed the role of openness to the global economy. Poor countries remain poor, they argued, because they have small domestic markets riddled with inefficiencies created by government restrictions on trade. Let these countries open themselves up to international trade and investment, the thinking went, and a rising tide of trade will pull them up from poverty. What was at stake was no longer some relatively minor efficiency gains—the standard argument for gains from trade—but a rapid convergence with the standards of living in the rich countries.

The apotheosis of this movement arrived in an article published in 1995 by the prominent economist Jeffrey Sachs and a co-author, Andrew Warner, both of them at Harvard at the time.[7] A long and elaborate piece, it was full of details on economic reform in the developing nations and the historical evolution of globalization. But the heart of the article was a statistical analysis with a striking finding. Sachs and Warner divided countries into two groups: those that were open to international trade and those that were closed. Their central result was that countries in the first group grew 2.45 percentage points faster over the longer term (in per capita terms) than those in the second. This is a remarkably large number. It meant that a developing country that was growing, say, at 2 percent per annum, could more than double its growth rate simply by opening itself to international trade.

Equally striking, the Sachs-Warner analysis implied that you could reap these benefits regardless of how poor your domestic policies were or how large your other disadvantages. A lousy government, say, or an ill-educated labor force, were of little significance. You could be extremely poor and have few industries, but those factors didn't matter either. Lowering barriers to trade alone would spur growth.[8]

These results depended crucially on the method Sachs and Warner had employed to classify countries as "open" and "closed."[9] For example, rapidly growing countries such as South Korea, Taiwan, Indonesia, and Mauritius were treated as open even though they had maintained high barriers on imports into the 1980s and had reduced these barriers only after they had acquired significant manufacturing capabilities. Sachs himself seemed to have a much more nuanced view, placing greater emphasis on the importance of promoting manufactured exports than on trade liberalization itself.[10] That, however, was not the focus of the statistical analysis. The message that technocrats and policy makers found in the research was loud and clear: If you want to catch up with the living standards of the advanced nations, there exists no instrument more potent than reducing your import tariffs and relaxing other restrictions on trade.[11]

So complete was the conversion that it became difficult to understand why the earlier generation of economists had been so skeptical of trade and so welcoming of government intervention. In an article celebrating the new consensus, Anne Krueger, one of its principal architects, would wonder how the principle of comparative advantage could have been so "blithely abandoned." "With hindsight," she wrote, "it is almost incredible that such a high fraction of economists could have deviated so far from the basic principles of international trade."[12] No leading Western economist in good professional standing during the eighties and nineties would dream of coming up with a plan like James Meade's; he would be considered a protectionist crank if he did.

The Sachs-Warner study and others, many of them carried out at the World Bank, became powerful artillery in the campaign by development agencies and technocrats to reshape development strategies. They fueled an obsessive drive for globalization on the part of developing country policy makers. The new consensus turned foreign trade and investment into the ultimate yardsticks for judging the adequacy of domestic economic and social policies—a key deformation produced by the quest for hyperglobalization. The best argument for addressing any domestic ill—whether crime, corruption, poor infrastructure, or low skills—was that it forestalled integration with the world economy.[13] Just mention "foreign investor sentiment" or "competitiveness in world markets," and policy makers would snap to attention. The pursuit of globalization became a substitute for development strategy, an end in itself, rather than an opportunity to be exploited strategically.

There were skeptical voices within academia, but few were interested in taking on this globalization mania in the real world. Many economists would say in private that the studies attributing such large growth effects to open trade lacked credibility. But they didn't want to appear to condone protectionism. The revisionists may have greatly exaggerated the growth-boosting effects of trade liberalization, but so what? Perhaps development strategies came to revolve too much around trade policies and trade agreements, but again, what's the big deal? Any move in the direction of open trade policies had to be a good thing.

When I presented a critique of the Sachs-Warner research and other similar work in front of a group of academics in 2000, the reception was emblematic. A prominent economist interrupted me to ask: "Why are you doing this?" I was stumped. Economists are a contentious lot, and I was used to having my methods or evidence questioned, but I had not encountered such incredulity before. The idea of free trade as an engine of growth had become such a sacred cow that someone who revisited the evidence needed to have his motives questioned.[14]

When Facts Are Not What They Seem

Trade fundamentalism appealed to many because the postwar evidence superficially seemed to bear it out. The phenomenal rise of South Korea, Taiwan, and other East and Southeast Asian nations on world markets had buried the idea, common in the 1950s and 1960s, that nascent industrial firms in poor nations wouldn't respond to trade incentives or would remain too weak to prosper in global markets. Meade himself had been overly pessimistic about Mauritius' export prospects. But the revisionists went much farther. They interpreted the East Asian experience as a triumph of markets over government and of free trade over controlled trade. Rampant state interventions were either overlooked or finessed as mutually offsetting, resulting in outcomes similar to what markets, left to their own devices, would have produced.[15] As a last resort, revisionists argued that East Asian economies would have grown even more rapidly in the absence of government interventions. We saw the difficulties this perspective ran into when we encountered the World Bank's report on *The East Asian Miracle* in the previous chapter.

The misdiagnosis of the experience of countries such as Brazil, Mexico, and Turkey, which had followed more inward-looking strategies, was equally problematic. Unlike East Asian countries or Mauritius, these countries had made little effort to push their firms to export, relying mostly on the domestic market to fuel growth. They had maintained highly restrictive trade regimes well into the 1980s. This was the strategy of "import-substituting industrialization" (ISI), and it had become the dominant model in Latin America, the Middle East, Africa, and parts of Asia (especially India) since the 1930s and following independence. As the name suggests, the strategy focused on replacing previously imported goods—initially simple consumer goods, but eventually more sophisticated capital goods as well—by domestic production. This goal was to be achieved through an array of government interventions, in the form of import protection, credit subsidies, tax incentives, and public investment. The strategy placed little emphasis or confidence in the ability of domestic firms to export and compete on world markets.

The revisionists painted a grim picture of ISI's record. By failing to take advantage of world markets and giving the state too large a role, they argued, these countries had severely handicapped their development. Once again, this depiction overshot the mark. To be sure, it was easy to dig up horror stories about the excesses of protectionism and state intervention. In some cases, trade barriers had distorted investment incentives so much that private entrepreneurs had found it profitable to set up plants where the cost of the inputs they were using exceeded the value of what they were producing.[16] Some countries, notably Argentina and India, did perform poorly.

Nonetheless, the overall record of ISI was in fact rather impressive. Brazil, Mexico, Turkey, and scores of other developing nations in Latin America, the Middle East, and Africa experienced faster rates of economic growth under ISI than at any other time in their economic history. Latin America grew at an annual average rate exceeding 2.5 percent per capita between 1945 and the early 1980s—a pace that far exceeds what the region has registered since 1990 (1.9 percent).[17] Two dozen countries in post-independence sub-Saharan Africa also grew quite rapidly until the mid- to late 1970s.

Industrialization drove this performance. ISI countries experienced rapid productivity growth as their economies diversified away from traditional agriculture into manufacturing activities. As surprising as it may seem, our best studies indicate that during the sixties and seventies economywide productivity grew more rapidly in import-substituting Latin America than it did in export-oriented East Asia.[18] Latin America's economies expanded at a slower clip than East Asia's not because they experienced slower technological progress but because they invested a lower share of their national income. Latin America has yet to reproduce such rates of productivity gain despite (or perhaps because of) two decades of economic liberalization and rapid integration into the world economy. To their credit, some of the ISI countries, notably Brazil, turned toward world markets during the seventies on the back of this industrialization. Even where ISI underperformed, it often bequeathed industrial capacities that would later prove very helpful. In India, for example, highly protected firms in pharmaceuticals, auto parts, and basic metals eventually became world-class players, and engineers employed in state-owned electronics companies formed the backbone of many of the IT firms that sprang up in Bangalore, India's answer to Silicon Valley.[19]

ISI acquired its bad reputation in part because it was associated with the debt crisis that engulfed Latin America in 1982. Revisionists viewed the crisis as a byproduct of ISI: an overextended state had produced large fiscal and external imbalances, while the incapacity to generate export revenues had made adjustment to the sudden stop in capital inflows that much more difficult. This oft-repeated narrative has major flaws.

Some of the most ardent champions of ISI managed in fact to avoid getting embroiled in a debt crisis. Think of India. India's policies had a major impact on the locus of economic activity, but they did not wreak havoc on macroeconomic balances—the balance between income and expenditures—or on external finances. And when fiscal expansion in the late 1980s threatened a Latin American–style crisis, Indian policy makers were quick to adjust macropolicies, unlike their Latin American counterparts. There is nothing in ISI that makes a foreign debt crisis more likely.

Outward orientation does nothing to make such crises less likely, either. The Asian financial crisis in 1997 and the Argentinean crisis in 2001–02 took place in economies that had given up on ISI policies—East Asia in the 1960s and Argentina in the 1990s—and, by the time of their crises, were highly open to international trade. Yet openness did little to protect the affected countries from the whiplash they suffered. As we have seen, financial crises have their own dynamic and don't particularly discriminate among countries with different trade strategies.

In Search of a Post–Washington Consensus Consensus

Today, the Washington Consensus is a "damaged brand," as John Williamson conceded as early as 2002.[20] Its disrepute comes not only from the ideological opposition it has engendered from the political left, but, more fundamentally, from its disappointing economic record. In their 1995 article, Sachs and Warner had written that "we find no cases to support the frequent worry that a country might open and yet fail to grow."[21] Even if their claim was true at the time, subsequent evidence clearly contradicted the assertion. The countries in Latin America and elsewhere that jettisoned ISI in favor of the Washington Consensus ended up, for the most part, with considerably lower rates of growth. Considering how misguided ISI policies seem by today's standards, this was quite an embarrassment for the proponents of the Washington Consensus. It would take a lot of explaining to square the disappointing outcomes with the revisionist narrative.[22] Jeffrey Sachs himself soon abandoned any pretense that trade openness alone can yield rapid growth or, for that matter, that it is even a major force. As he spent more time in Africa, he would increasingly focus on domestic constraints on development: low levels of education, poor health standards, dismal agricultural productivity, and inadequate investment in public infrastructure.[23]

The failure of the Washington Consensus left economists with a conundrum. Repudiating the specific reforms on the agenda was not an attractive option. Trade liberalization, deregulation, privatization, and the other reforms still seemed eminently reasonable: they would make poor nations' policies look more like those of the advanced market economies. An explicit rejection of these reforms would have forced economists to abandon some of their most fundamental tenets. The problem with the Washington Consensus had to lie elsewhere.

The rehabilitation took the form of retaining the Washington

Consensus but expanding it to include a wide range of additional reforms. There was nothing wrong with the Washington Consensus itself; it just had not been ambitious enough. The failure showed, the new story line went, that much more profound institutional reforms were needed to ensure the Washington Consensus would produce the advertised results. The actual reforms undertaken have been uneven and incomplete, an IMF report complained in 2005: "More progress was made with measures that had low up-front costs, such as privatization, relative to reforms that promised greater long-term benefits, such as improving macroeconomic and labor market institutions, and strengthening legal and judicial systems."[24] Anne Krueger captured the verdict in the title of a 2004 speech: "Meant Well, Tried Little, Failed Much."[25]

Developing countries had to work harder; so the thinking went. It wasn't enough to slash import tariffs and eliminate barriers to trade; open trade policies had to be underpinned by extensive reforms in public administration, by labor market "flexibility," and by international trade agreements. Macroeconomic stability had to be cemented by reforming fiscal institutions, giving central banks independence, and of course by better politics. Property rights required extensive reforms in governance and legal regimes. Free capital flows added their own long list of regulatory, supervisory, and macroeconomic prerequisites. Policy makers received a veritable laundry list of reforms, many of which required institutional changes that had taken developed countries decades, if not centuries, to accomplish.

The new reforms were called "second-generation reforms," to distinguish them from the earlier, simpler commandments. These would eventually morph into an impossibly broad and ambitious agenda under the general heading of "governance reforms." This open-ended agenda offered little help to policy makers in the developing world. Telling poor countries in Africa or Latin America that they should set their sights on the institutions of the United States or Sweden is like telling them that the only way to develop

is to become developed. This is hardly useful policy advice; but it
made for excellent cover when the advice went awry. As one propo-
nent of trade reform would put it: "Of course, openness to trade
is not by itself sufficient to promote growth—macroeconomic and
political stability *and other policies* are needed as well" (emphasis
mine).[26] In the end there is always something that the recipient of
the advice can be faulted for not having done properly.

While the World Bank and most development economists
focused on augmenting and enlarging the Washington Consensus, other efforts centered on the United Nations took a different
tack. The UN Millennium Project, led by Jeffrey Sachs, explicitly
rejected the Washington Consensus and recommended large-
scale public investments in health and infrastructure for Africa,
financed by foreign aid. The UN Millennium Development Goals,
a blueprint agreed to by the world's nations in 2000, set concrete
targets to be achieved by 2015, including halving extreme poverty
(defined as incomes below $1 a day), stopping the spread of HIV/
AIDS, and providing universal access to primary education.

In contrast to these holistic approaches encompassing a very
long list of reforms, others attempted to come up with a new big
fix. The hedgehogs' big idea this time was not trade; it had to be
something else. But the reasoning took a similar form: "Poor countries are poor primarily because they lack X: give them X and we
will have solved the problem of world poverty." For the Peruvian
economist and activist Hernando de Soto, X was formal titles to
property. Give poor people a piece of paper which gives them legal
ownership rights over their house or their land, he thought, and
you will turn them into entrepreneurs and successful capitalists.[27]
For the Bangladeshi economist and banker Muhammad Yunus, X
was credit. Give each entrepreneur a small loan (a "microcredit"),
he argued, and you will unleash a process of growth and development from below.[28] Both of these ideas inspired active movements
and found large numbers of practitioners worldwide.

Despite their obvious differences, what all of these strategies

presume is that all developing countries suffer from the same ail-
ments and require broadly similar treatment, and that we know
enough about the nature of the remedies to mount a bold, ambitious, and often costly effort to eradicate world poverty. None
of this need be true. After all, governmental and international
efforts to spur development have failed more often than they have
succeeded. A much less confident perspective might posit that we
have little clue about what works in different settings or why.

William Easterly, the former World Banker and foreign aid foe,
has taken this line of thought to its most extreme form. Trying to
force development from above by applying some grand scheme
dreamt up in the halls of academe or the corridors of Washington,
Easterly would argue, is simply futile.[29] Development experts have
nothing useful to tell policy makers, except possibly how to avoid
gross errors. The best we can do is ensure that an overconfident
and overintrusive state does not stay in the way of development
bubbling up from below.

In a world where globalization can just as easily condemn you to
dependence on exports of commodities as it fosters rapid growth
through industrialization, the wait for development to take place
on its own could take a very long time. Easterly's argument coun-
sels despair rather than hope. Fortunately, though, there is a
middle way.

Different Strokes for Different Folks

When I visited a Latin American country a few years back, a proud
economics minister told me that his government had already completed all the second-generation reforms, and that they were now
embarking on "third-generation reforms." The economy had been
opened to trade and capital flows, markets deregulated, public
enterprises privatized, and macroeconomic imbalances eliminated. The tax regime, banking regulations, social security institu-

tions, fiscal rules, and judicial system had all been reformed in line with "best-practice" standards. Labor markets were as "flexible"—that is, free of regulations—as they come. Yet the economy was barely growing. What was the problem? Was it that all the necessary reforms had not yet been implemented, or was it something more fundamental about the development strategy in place?

The difficulty that this country confronted typifies the shortcomings of the laundry list approach to reform. The agenda presumes that all developing nations suffer from the same problems, and that all of the problems are equally important. It is a ready-made, undifferentiated program that fails to target an economy's most severe bottlenecks. At best, it forces policy makers to spread themselves too thin in pursuit of a very ambitious set of reforms. At worst, it can backfire when otherwise well-intentioned reforms end up aggravating problems elsewhere in the economy.

Once we begin to think in terms of specific bottlenecks and their relative importance, we are in fact on our way to a more effective strategy for growth, one that is based on the fox's more grounded approach. Suppose you have an old clunker of a car that no longer drives. Sprucing it up with new fenders, different headlights, a shinier coat of paint, and a more powerful engine may make it look like a better car. But it is not clear that these improvements will make it go. A far better strategy would be to try to identify the immediate source of the trouble. If the problem is a flat tire, replace the tire and then drive on. If the problem is with the ignition system, then fix the ignition. Eventually, the car will need new headlights and a fresh coat of paint, and possibly even a new engine. But you can get a lot more mileage out of the car, at less cost, if you tackle one problem at a time instead of attempting a long list of renovations suggested by a mechanic who has not even examined the car.

So it is with growth strategies, too. Poor countries suffer from multiple shortcomings, but not all of them need to be addressed at the same time for their economies to enjoy rapid growth for a while. The trick is to identify the most binding constraints that prevent entrepreneurs from investing in the modern industries and services that fuel economic growth. The most pressing problem could be a shortage of finance. It could be government practices (such as high taxes or corruption) that depress private profits. It could be high inflation or public debt that increases risk. Or it could be learning spillovers associated with infant industries that prevent private entrepreneurs from reaping the full social value of their investments.[30]

Each one of these constraints, as well as an almost endless number of others that might exist, will call for a different approach. For example, if the chief constraint is that trade restrictions have cut off the private sector from imported inputs and technologies, trade opening would clearly be a priority. If, on the other hand, the problem is macroeconomic instability fed by large fiscal deficits, a conventional stabilization program (consisting of government expenditure cuts and tax increases) will do wonders for growth even in the absence of trade opening or large-scale institutional reform. In this instance, cuts in import tariffs may actually make things worse by aggravating the fiscal deficit. Similarly, if the main constraint lies in inadequate entrepreneurial incentives because much of the benefit of investments in technology spills over to other firms, some kind of incentive package for the private sector may be required. Moves toward trade liberalization would threaten to aggravate the underlying problem in this last instance by depressing profitability in industry even further.

These examples illustrate how policies that would normally be desirable in well-functioning advanced market economies can produce perverse effects in the second-best environment of developing nations. International capital flows is an important area where such effects have played out. Leaving aside financial crises for a moment, a large capital inflow is a great idea when the most severe obstacle blocking domestic investment is insufficient credit. But when investment is constrained primarily by low profitability, which is the situation in many, if not most, emerging economies, a capital inflow aggravates the problem instead of making it better. It makes dollars plentiful and their price low, reducing the competitiveness of domestic industries on global markets.[31] In a second-best world, increasing transaction costs on international finance may make sense.

There are diverse ways in which a particular constraint can be lifted, some more attuned to domestic circumstances than others. If you want to increase the economy's outward orientation, this can be achieved via export subsidies (as in South Korea and Taiwan), via an export-processing zone (as in Mauritius), via Special Economic Zones (as in China)—or via free trade (as in Hong Kong) for that matter. Domestic industries can be promoted through subsidized credit (South Korea), tax incentives (Taiwan), or trade protection (Brazil, Mexico, and Turkey). Property rights can be enhanced by importing and adapting foreign legal codes (as in Japan during the Meiji Restoration) or by developing domestic variants (as in China and Vietnam). Countries need room to experiment with alternative, often unorthodox arrangements. Whether you choose to fix your car's flat tire by replacing it or by patching it up depends on whether you have a spare in the trunk or there is a garage nearby.

Governments do not need to do a whole lot to unleash rapid growth—at least for a while—as long as the little they do lifts the most binding constraints they face. India's remarkable economic performance in recent years provides a perfect example. The mythology around India's economic miracle holds that India took off after a wave of economic liberalization that started in 1991. In fact, India's growth acceleration took place a decade earlier, in the early 1980s, with tentative and relatively minor reforms aimed at reversing the long-held anti-business attitudes of the Indian state. The Congress Party under Indira Gandhi and (after her death in 1984) Rajiv Gandhi began to woo private business and the industrial establishment, in large part to neutralize the perceived political threat from the private-sector-oriented Janata Party which had trounced Congress in the 1977 election.[32]

This attitudinal change and concomitant small adjustments on the part of the central government—such as the reduction in some business taxes and the easing of access to imported inputs—had remarkably powerful effects on economic activity. India's growth rate, which many observers had considered immutably fixed, more than doubled, from less than 2 percent (in per capita terms) to closer to 4 percent during the 1980s.[33] Yet few of the obstacles in the standard litany of what holds India back had been removed. Bureaucratic inefficiency and red tape were still a nightmare, trade barriers remained high, and the infrastructure was in very poor shape.

When a country lies so much below its potential, it doesn't require much to unleash economic growth. And so it was with India, which had accumulated some significant strengths during long decades of repression of much private-sector activity. Once India's private sector was unleashed, previous investments in industry and technical education paid off. India would eventually open up its economy; but unlike Latin America it did so cautiously, gradually, and more than a decade after the pickup in growth.

A constraint will cede its place to others once it is successfully lifted. A selective approach therefore requires being ready to address the next set of constraints. It requires flexible policies and willingness to change course as circumstances demand. Countries that have grown in a sustained fashion are those where this strategy has been applied consistently over the longer run. China once again provides the leading example. Chinese policy reformers employed a strategic and sequential approach that targeted one set of supply-side constraints after another. They started out in agriculture in the late seventies, moved to industry in the eighties, then to foreign trade in the nineties, and are now struggling with the finance sector. China's leaders have not yet furnished the complete institutional underpinnings for a modern market economy. Most conspicuously missing are representative political institutions. In the meantime at least they have turned their country from a basket case into a middle-income economy and have lifted half a billion people from extreme poverty.

How ironic and sad, then, that globalization's rules have evolved to make it more difficult, rather than easier, for other countries to emulate the success of countries like Mauritius, South Korea, Taiwan, India, and China. The rules of the WTO, the practices of the IMF, and the recommendations of Western policy advisers have had the collective effect of shrinking the policy space within which similar homegrown, sequential approaches could be devised and implemented—all in the name of spreading the benefits of globalization.

The South African Predicament

Nearly half a century after Meade's visit to Mauritius, a group of colleagues and I were invited by South Africa's finance minister at the time, Trevor Manuel, to provide assistance on the country's growth strategy. Manuel, a former resistance leader, was largely self-taught in economics, but he was so well versed in the economics literature that he could cite my latest papers within days of them being posted online. He knew that South Africa was underperforming relative to other nations and to its own potential.

South Africa in 2005 looked of course very different from Mauritius in 1960. A middle-income country with a fairly diversified economy, it was highly integrated with world markets and had a sophisticated financial sector. But the central challenge South Africa confronted was the same: where would the jobs needed to employ the large surplus of low-skilled workers come from?

South Africa had undergone a remarkable political and economic transformation since its democratic transition in 1994. Following the end of white minority rule, it had managed to avoid

a descent into acrimonious recrimination, endless redistribution, and populism that would have decimated the economy and
turned the country into a sham democracy. The African National
Congress government had managed to create a stable, peaceful,
and racially balanced political regime with an exemplary record
of civil liberties and political freedoms. Economic policy had also
been prudent and cautious, following the general dictates prevailing during the 1990s. The economy was opened to trade and
capital flows. The government pursued cautious fiscal policies. An
independent central bank focused on fighting inflation.

If the world were fair, political restraint and economic recti-
tude of this magnitude would have produced a booming South
African economy operating at full employment. Unfortunately,
growth had been measly since 1994, at less than 2 percent per year
per capita; private investment had remained low; and most important, unemployment had risen to 26 percent. Counting discouraged workers, the unemployment rate stood closer to 40 percent.
These are some of the highest unemployment rates ever recorded.
As would be expected, unemployment was heavily concentrated
among the young, unskilled, and black population.

The economy had not been able to generate enough work at
reasonable wages for the large number of job seekers, both new
entrants into the labor market and workers released from shrinking sectors (mining and agriculture). The mismatch between a
slow rise in labor demand and a rapid rise in labor supply meant
one of two things: either wages would fall to rock-bottom levels, or
there would be high unemployment. The South African government had chosen unemployment, but had also instituted a relatively generous system of public financial assistance to prop up the
living standards of the poor and unemployed.

Going forward, the only way to create well-paying jobs for the
unemployed was to significantly expand manufacturing production. Agriculture and mining were unlikely to revive, and service
industries such as finance (which had been doing reasonably well)

employed mostly skilled workers. This in turn required increasing the profitability of manufacturing in South Africa, which would stimulate private investment in the sector. Ultimately, the solution had to match the one that Meade had advocated for Mauritius.[34]

South Africa had to meet this challenge in a world where the rules of the game were quite different. China's rise as a low-cost exporter had made competing in manufactures much more difficult. South Africa's import tariffs had been slashed and international agreements made it difficult or impossible to raise them significantly. Even though the government subsidized certain manufacturing industries, such as autos, these programs were already pushing the boundaries of WTO law. And the country's independent central bank and liberal regime of capital flows made it impossible to contemplate a devaluation of the currency (the rand) to provide manufactured exports a boost in profitability.

In the end, my colleagues and I recommended an eclectic mix of policies. We advocated a tighter fiscal policy that would leave room for the central bank to reduce interest rates and let the rand depreciate. We proposed a temporary jobs subsidy to reduce the cost to employers of hiring young school-leavers. And we recommended a new approach to industrial policy which we thought would be more effective, more market-friendly, and less likely to be challenged in the WTO.

The traditional approach to industrial policy consists of a list of sectors to be promoted along with a list of instruments for promotion (for example, tariff protection, tax rebates, R&D subsidies, cheap credit, industrial zones). Our approach, by contrast, was process-oriented. It focused on repositioning existing institutions—such as the Department of Trade and Industry or the Industrial Development Corporation—into foci of business-government dialogue. The dialogue would seek to identify bottlenecks and opportunities in industrial activities, few of which could be known beforehand, and to respond quickly and with a variety of policies to the prospects that the dialogue identified.[35]

Would these proposals help? It is difficult to know. No doubt some would fail, and others would need revision before they became fully effective. What matters ultimately is having a government that understands the nature of the challenge and is willing to try different solutions to overcome it. By 2009, South Africa had elected a new president, Jacob Zuma, and installed a new government. Government officials were warning about the risk of deindustrialization and talking about industrial policy as the central plank of South Africa's response to the global financial crisis.[36]

A New Narrative for Development

As early as 1791, Alexander Hamilton had argued that those who believed that modern industries would develop on their own, without support from government, were mistaken.[37] There were too many obstacles, not the least competition from more advanced nations, for these industries to arise spontaneously and naturally in the United States. Hamilton argued equally strongly against those who thought government efforts would necessarily make things worse rather than better. It wasn't a matter of whether the government should intervene, but of how.

Trade fundamentalists overlooked the insights of Hamilton and of countless other economists since. They fundamentally misunderstood the nature of the challenges faced by developing nations. Economic growth and development are possible only through the accumulation of capabilities over time, in areas ranging from skills and technologies to public institutions. Globalization on its own does not generate these capabilities; it simply allows nations to leverage better those that they already possess. That is why the world's successful globalizers—East Asian nations in our times—enhance their domestic productive capacities before they lay themselves bare to the gales of international competition.

That industrial policy, in whatever guise, is once again considered acceptable, and indeed necessary, speaks volumes about how far we have retreated from the trade fundamentalism of the 1990s. But it is too early to declare victory. The precepts of trade fundamentalism remain ingrained in WTO rules and in the practices of other multilateral institutions, as well as in the consciousness of too many technocrats and policy makers.

This reflects in large part the absence of an alternative narrative that has sufficient appeal. The older, second-best tradition of thinking on development strategy, closer to the fox's approach than the hedgehog's, got the essentials right, but it looks worn and jaded. Reinvigorating it requires recalibrating the balance between states and markets while retaining its essence.

9

The Political Trilemma of the World Economy

n 1990, Argentina couldn't have been in a worse economic mess. In almost perpetual crisis since the seventies, the country reeled under hyperinflation and a crushing debt burden. Incomes had shrunk 25 percent from their levels a decade earlier and private investment had come to a virtual standstill. Prices were rising at unprecedented rates, even by Argentina's demanding standards. In March 1990, inflation climbed to more than 20,000 percent (on an annualized basis), sowing chaos and confusion. Struggling to cope, Buenos Aires' world-weary residents took refuge in gallows humor. With prices soaring by the minute, they told themselves, at least it had become cheaper to take a cab than a bus. With the cab you paid at the end of the ride instead of the beginning!

Can You Save an Economy by Tying It to the Mast of Globalization?

Domingo Cavallo thought he knew the real problem. For too long, Argentina's governments had changed the rules of the game whenever it suited them. Too much governmental discretion had resulted in a complete loss of confidence in Argentine policy makers. The private sector had responded by withholding its invest-ment and fleeing the domestic currency. To restore credibility with domestic and foreign investors, the government needed to commit itself to a clear set of rules. In particular, strict monetary discipline was required to prevent governments from printing money at will.[1]

Cavallo, an economist with a PhD from Harvard, was foreign minister in the administration of President Carlos Menem. He would get the chance to execute his plan when Menem put him in charge of the economy in February 1991. The linchpin of Cav-allo's strategy was the Convertibility Law, which legally anchored the Argentine currency to the U.S. dollar at 1 peso per dollar and prohibited restrictions on foreign payments. The Convertibility Law effectively forced Argentina's central bank to operate by gold standard rules. Henceforth the domestic money supply could be increased and interest rates lowered only if dollars were flowing into the economy. If dollars were moving the other way, the money supply would have to be cut and interest rates raised. No more mucking around with monetary policy.

In addition, Cavallo accelerated the privatization, deregula-tion, and opening up of the Argentine economy. He believed open economy rules and deep integration would reinforce business con-fidence by precluding discretionary interventions and the hijack-ing of policy by special interests. With policy on automatic pilot, investors would have little fear that the rules would be changed on them. By the early 1990s, Argentina's record in trade liberaliza-tion, tax reform, privatization, and financial reform was second to none in Latin America.

Cavallo envisioned globalization as both a harness and an engine for Argentina's economy. Globalization provided not just discipline and an effective shortcut to credibility in economic poli-cies. It would also unleash powerful forces to propel the economy forward. With lack of confidence and other transaction costs out of the way, foreign capital would flow into the country, allowing domestic investment to rise and the economy to take off. Imports from abroad in turn would force domestic producers to become more competitive and productive. Deep integration with the world economy would solve Argentina's short- and long-term problems.

This was the Washington Consensus taken to an extreme, and it turned out to be right about the short term, but not the long term. Cavallo's strategy worked wonders on the binding constraint of the moment. The Convertibility Law eliminated hyperinflation and restored price stability practically overnight. It generated credibility and confidence—at least for a while—and led to large capital inflows. Investment, exports, and incomes all rose rapidly. As we saw in chapter Six, Argentina became a poster child for multilateral organizations and globalization enthusiasts in the mid-1990s, even though policies like the Convertibility Law had clearly not been part of the Washington Consensus. Cavallo became the toast of the international financial community.

By the end of the decade, the Argentine nightmare had returned with a vengeance. Adverse developments in the world economy set the stage for an abrupt reversal in investors' views on Argentina. The Asian financial crisis hit the country hard by reducing international money managers' appetite for emerging markets, but the real killer was the Brazilian devaluation in early 1999. The devaluation reduced the value of the Brazilian currency by 40 percent against the dollar, allowing Brazilian exporters to charge much lower dollar prices on foreign markets. Since Brazil is Argentina's chief global competitor, Brazil's cost advantage left the Argentinean peso looking decidedly overvalued. Doubts about Argentina's ability to service its external debt multiplied, confidence collapsed, and before too long Argentina's creditworthiness had slid below some African countries'.

Cavallo's relations with Menem had soured in the meantime and he had left office in 1996. President Fernando de la Rúa, who succeeded Menem, invited Cavallo back to the government in March 2001 in an effort to shore up confidence. Cavallo's new efforts proved ineffective. When his initial tinkering with the trade and currency regime produced meager results, he was forced to resort to austerity policies and sharp fiscal cutbacks in an economy where one worker out of five was already out of a job. He launched a "zero-deficit" plan in July and enforced it with cuts in government salaries and pensions of up to 13 percent. The financial panic went from bad to worse. Fearing that the peso would be devalued, domestic depositors rushed to pull their money out of banks, which in turn forced the government to limit cash withdrawals.

The fiscal cuts and the restriction on bank withdrawals sparked mass protests. Unions called for nationwide strikes, rioting enveloped major cities, and looting spread. Just before Christmas, Cavallo and de la Rúa resigned in rapid succession.[2] Starved of funds, the Argentinean government was eventually forced to freeze domestic bank accounts, default on its foreign debt, reimpose capital controls, and devalue the peso. Incomes shrunk by 12 percent in 2002, the worst drop in decades. The experiment with hyperglobalization had ended in colossal failure.

What went wrong? The short answer is that domestic politics got in the way of hyperglobalization. The painful domestic economic adjustments required by deep integration did not sit well with domestic constituencies, and politics ultimately emerged victorious.

The Inevitable Clash Between Politics and Hyperglobalization

The economic story behind Argentina's economic collapse is fairly straightforward in hindsight. Argentina's policy makers had succeeded in removing one binding constraint—monetary mismanagement—but eventually ran into another—an uncompetitive currency. Had the government abandoned the Convertibility Law or reformed it in favor of a more flexible exchange rate, say in 1996, the confidence crisis that engulfed the country later might have been averted. But Argentina's policy makers were too wedded to the Convertibility Law. They had sold it to their public as the central plank of their growth strategy, making it virtually impossible to step back. Pragmatism would have served the country better than ideological rigidity.

But there is a deeper political lesson in Argentina's experience, one that is fundamental to the nature of globalization. The country had bumped against one of the central truths of the global economy: National democracy and deep globalization are incompatible. Democratic politics casts a long shadow on financial markets and makes it impossible for a nation to integrate deeply with the world economy. Britain had learned this lesson in 1931, when it was forced to get off gold. Keynes had enshrined it in the Bretton Woods regime. Argentina overlooked it.

The failure of Argentina's political leaders was ultimately a matter not of will but of ability. Their commitment to the Convertibility Law and to financial market confidence could not have been doubted. Cavallo knew there was little alternative to playing the game by financial markets' rules. Under his policies, the Argentine government was willing to abrogate contracts with virtually all domestic constituencies—public employees, pensioners, provincial governments, bank depositors—so as not to skip one cent of its obligations to foreign creditors.

What sealed Argentina's fate in the eyes of financial markets was not what Cavallo and de la Rúa were doing, but what the Argentine people were willing to accept. Investors and creditors grew increasingly skeptical that the Argentine Congress, provinces, and ordinary people would tolerate austerity policies long discredited in advanced industrial countries. In the end, the markets were right. When globalization collides with domestic politics, the smart money bets on politics.

Remarkably, deep integration cannot sustain itself even when its requirements and goals are fully internalized by a country's political leadership. For Cavallo, Menem, and de la Rúa, globalization was not a constraint to be respected willy-nilly; it was their ultimate objective. Yet they could not keep domestic political pressure from unraveling their strategy. The lesson for other countries is sobering. If hyperglobalization could not be made to work in Argentina, might it ever work in other settings?[3]

In his ode to globalization, *The Lexus and the Olive Tree*, Tom Friedman famously described how the "electronic herd"—financiers and speculators who can move billions of dollars around the globe in an instant—forced all nations to don a "Golden Straitjacket." This defining garment of globalization, he explained, stitched together the fixed rules to which all countries must submit: free trade, free capital markets, free enterprise, and small government. "If your country has not been fitted for one," he wrote, "it will soon." When you put it on, he continued, two things happen: "your economy grows, and your politics shrink." Since globalization (which to Friedman meant deep integration) does not permit nations to deviate from the rules, domestic politics is reduced to a choice between Coke and Pepsi. All other flavors, especially local ones, are banished.[4]

Friedman was wrong to presume that deep integration rules produce rapid economic growth, as we have already seen. He was also wrong to treat his Golden Straitjacket as an established reality. Few countries' leaders put on the Golden Straitjacket more willingly than Argentina's (who then also threw the keys away for good measure). As the unraveling of the Argentine experiment shows, in a democracy, domestic politics win out eventually. The only exceptions are small nations that are already part of a larger political grouping such as the European Union; we will look at the case of Latvia in the next chapter. When push comes to shove, democracy shrugs off the Golden Straitjacket.

Nevertheless, Friedman's central insight remains valid. There *is* a fundamental tension between hyperglobalization and democratic politics. Hyperglobalization *does* require shrinking domestic politics and insulating technocrats from the demands of popular groups. Friedman erred when he overstated the economic benefits of hyperglobalization and underestimated the power of politics. He therefore overestimated the long-run feasibility, as well as desirability, of deep integration.

When Hyperglobalization Impinges on Democratic Choices

We cherish our democracy and national sovereignty, and yet we sign one trade agreement after another and treat free capital flows as the natural order of things. This unstable and incoherent state of affairs is a recipe for disaster. Argentina in the 1990s gave us a vivid and extreme example. However, one does not have to live in a badly governed developing country ravaged by speculative capital flows to experience the tension on an almost daily basis. The clash between globalization and domestic social arrangements is a core feature of the global economy. Consider a few illustrations of how globalization gets in the way of national democracy.

Labor standards. Every advanced economy has detailed regulations that cover employment practices. These regulations dictate who can work, the minimum wage, the maximum hours of work, the nature of working conditions, what the employer can ask the worker to do, and how easily the worker can be fired. They guarantee the worker's freedom to form unions to represent his or her interests and set the rules under which collective bargaining can take place over pay and benefits.

From a classical liberal standpoint, most of these regulations make little sense. They interfere with an individual's right to enter into contracts of his or her choosing. If you are willing to work for 70 hours a week below the minimum wage under unsafe conditions and allow the employer to dismiss you at will, why should the state prevent you from accepting such terms? Similarly, if you think it is a good thing for your fourteen-year-old daughter to get a full-time job in a factory, why should the government tell you otherwise? According to classical liberal doctrine, people are the best judge of their own interests (and the interests of their family members), and voluntary contracts, entered freely, must leave both parties better off.

Labor markets were once governed by this doctrine.[5] Since the 1930s, however, U.S. legislation and the courts have recognized that what may be good for an individual worker may not be good for workers *as a whole*. Without regulations that enforce societal norms of decent work, a prospective employee with little bargaining power may be forced to accept conditions that violate those norms. By accepting such a contract, the employee also makes it harder for other workers to achieve higher labor standards. Thus employers must be prohibited from offering odious contracts even if some workers are willing to accept them. Certain forms of competition have to be ruled out. You may be willing to work for 70 hours a week below the minimum wage. But my employer cannot take advantage of your willingness to work under these conditions and offer my job to you.

Consider how international trade affects this understanding. Thanks to outsourcing, my employer can now do what he previously could not. Domestic labor laws still prohibit him from hiring you in my place and putting me to work under conditions that violate those laws. But this no longer matters. He can now replace me with a worker in Indonesia or Guatemala who will work willingly under those same substandard conditions or worse. To economists, this is not just legal; it is a manifestation of the gains from trade. Yet the consequences for me and my job do not depend on the citizenship of the worker bidding down my labor standards. Why do national regulations protect me from downward competition in employment practices from a domestic worker but not a foreign one? Why should we allow international markets to erode domestic labor regulations through the back door when we do not allow domestic markets to do the same?

The inconsistency is further highlighted by considering whether a society would condone allowing those Indonesian and Guatemalans to be employed *at home* as guest workers under the same labor standards they face in their native countries. Even most free traders would object to such a practice. There should be a single set of labor standards in a country, they will say, applied to all workers regardless of the passport they carry. But why? Outsourcing jobs through trade has exactly the same consequences, for all concerned, as allowing migrant workers to toil under a lower set of standards.

How significant are these issues in the real world? Less than many labor advocates claim, but more than free traders are willing to admit. Wage levels are determined first and foremost by labor productivity. Differences in productivity account for between 80 to 90 percent of the variation in wages around the world. This puts a significant damper on the potential of outsourcing to undermine employment practices in the advanced countries. An employer's threat to outsource my job to someone who earns half my wage does not pose much danger to me when that foreign worker also has half my productivity.

But 80 to 90 percent is not 100 percent. The political and social institutions that frame labor markets exert some independent influence on labor earnings, quite separate from the powerful effects of productivity. Labor regulations, unionization levels, and more broadly the political rights exercised by workers shape the bargains between workers and their employers and determine how the economic value created by firms is shared between them. These arrangements can move wage levels up or down in any country by 40 percent or more.[6] It is here that outsourcing, or the threat thereof, can play a role. Moving jobs to where workers enjoy fewer rights—or threatening to do so—*can be* beneficial to employers. Within limits, it can be used as a lever for extracting concessions on wages and employment practices from domestic workers.

There aren't easy solutions to these conundrums. An employer's freedom to choose where he wants to operate is a competing value that surely deserves attention. The interests of the Guatemalan or Indonesian workers may collide with the interests of domestic workers. We cannot however pretend that outsourcing does not create serious difficulties for domestic labor standards.

Corporate tax competition. The international mobility of firms and of capital also restricts a nation's ability to choose the tax structure that best reflects its needs and preferences. In particular, this mobility puts downward pressure on corporate tax rates and shifts the tax burden from capital, which is internationally mobile, to labor, which is much less so.

The logic is obvious and figures regularly in the arguments of those who push for lower taxes on business. Senator John McCain invoked it prominently in his pre-election debate with Barack Obama when he compared America's corporate tax rate of 35 percent to Ireland's 11 percent. "Now, if you're a business person, and you can locate any place in the world," McCain noted, then obviously "you go to the country where it's 11 percent tax versus 35 percent."[7] McCain got his number for Ireland wrong: the Irish corporate tax rate is 12.5 percent, not 11 percent; but note that he accepted (and cherished) the constraint imposed by globalization. It enabled him to fortify his argument for lower taxes by appealing to their inevitability, courtesy of globalization.

There has been a remarkable reduction in corporate taxes around the world since the early 1980s. The average for the member countries of the OECD countries, excluding the United States, has fallen from around 50 percent in 1981 to 30 percent in 2009. In the United States, the statutory tax on capital has come down from 50 percent to 39 percent over the same period.[8] Competition among governments for increasingly mobile global firms—what economists call "international tax competition"—has played a role in this global shift. The arguments of McCain and countless other conservative politicians who have used globalization to advance their agendas provide still more evidence of this role.

A detailed economic study on OECD tax policies finds that when other countries reduce their average statutory corporate tax rate by 1 percentage point the home country follows by reducing its tax rate by 0.7 percentage points. You either stand your ground and risk seeing your corporations depart for lower tax jurisdictions, or you respond in kind. Interestingly, the same study finds that international tax competition takes place only among countries that have removed their capital controls. When such controls are in place, capital and profits cannot move as easily across national borders and there is no downward pressure on capital taxes. The removal of capital controls appears to be the main factor driving the reduction in corporate tax rates since the 1980s.[9]

The problem has become a big enough headache for tax agencies that efforts are under way within the OECD and European Union to identify and roll back instances of so-called "harmful tax competition." To date, these activities have only focused on tax havens in a number of microstates ranging from Andorra to Vanuatu. The real challenge is to safeguard the integrity of each nation's corporate tax regime in a world where enterprises and their capital are footloose. This challenge remains unaddressed.

Health and safety standards. Most people would subscribe to the principle that nations ought to be free to determine their own standards with respect to public health and safety. What happens when these standards diverge across countries, either by design or because of differences in their application? How should goods and services be treated when they cross the boundaries of jurisdictions with varying standards?

WTO jurisprudence on this question continues to evolve. The WTO allows countries to enact regulations on public health and safety grounds that may run against their general obligations under the trade rules. But these regulations need to be applied in a way that does not overtly discriminate against imports and must not smack of disguised protectionism. The WTO's Agreement on Sanitary and Phytosanitary (SPS) Measures recognizes the right of nations to apply measures that protect human, animal, or plant life or health, but these measures must conform to international standards or be based on "scientific principles." In practice, disputes in these areas hang on the interpretation of a group of judges in Geneva about what is reasonable or practical. In the absence of bright lines that demarcate national sovereignty from international obligations, the judges often claim too much on behalf of the trade regime.

In 1990, for example, a GATT panel ruled against Thailand's ban on imported cigarettes. Thailand had imposed the ban as part of a campaign to reduce smoking, but continued to allow the sale of domestic cigarettes. The Thai government argued that imported cigarettes were more addictive and were more likely to be consumed by young people and by women on account of their effective advertising. The GATT panel was unmoved. It reasoned that the Thai government could have attained its public health objectives at less cost to trade by pursuing alternative policies. The government might have resorted to restrictions on advertising, labeling requirements, or content requirements, all of which could be applied in a non-discriminatory manner.

The GATT panel was surely correct about the impact of the Thai ban on trade. But in reaching their decisions, the panelists second-guessed the government about what is feasible and practical. As the legal scholars Michael Trebilcock and Robert Howse put it, "the Panel simply ignored the possibility that the alternative measures might involve high regulatory and compliance costs, or might be impracticable to implement effectively in a developing country."[10]

The hormone beef case from chapter Four also raises difficult issues. In this instance, the European Union ban on beef reared on certain growth hormones was not discriminatory; it applied to

imported and domestic beef alike. It was also obvious that there
was no protectionist motive behind the ban, which was pushed by
consumer lobbies and interests in Europe alarmed by the potential
health threats. Nonetheless, the WTO Panel and appellate body
both ruled against the European Union, arguing that the ban violated the requirement in the SPS Agreement that policies be based
on "scientific evidence." There was indeed scant positive evidence
to date that growth hormones posed any health threats. Instead,
the European Union had applied a broader principle not explicitly
covered by the WTO, the "precautionary principle," which permits
greater caution in the presence of scientific uncertainty.[11]

The precautionary principle reverses the burden of proof.
Instead of asking, "Is there reasonable evidence that growth hormones or GMOs have adverse effects?" it requires policy makers to ask, "Are we reasonably sure that they do *not*?" In many
unsettled areas of scientific knowledge, the answer to both questions can be no. The precautionary principle makes sense in cases
where adverse effects can be large and irreversible. As the European Commission argued (unsuccessfully), policy here cannot be
made purely on the basis of science. Politics, which aggregates a
society's risk preferences, must play the determinative role. The
WTO judges did acknowledge a nation's right to apply its own risk
standards, but ruled that the European Union's invocation of the
precautionary principle did not satisfy the criterion of "scientific
evidence." Instead of simply ascertaining whether the science was
taken into account, the rules of the SPS Agreement forced them
to use an international standard on *how* scientific evidence should
be processed.

If the European Union, with its sophisticated policy machinery,
could not convince the WTO that it should have leeway in determining its own standards, we can only imagine the difficulties that
developing nations face. For poor nations, even more than rich
ones, the rules imply a single standard.

Ultimately, the question is whether a democracy is allowed to determine its own rules—and make its own mistakes. The European Union regulations on beef (and, in a similar case in 2006, on biotech) did not discriminate against imports, which makes international discipline designed to promote trade even more problematic. As I will argue later, international rules can and should require certain procedural safeguards for domestic regulatory proceedings (such as transparency, broad representation, and scientific input) in accord with democratic practices. The trouble occurs when international tribunals contradict domestic proceedings on *substantive* matters (in the beef case, how to trade off economic benefits against uncertain health risks). In this instance, trade rules clearly trumped democratic decision making within the European Union.

"Regulatory takings." There are thousands of bilateral investment treaties (BITs) and hundreds of bilateral or regional trade agreements (RTAs) currently in force. Governments use them to promote trade and investment links in ways that go beyond what the WTO and other multilateral arrangements permit. A key objective is to provide a higher level of security to foreign investors by undertaking stronger external commitments.

BITs and RTAs usually allow foreign investors to sue host governments in an international tribunal for damages when new domestic regulations have adverse effects on the investors' profits. The idea is that the change in government regulations amounts to expropriation (it reduces the benefits that were initially granted to the investors under the BIT or RTA), and therefore requires compensation. This is similar to the U.S. doctrine of "regulatory takings," which however has never been accepted legal practice within the United States. The treaties include a general exception to allow governments to pursue policies in the interests of the public good, but since these cases are judged in international courts, different standards can apply. Foreign investors may end up receiving rights that domestic investors do not have.[12]

Such cases have been prominent under the North American Free Trade Agreement or NAFTA of 1992, particularly in the area of environmental regulation. Foreign investors have won damages against the Canadian and Mexican governments in several instances. In 1997, a U.S. firm challenged a Mexican municipality's refusal to grant a construction permit for a toxic waste facility and was awarded $15.6 million in damages. The same year, a U.S. chemical company challenged a Canadian ban on a gasoline additive and received $13 million in a settlement.[13]

Perhaps the most worrying case to date involves a suit brought against the South African government in 2007 by three Italian mining companies. The companies charge that South Africa's affirmative action program, called Black Economic Empowerment, violates the rights provided to them under existing bilateral investment treaties. The program aims to reverse South Africa's long history of racial discrimination and is an integral element in the country's democratic transition. It requires that mining companies alter their employment practices and sell a minority share to black partners. The Italian companies have asked for $350 million in return for what they assert is an expropriation of their South African operations.[14] If they win, they will have achieved an outcome beyond the reach of any domestic investor.

Industrial policies in developing nations. Probably the most significant external constraint that developing nations face as a consequence of hyperglobalization are the restrictions on industrial policies that make it harder for countries in Latin America, Africa, and elsewhere to emulate the development strategies that East Asian countries have employed to such good effect.

Unlike GATT, which left poor nations essentially free to use any and all industrial policies, the WTO imposes several restrictions. Export subsidies are now illegal for all but the poorest nations, denying developing nations the benefit of export-processing zones of the type that Mauritius, China, and many Southeast Asian nations have used.[15] Policies that require firms to use more local inputs (so-called "domestic content requirements") are also illegal, even though such policies helped China and India develop into world-class auto parts suppliers. Patent and copyright laws must now comply with minimum international standards, ruling out the kind of industrial imitation that was crucial to both South Korea and Taiwan's industrial strategies during the 1960s and 1970s (and indeed to many of today's rich countries in earlier periods).[16] Countries that are not members of the WTO are often hit with more restrictive demands as part of their negotiations to join the organization.

The WTO's Agreement on Intellectual Property Rights (TRIPS) deserves special mention. This agreement significantly impairs the ability of developing nations to reverse-engineer and copy the advanced technologies used in rich countries. As the Columbia economist and expert on technology policy Richard Nelson notes, copying foreign technology has long been one of the most important drivers of economic catch-up.[17] TRIPS has raised considerable concern because it restricts access to essential medicines and has adverse effects on public health. Its detrimental effects on technological capabilities in developing nations have yet to receive similar attention, though they may be of equal significance.

Regional or bilateral trade agreements typically extend the external constraints beyond those found in the WTO. These agreements are in effect a means for the United States and the European Union to "export their own regulatory approaches" to developing nations.[18] Often they encompass measures which the United States and the European Union have tried to get adopted in the WTO or other multilateral forums, but have failed. In particular in its free trade agreements with developing countries, the United States aggressively pushes for restrictions on their governments' ability to manage capital flows and shape patent regulations. And even though the IMF now exercises greater restraint, its programs with individual developing countries still contain many detailed requirements on trade and industrial policies.[19]

Developing nations have not completely run out of room to pursue industrial strategies that promote new industries. Determined governments can get around many of these restrictions, but few governments in the developing world are not constantly asking themselves if this or that proposed policy is WTO-legal.

The Trilemma

How do we manage the tension between national democracy and global markets? We have three options. We can *restrict democracy* in the interest of minimizing international transaction costs, disregarding the economic and social whiplash that the global economy occasionally produces. We can *limit globalization*, in the hope of building democratic legitimacy at home. Or we can *globalize democracy*, at the cost of national sovereignty. This gives us a menu of options for reconstructing the world economy.

The menu captures the fundamental political trilemma of the world economy: we cannot have hyperglobalization, democracy, and national self-determination all at once. We can have at most two out of three. If we want hyperglobalization and democracy, we need to give up on the nation state. If we must keep the nation state and want hyperglobalization too, then we must forget about democracy. And if we want to combine democracy with the nation state, then it is bye-bye deep globalization. The figure below depicts these choices.

Why these stark trade-offs? Consider a hypothetical fully globalized world economy in which all transaction costs have been eliminated and national borders do not interfere with the exchange of goods, services, or capital. Can nation states exist in such a world? Only if they focus exclusively on economic globalization and on

The Political Trilemma of the World Economy

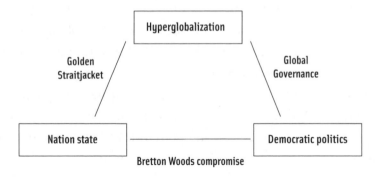

Figure 9-1: Pick two, any two

becoming attractive to international investors and traders. Domestic regulations and tax policies would then be either brought into alignment with international standards, or structured so that they pose the least amount of hindrance to international economic integration. The only services provided by governments would be those that reinforce the smooth functioning of international markets.

We can envisage a world of this sort, and it is the one Tom Friedman had in mind when he coined the term "Golden Straitjacket." In this world, governments pursue policies that they believe will earn them market confidence and attract trade and capital inflows: tight money, small government, low taxes, flexible labor markets, deregulation, privatization, and openness all around. "Golden Straitjacket" evokes the era of the gold standard before World War I. Unencumbered by domestic economic and social obligations, national governments were then free to pursue an agenda that focused exclusively on strict monetary rules.

External restraints were even more blatant under mercantilism and imperialism. We cannot properly speak of nation states before the nineteenth century, but the global economic system operated along strict Golden Straitjacket lines. The rules of the game—open borders, protection of the rights of foreign merchants and investors—were enforced by chartered trading companies or imperial powers. There was no possibility of deviating from them.

We may be far from the classical gold standard or chartered trading companies today, but the demands of hyperglobalization require a similar crowding out of domestic politics. The signs are familiar: the insulation of economic policy-making bodies (central banks, fiscal authorities, regulators, and so on), the disappearance (or privatization) of social insurance, the push for low corporate taxes, the erosion of the social compact between business and labor, and the replacement of domestic developmental goals with the need to maintain market confidence. Once the rules of the game are dictated by the requirements of the global economy, domestic groups' access to, and their control over, national economic policy making must inevitably become restricted. You can have your globalization and your nation state too, but only if you keep democracy at bay.

Must we give up on democracy if we want to strive for a fully globalized world economy? There is actually a way out. We can drop nation states rather than democratic politics. This is the "global governance" option. Robust global institutions with regulatory and standard-setting powers would align legal and political jurisdictions with the reach of markets and remove the transaction costs associated with national borders. If they could be endowed with adequate accountability and legitimacy in addition, politics need not, and would not, shrink: it would relocate to the global level.

Taking this idea to its logical conclusion, we can envisage a form of global federalism—the U.S. model expanded on a global scale. Within the United States a national constitution, federal government, federal judiciary, and large number of nationwide regulatory agencies ensure that markets are truly national despite many differences in regulatory and taxation practices among individual states. Or we can imagine alternative forms of global governance, not as ambitious as global federalism and built around new mechanisms of accountability and representation. A major move in the direction of global governance, in whatever form, necessarily would entail a significant diminution of *national* sovereignty. National governments would not disappear, but their powers would be severely circumscribed by supranational rulemaking and enforcing bodies empowered (and constrained) by democratic legitimacy. The European Union is a regional example of this.

This may sound like pie in the sky, and perhaps it is. The historical experience of the United States shows how tricky it can be to establish and maintain a political union in the face of large differences in the constituent parts. The halting way in which political institutions within the European Union have developed, and the persistent complaints about their democratic deficit, also indicate the difficulties involved—even when the union comprises a group of nations at similar income levels and with similar historical trajectories. Real federalism on a global scale is at best a century away.

The appeal of the global governance model, however wishful, cannot be denied. When I present my students with the trilemma and ask them to pick one of the options, this one wins hands-down. If we can simultaneously reap the benefits of globalization and democracy, who cares that national politicians will be out of a job? Yes, there are practical difficulties with democratic global governance, but perhaps these are exaggerated, too. Many political theorists and legal scholars suggest that democratic global governance can grow out of today's international networks of policy makers, as long as these are held in check by new mechanisms of accountability of the type we shall consider in the next chapter.

I am skeptical about the global governance option, but mostly on substantive rather than practical grounds. There is simply too much diversity in the world for nations to be shoehorned into common rules, even if these rules are somehow the product of democratic processes. Global standards and regulations are not just impractical; they are undesirable. The democratic legitimacy constraint virtually ensures that global governance will result in the lowest common denominator, a regime of weak and ineffective rules. We then face the big risk of too little governance all around, with national governments giving up on their responsibilities and no one else picking up the slack. But more on this in the next chapter.

The only remaining option sacrifices hyperglobalization. The Bretton Woods regime did this, which is why I have called it the Bretton Woods compromise. The Bretton Woods–GATT regime allowed countries to dance to their own tune as long as they removed a number of border restrictions on trade and generally treated all their trade partners equally. They were allowed (indeed encouraged) to maintain restrictions on capital flows, as the architects of the postwar economic order did not believe that free capital flows were compatible with domestic economic stability. Developing country policies were effectively left outside the scope of international discipline.

Until the 1980s, these loose rules left space for countries to follow their own, possibly divergent paths of development. Western Europe chose to integrate as a region and to erect an extensive welfare state. As we have seen, Japan caught up with the West using its own distinctive brand of capitalism, combining a dynamic export machine with large doses of inefficiency in services and agriculture. China grew by leaps and bounds once it recognized the importance of private initiative, even though it flouted every other rule in the guidebook. Much of the rest of East Asia generated an economic miracle by relying on industrial policies that have since been banned by the WTO. Scores of countries in Latin America, the Middle East, and Africa generated unprecedented economic growth rates until the late 1970s under import-substitution policies that insulated their economies from the world economy. As we saw, the Bretton Woods compromise was largely abandoned in the 1980s as the liberalization of capital flows gathered speed and trade agreements began to reach behind national borders.

The world economy has since been trapped in an uncomfortable zone between the three nodes of the trilemma. We have not squarely faced up to the tough choices that the trilemma identifies. In particular, we have yet to accept openly that we need to lower our sights on economic globalization if we want the nation state to remain the principal locus of democratic politics. We have no choice but to settle for a "thin" version of globalization—to reinvent the Bretton Woods compromise for a different era.

We cannot simply bring back wholesale the approaches of the 1950s and 1960s. We will have to be imaginative, innovative, and willing to experiment. In the last part of the book, I will provide some ideas on how to move forward. But the first order of business is getting the big picture right. The necessary sort of policy experimentation will not be unleashed until we change our narrative.

Smart Globalization *Can* Enhance National Democracy

Each of the cases I discussed previously embodies a trade-off between removing transaction costs in the international economy and maintaining domestic differences. The greater the emphasis on deep economic integration, the less the room for national differences in social and economic arrangements, and the smaller the space for democratic decision making at the national level.

More restrained forms of globalization need not embrace the assumptions inherent in deep integration. By placing limits on globalization, the Bretton Woods regime allowed the world economy and national democracies to flourish side by side. Once we accept restraints on globalization, we can in fact go one step further. We can envisage global rules that actually *enhance* the operation of national democracies.

There is indeed nothing inherently contradictory between having a global rule–based regime and national democracy. Democracy is never perfect in practice. As the Princeton political scientists Robert Keohane, Stephen Macedo, and Andrew Moravcsik have argued, well-crafted external rules may enhance both the quality and legitimacy of democratic practices. Democracies, these authors note, do not aim simply to maximize popular participation. Even when external rules constrain participation at the national level, they may provide compensating democratic benefits such as improving deliberation, suppressing factions, and ensuring minority representation. Democratic practices can be enhanced by procedural safeguards that prevent capture by interest groups and ensure the use of relevant economic and scientific evidence as part of the deliberations. Besides, entering into binding international commitments is a *sovereign* act. Restricting it would be like preventing Congress from delegating some of its rulemaking powers to independent regulatory agencies.[20]

While international commitments can enhance national democracy, they will not necessarily do so. The hyperglobalization agenda, with its focus on minimizing transaction costs in the international economy, clashes with democracy for the simple reason that it seeks not to improve the functioning of democracy but to accommodate commercial and financial interests seeking market access at low cost. It requires us to buy into a narrative that gives predominance to the needs of multinational enterprises, big banks, and investment houses over other social and economic objectives.[21] Hence this agenda serves primarily those needs.

We have a choice in how we overcome this defect. We can globalize democratic governance along with markets; or we can rethink trade and investment agreements to expand space for democratic decision making at the national level. I discuss each of these strategies in turn in the following two chapters.

10

Is Global Governance Feasible?
Is It Desirable?

The nation state is passé. Borders have disappeared. Distance is dead. The earth is flat. Our identities are no longer bound by our places of birth. Domestic politics is being superseded by newer, more fluid forms of representation that transcend national boundaries. Authority is moving from domestic rule-makers to transnational networks of regulators. Political power is shifting to a new wave of activists organized around international non-governmental organizations. The decisions that shape our economic lives are made by large multinational companies and faceless international bureaucrats.

How many times have we heard these or similar statements, heralding or decrying the dawn of a new era of global governance?

And yet look at the way events have unfolded in the recent crisis of 2007–08. Who bailed out the global banks to prevent the financial crisis from becoming even more cataclysmic? Who pumped in the liquidity needed to soothe international credit markets? Who stimulated the global economy through fiscal expansion? Who provided unemployment compensation and other safety nets for the workers who lost their jobs? Who is setting the new rules on compensation, capital adequacy, and liquidity for large banks? Who gets the lion's share of the blame for everything that went wrong before, during, and after?

The answer to each one of these questions is the same: *national governments.* We may think we live in a world whose governance has been radically transformed by globalization, but the buck still stops with domestic policy makers. The hype that surrounds the decline of the nation state is just that: hype. Our world economy may be populated by a veritable alphabet soup of international agencies— everything from ADB to WTO[1]—but democratic decision making remains firmly lodged within nation states. "Global governance" has a nice ring to it, but don't go looking for it anytime soon. Our complex and variegated world allows only a very thin veneer of global governance—and for very good reasons, too.

Overcoming the Tyranny of Nation States

It's no longer just cranks and wide-eyed utopians who entertain the idea of global government. Many economists, sociologists, political scientists, legal scholars, and philosophers have joined the search for new forms of governance that leave the nation state behind. Of course, few of these analysts advocate a truly global version of the nation state; a global legislature or council of ministers is too much of a fantasy. The solutions they propose rely instead on new conceptions of political community, representation, and accountability. The hope is that these innovations can replicate many of constitutional democracy's essential functions at the global level.

The crudest form of such global governance envisages straightforward delegation of national powers to international technocrats. It involves autonomous regulatory agencies charged with solving what are essentially regarded as "technical" problems arising from uncoordinated decision making in the global economy. For obvious reasons, economists are particularly enamored of such arrangements. For example, when the European economics network VoxEU.org solicited advice from leading economists on how to address the frailties of the global financial system in the wake of the 2008 crisis, the proposed solutions often took the form of tighter international rules administered by some kind of technocracy: an international bankruptcy court, a world financial organization, an international bank charter, an international lender of last resort, and so on.[2] Jeffrey Garten, under secretary of commerce for international trade in the Clinton administration, has long called for the establishment of a global central bank.[3] Economists Carmen Reinhart and Ken Rogoff have proposed an international financial regulator.

These proposals may seem like the naive ruminations of economists who don't understand politics, but in fact they are often based on an explicit political motive. When Reinhart and Rogoff argue for an international financial regulator, their goal is as much to fix a political failure as it is to address economic spillovers across nations; perhaps the political motive even takes precedence over the economic one. They hope to end political meddling at the national level that they perceive has emasculated domestic regulations. They write: "a well-endowed, professionally staffed international financial regulator—operating without layers of political hacks—would offer a badly needed counterweight to the powerful domestic financial service sector."[4] The political theory that underpins this approach holds that delegating regulatory powers to an insulated and autonomous global technocracy leads to better governance, both global and national.

In the real world, delegation requires legislators to give up their prerogative to make the rules and reduces their ability to respond to their constituents. As such, it typically takes place under a narrow set of conditions. In the United States, for example, Congress delegates rulemaking powers to executive agencies only when its political preferences are quite similar to the president's and when the issues under consideration are highly technical.[5] Even then, delegation remains partial and comes with elaborate accountability mechanisms. Delegation is a *political* act. Hence, many preconditions have to be satisfied before delegation to supranational bodies can become widespread and sustainable. We would need to create a "global body politic" of some sort, with common norms, a transnational political community, and new mechanisms of accountability suited to the global arena.

Economists don't pay much attention to these prerequisites, but other scholars do. Many among them see evidence that new models of global governance are indeed emerging. Anne-Marie Slaughter, a scholar of international relations at Princeton, has focused on transnational networks populated by regulators, judges, and even legislators. These networks can perform governance functions even when they are not constituted as intergovernmental organizations or formally institutionalized. Such networks, Slaughter argues, extend the reach of formal governance mechanisms, allow persuasion and information sharing across national borders, contribute to the formation of global norms, and can generate the capacity to implement international norms and agreements in nations where the domestic capacity to do so is weak.[6]

The governance of financial markets is in fact the arena where such networks have advanced the furthest and which provides Slaughter's most telling illustrations. The International Organization of Securities Commissions (IOSCO) brings together the world's securities regulators and issues global principles. The Basel Committee on Banking Supervision performs the same role for banking regulators. These networks have small secretariats (if any at all) and no enforcement power. Yet they certainly exert influence through their standard-setting powers and legitimacy—at least in the eyes of regulators. Their deliberations often become a reference point in domestic discussions. They may not entirely substitute for nation states, but they end up creating internationally intertwined networks of policy makers.

To achieve legitimacy, global governance must transcend exclusive clubs of regulators and technocrats. Can these networks go beyond narrowly technical areas and encompass broader social purposes? Yes, says John Ruggie, the Harvard scholar who coined the term "embedded liberalism" to describe the Bretton Woods regime. Ruggie agrees that transnational networks have undermined the traditional model of governance based on nation states. To right this imbalance, he argues, we need greater emphasis on corporate social responsibility at the global level. An updated version of embedded liberalism would move beyond a state-centered multilateralism to "a multilateralism that actively embraces the potential contributions to global social organization by civil society and corporate actors." These actors can advance new global norms—on human rights, labor practices, health, anti-corruption, and environmental stewardship—and then enshrine them in the operations of large international corporations and policies of national governments. Multinational corporations' funding of HIV/AIDS treatment programs in poor nations represents one prominent example.

The United Nation's Global Compact, which Ruggie had a big hand in shaping, embodies this agenda. The Compact aims to transform international corporations into vehicles for the advancement of social and economic goals. Such a transformation would benefit the communities in which these corporations and their affiliates operate. But, as Ruggie explains, there would be additional advantages. Improving large corporations' social and environmental performance would spur emulation by other, smaller firms. It would alleviate the widespread concern that international competition creates a race to the bottom in labor and environmental standards at the expense of social inclusion at home. And it would allow the private sector to shoulder some of the functions that states are finding increasingly difficult to finance and carry out, as in public health and environmental protection, narrowing the governance gap between international markets and national governments.[7]

Arguments on behalf of new forms of global governance—whether of the delegation, network, or corporate social responsibility type—raise troubling questions. To whom are these mechanisms supposed to be accountable? From where do these global clubs of regulators, international non-governmental organizations, or large firms get their mandates? Who empowers and polices them? What ensures that the voice and interests of those who are less globally networked are also heard? The Achilles' heel of global governance is lack of clear accountability relationships. In a nation state, the electorate is the ultimate source of political mandates and elections the ultimate vehicle for accountability. If you do not respond to your constituencies' expectations and aspirations, you are voted out. Global electoral accountability of this sort is too far-fetched a notion. We would need different mechanisms.[8]

Probably the best argument for an alternative *global* conception of accountability comes from two distinguished political scientists, Joshua Cohen and Charles Sabel. These scholars begin by arguing that the problems global governance aims to solve don't lend themselves to traditional notions of accountability. In the traditional model, a constituency with well-defined interests empowers its representative to act on behalf on those interests. Global regulation presents challenges that are new, often highly technical, and subject to rapidly evolving circumstances. The global "public" typically has only a hazy notion of what problems need solving and how to solve them.

In this setting, accountability hinges on the international regulator's ability to provide "a good explanation" for what she chooses to do. "Questions are decided by argument about the best way to address problems," write Cohen and Sabel, "not [by] simply exertions of power, expressions of interest, or bargaining from power positions on the basis of interests."[9] There is no presumption here that the solutions will be "technocratic" ones. Even when values and interests diverge and disagreement prevails, the hope is that the process of transnational deliberation will generate the explanations that all or most can acknowledge as legitimate. Global rulemaking becomes accountable to the extent that the reasoning behind the rules is found to be compelling by those to whom the rules would apply.

Cohen and Sabel's scheme provides room, at least in principle, for variation in institutional practices across nation states within an overall framework of global cooperation and coordination. A country and its policy makers are free to experiment and implement different solutions as long as they can explain to their peers— policy makers in the other countries—why they have arrived at those solutions. They must justify their choices publicly and place them in the context of comparable choices made by others. A skeptic may wonder, however, if such mechanisms will not lead instead to widespread hypocrisy as policy makers continue with business-as-usual while rationalizing their actions in loftier terms.

Ultimately, Cohen and Sabel hope that these deliberative processes would feed into the development of a global political community, in which "dispersed peoples might come to share a new identity as common members of an organized global populace."[10] It is difficult to see how their conception of global governance would work in the absence of such a transformation in political identities. At the end of the day, global governance requires individuals who feel that they are global citizens.

Maybe we are not too far from that state of affairs. The Princeton ethicist Peter Singer has written powerfully about the development of a new global ethic that follows from globalization. "If . . . the revolution in communications has created a global audience," he writes, "then we might need to justify our behavior to the whole world."[11] The economist and philosopher Amartya Sen has argued that it is quite misleading to think of ourselves as bound by a single, unchanging identity—ethnic, religious, or national— with which we are born. Each one of us has multiple identities, based on our profession, gender, occupation, class, political leanings, hobbies and interests, sports teams we support, and so on.[12] These identities do not come at the expense of each other, and we freely choose how much weight we put on them. Many identities cross national boundaries, allowing us to form transnational associations and define our "interests" across a broad geography. This flexibility and multiplicity creates room, in principle, for the establishment of a truly global political community.

There is much that is attractive in these ideas about the potential for global governance. As Sen puts it, "there is something of a tyranny of ideas in seeing the political divisions of states (primarily, national states) as being, in some way, fundamental, and in seeing them not only as practical constraints to be addressed, but as divisions of basic significance in ethics and political philosophy."[13] Furthermore, political identity and community have been continuously redefined over time in ever more expansive terms. Human associations have moved from the tribal and local to city states and then on to nation states. Shouldn't a global community be next?

The proof of the pudding is in the eating. How far can these emergent forms of global governance go and how much globalization can they support? A good place to start is the European Union, which has traveled further along the road of transnational governance than any other collection of nation states.

European Union: The Exception That Tests the Rule

When Cohen and Sabel were developing their ideas on global governance through deliberation, they had one concrete example in mind: the European Union. The European experiment shows both the potential and the limitations of these ideas.

European nations have achieved an extraordinary amount of economic integration among themselves. Nowhere is there a better approximation of deep integration or hyperglobalization, albeit at the regional level. Underneath Europe's single market lies an enormous institutional artifice devoted to removing transaction costs and harmonizing regulations. EU members have renounced barriers on the movement of goods, capital, and labor. But beyond that they have signed on to 100,000-plus pages of EU-wide regulations—on everything from science policy to consumer protections—that lay out common standards and expectations. They have set up a European Court of Justice that assiduously enforces these regulations. They have empowered an administrative arm in the form of the European Commission to propose new laws and implement common policies in external trade, agriculture, competition, regional assistance, and many other areas. They have established a number of programs to provide financial assistance to lagging regions of the Union and foster economic convergence. Sixteen of the members have adopted a common currency (the euro) and succumbed to a common monetary policy administered by the European Central Bank. In addition to all this, the EU has many specialized agencies that are too numerous to list here.

The EU's democratic institutions are less well developed. The directly elected European Parliament operates mostly as a talking shop rather than as a source of legislative initiative or oversight. Real power lies with the Council of Ministers, which is a collection of ministers from national governments. How to establish and maintain democratic legitimacy and accountability for Europe's extensive supranational setup has long been a thorny question. Critics from the right blame EU institutions for overreaching while critics from the left complain about a "democratic deficit."

European leaders have made significant efforts in recent years to boost the *political* infrastructure of the European Union, but it has been a bumpy and arduous road. An ambitious effort to ratify a European Constitution failed after voters in France and The Netherlands rejected it in 2005. In the wake of this failure came the Lisbon Treaty, which entered into force in December 2009—but only after the United Kingdom, Poland, Ireland, and the Czech Republic secured exclusions from some of the requirements of the treaty. The treaty reforms the voting rules in the Council of Ministers, gives more power to the European Parliament, renders the European Union's human rights charter legally binding, and establishes a new executive position in the form of the president of the European Council.

As the opt-outs received by Britain and others suggest, there remain significant differences among member states on the desirability of turning Europe into a true political federation. Britain zealously guards its distinctive constitution and legal system from the encroachment of EU rules or institutions. In many areas such as financial regulation and monetary policy, it has little interest in bringing its practices in line with those of the others. Britain's interest in Europe remains primarily economic. Its minimalist approach to European institution building contrasts sharply with France's and Germany's occasionally more ambitious federalist goals.

As important as these broad debates over the European Union's constitutional architecture may be, much of the organization's real work gets done under an informal, evolving set of practices that Charles Sabel calls "experimentalist governance." The member states and the higher-level EU institutions decide on the goals to be accomplished. These could be as ambitious and ill-defined as "social inclusion" or as narrow as "a unified energy grid." National regulatory agencies are given freedom to advance these goals in the ways they see fit, but the quid pro quo is that they must report their actions and results in what are variably called forums, networked agencies, councils of regulators, or open methods of coordination. Peer review allows national regulators to compare their approaches to those of others and revise them as necessary. Over time, the goals themselves are updated and altered in light of the learning that takes place in these deliberations.[14]

Experimentalist governance helps create Europe-wide norms and contributes to building transnational consensus around common approaches. They need not necessarily result in complete homogenization. Where differences continue to exist, they do so in the context of mutual understanding and accountability, so that they are much less likely to turn into sources of friction. The requirement that national practices be justified renders national differences easier to accommodate.

The members of the European Union may seem like a diverse bunch, but compared to the nations that make up the world economy they are a model of concord. These twenty-seven nations are bound together by a common geography, culture, religion, and history. Excluding Luxembourg, where measured income per head is very high, the richest among them (Ireland, in 2008) is only 3.3 times wealthier than the poorest (Bulgaria), compared to a multiple of almost 190 across the world. EU members are driven by a strong sense of strategic purpose that extends considerably beyond economic integration. European unity in fact looms larger as a political goal than it does as an economic one.

Despite all these comparative advantages, the European Union's institutional evolution has progressed slowly and large differences remain among the member states. Most telling is the well-recognized tension between deepening the Union and expanding it to incorporate new members. Consider the long-simmering debate over Turkey. French and German opposition to Turkey's entrance into the European Union derives in part from cultural and religious reasons. But the fear that Turkey's divergent political traditions and institutions would greatly hamper European political integration also plays a large role. Britain, on the other hand, welcomes anything that would temper French and German ambitions for a *political* Europe, and for that reason supports eventual membership for Turkey. Everyone understands that the deepening of Europe's political integration becomes more problematic as the number of members increases and the European Union's composition becomes more diverse.

Europe's own dilemma is no different from that faced by the world economy as a whole. As we saw in previous chapters, deep economic integration requires erecting an extensive transnational governance structure to support it. Ultimately, the European Union will either bite the political bullet or resign itself to a more limited economic union. Those who push for a political Europe stand a greater chance of achieving a truly single European market than those who want to limit the conversation to the economic level. But political advocates have yet to win the argument. They face great opposition both from their national electorates and from other political leaders with differing visions.

Thus Europe has become a halfway house—economically more integrated than any other region of the world, but with a governance structure that remains a work in progress. It has the potential to turn itself into a true economic union, but it is not there yet. When European economies come under stress, the responses are overwhelmingly national.

The governance gaps became particularly obvious during the crisis of 2008 and its aftermath. Europe's banks are supervised by national regulators. When they started going bust, there was practically no coordination among EU governments. Bailouts of banks and other firms were carried out separately by individual governments, often in ways that harmed other EU members. There was also no coordination in the design of recovery plans and fiscal stimulus programs, even though there are clear spillovers (German firms benefit from a French fiscal stimulus almost as much as French firms do, given how intertwined the two economies are). When European leaders finally approved a "common" framework for financial oversight in December 2009, Britain's finance minister underscored the limited nature of the agreement by emphasizing that "responsibility lies with national regulators."[15]

The poorer and worse-hit members of the European Union could count on only grudging support from Brussels. Latvia, Hungary, and Greece were forced to turn to the IMF for financial assistance as a condition for getting loans from richer EU governments.[16] (Imagine what it would look like if Washington were to require California to submit to IMF monitoring in order to benefit from Federal Recovery Funds.) Others dealing with crushing economic problems were left to fend for themselves (Spain and Portugal). In effect, these countries had the worst of both worlds: economic union prevented their resort to currency devaluation for a quick boost to their competitiveness, while the lack of political union precluded their receiving much support from the rest of Europe.

In light of all this it would be easy to write off the European Union, but that would be too harsh a judgment. Membership in the Union did make a difference to the willingness of smaller countries to live by hyperglobalization rules. Consider Latvia, the small Baltic country, which found itself experiencing economic difficulties similar to those Argentina had lived through a decade earlier. Latvia had grown rapidly since joining the European Union in 2004 on the back of large amounts of borrowing from European banks and a domestic property bubble. It had run up huge current account deficits and foreign debts (20 percent and 125 percent of GDP, respectively, by 2007). Predictably, the global economic crisis and the reversal in capital flows in 2008 left the Latvian economy in dire straits. As lending and property prices collapsed, unemployment rose to 20 percent and GDP declined by 18 percent in 2009. In January 2009, the country had its worst riots since the collapse of the Soviet Union.

Latvia had a fixed exchange rate and free capital flows, just like Argentina. Its currency had been pegged to the euro since 2005. Unlike Argentina, however, the country's politicians managed to tough it out without devaluing the currency and introducing capital controls (the latter would have explicitly broken EU rules). By early 2010, it looked as if the Latvian economy had begun to stabilize.[17] The difference with Argentina was that Latvia's membership in a larger political community changed the balance of costs and benefits of going it alone. The right to free circulation of labor within the European Union allowed many Latvian workers to emigrate, serving as a safety valve for an economy under duress. Brussels prevailed on European banks to support their subsidiaries in Latvia. Most important, the prospect of adopting the euro as the domestic currency and joining the Eurozone compelled Latvian policy makers to foreclose any options—such as devaluation—that would endanger that objective, despite the very high short-term economic costs.

For all its teething problems, Europe should be viewed as a great success considering its progress down the path of institution building. For the rest of the world, however, it remains a cautionary tale. The European Union demonstrates the difficulties of achieving a political union robust enough to underpin deep economic integration even among a comparatively small number of like-minded countries. At best, it is the exception that tests the rule. The European Union proves that transnational democratic governance is workable, but its experience also lays bare the demanding requirements of such governance. Anyone who thinks global governance is a plausible path for the world economy at large would do well to consider Europe's experience.

Would Global Governance Solve Our Problems?

Let's give global governance enthusiasts the benefit of the doubt and ask how the mechanisms they propose would resolve the tensions that hyperglobalization generates.

Consider how we should deal with the following three challenges:

1. Chinese exports of toys to the United States are found to contain unsafe levels of lead.
2. The subprime mortgage crisis in the United States spreads to the rest of the world as many of the securities issued by U.S. banks and marketed in foreign countries turn out to be "toxic."
3. Some of the goods exported from Indonesia to the United States and Europe are manufactured using child labor.

In all three cases, a country exports a good, service, or asset that causes problems for the importing country. Chinese exports of lead-tainted toys endanger the health of American children; U.S. exports of mispriced mortgage-based assets endanger financial stability in the rest of the world, and Indonesian exports of child-labor services threaten labor standards and values in the United States and Western Europe. Prevailing international rules do not provide clear-cut solutions for these challenges, so we need to think our way through them. Can we address them through markets alone? Do we need specific rules, and if so, should they be national or global? Might the answers differ across these three areas?

Consider the similarities between these problems, even though they are drawn from quite different domains of the world economy. At the core of each is a dispute about standards, with respect to lead content, rating of financial securities, and child labor. In all three cases there are differences in the standards applied (or desired) by the exporting and importing countries. Exporters may have lower standards and therefore possess a competitive advantage in the markets of the importing countries. However, purchasers in the importing country cannot directly observe the standard under which the exported good or service has been produced. A consumer cannot tell easily whether the toy contains lead paint or has been manufactured using child labor under exploitative conditions; nor can a lender fully identify the risk characteristics of the bundled assets it holds. Everything else held constant, importers are less likely to buy the good or the service in question if it contains lead paint, has been made by children, or is likely to cause financial havoc.

At the same time, consumers' preferences vary. Each one of us probably places somewhat different weights on upholding the standard versus obtaining other benefits, such as a low price. You may be willing to pay an extra $2 for a T-shirt certified as child-labor-free, but I may want to pay no more than $1. You may be willing to trade off some extra risk for additional yield on a security, while I am more conservative in my investment philosophy. Some may be willing to purchase lead-tainted toys if it makes a big enough difference to the price, while others would consider it abhorrent. For this reason, any standard creates gainers and losers when applied uniformly.

How do we respond to these three challenges? The default option is to neglect them until they loom too large to ignore. We may choose this option for several reasons. First, we may trust the standard applied in the exporting country. The credit rating agencies in the United States are supposedly the best in the world, so why would any country worry about buying triple-A-rated U.S. mortgage securities? Chinese lead regulations are, on paper, more stringent than those in the United States, so why get concerned about the health hazards of Chinese toys? Second, we may think standards and regulations in foreign countries are none of our business. Buyers simply beware. Third, we may actually think that differences in regulatory standards are a source of comparative advantage—and hence of gains from trade—just like differences in productivity or skills across nations. If lax labor standards enable Indonesia to sell us cheaper goods, this is just another manifestation of the benefits of globalization.

These shortsighted arguments undercut the efficiency of the global economy and ultimately undermine its legitimacy. The challenges presented raise legitimate concerns and deserve serious responses. Consider therefore some of the possibilities.

Global standards. We may be tempted to seek global standards by which all countries would have to abide. We might require compliance with core labor standards of all producers, a common set of banking regulations, and uniform product safety codes. This is the global governance solution par excellence. In many areas we are gravitating toward this kind of approach, as we have seen, but obvious limitations remain. Nations are unlikely to agree on the appropriate standards, and often for very good reasons.

Labor standards offer the easiest example. The argument that rich countries' restrictions on child labor may be a poor fit for developing countries has long prevented a global consensus from emerging. Child labor of the type that activists in rich nations object to is often an unavoidable consequence of poverty. Preventing young children from working in factories may end up doing more harm than good if the most likely alternative for the children is not going to school but employment in domestic trades that are even more odious (prostitution is an oft-mentioned illustration). This argument against homogenization applies to other labor regulations too, such as maximum hours of work or minimum wages. More broadly, as long as basic human rights such as non-discrimination and freedom of association are not violated, nations ought to be free to choose the labor standards that best fit their own circumstances and social preferences. Common standards are costly, even if they may facilitate acceptance of certain kinds of imports in the rich countries.

This is also true in the area of financial regulation. What is "safe" for the United States may not be "safe enough" for France or Germany. The United States may accept happily a bit more risk than the other two countries as the price of financial innovation. On the other hand, the U.S. may want its banks to have higher capital requirements as a cushion against risk taking than French or German policy makers think necessary. In each case, neither position is necessarily right and the other wrong. Nations have different views because they have different preferences and circumstances.

Product safety rules seem the easiest to organize around a common standard, but even here there are important constraints. Note first that Chinese lead paint standards are in fact quite stringent. The problem arises not from differences in standards as written, but from differences in standards as practiced. As in most developing countries, the Chinese government has trouble enforcing and monitoring product standards. These difficulties often arise not from lack of willingness, but from lack of ability stemming from administrative, human resource, and financial constraints. No global standard can change this underlying reality. Perhaps, as Slaughter suggests, participation in global networks can help Chinese regulators improve by enabling information sharing and transfer of "best practices." Don't hold your breath. Improving domestic institutions is a long, drawn-out process over which foreigners typically have a very limited influence.

Even if nations were to agree on global standards, they may end up converging on the wrong set of regulations. Global finance provides an apt illustration. The Basel Committee on Banking Supervision, the global club of bank regulators, has been widely hailed as the apogee of international financial cooperation, but has produced largely inadequate agreements.[18] The first set of recommendations (Basel I) encouraged risky short-term borrowing and may have played a role in precipitating the Asian financial crisis. The second (Basel II) relied on credit rating agencies and banks' own models to generate risk weights for capital requirements, and is now widely viewed as inappropriate in light of the recent financial crisis. By neglecting the fact that the risks created by an individual bank's actions depend on the liquidity of the system as a whole, the Basel Committee's standards have, if anything, magnified systemic risks. In light of the great uncertainty about the merits of different regulatory approaches, it may be better to let a variety of regulatory models flourish side by side.

Market-based solutions. There is a more market-friendly alternative. Instead of mandating adherence to global standards, it entails mandating provision of *information*. If we enhance the information available to importers about the standards under which goods and services have been produced, every buyer can then make the decision that best fits his or her circumstances.

Consider child labor. We can imagine a system of certification and labeling that lets consumers in the advanced nations distinguish between imported goods that have been produced by children and those that have not. There are already many such labeling schemes in operation. RugMark, for example, is an international non-governmental organization that certifies that no child labor has been used in carpets from India and Nepal. Presumably, child-labor-free products cost more to produce and are more expensive. Consumers can express their preferences through the products they want to buy. Those who oppose the use of child labor can pay extra and buy the appropriately labeled goods while others remain free to consume the cheaper product. An attractive feature of labeling is that it doesn't impose a common standard on everyone in the importing country. I don't have to pay for your high standard if a lower one is good enough for me.

This would seem like a good solution, especially since it makes limited demands on global governance. And there may be certain areas where it makes a lot of sense. But as a generic solution, it falls far short.

Until the recent financial crisis we would have pointed to credit rating agencies as a successful instance of labeling. These agencies functioned, in principle, in the way that labeling is supposed to work. If you were risk-averse, you could restrict yourself to triple-A-rated, low-yield securities. If you wanted more yield, at the expense of higher risk, you could invest in lower-rated securities instead. These ratings allowed investors, again in principle, to decide where they wanted to be on the risk spectrum. The government did not need to micromanage portfolio decisions.

We have learned since that the information conveyed by credit ratings was not nearly as meaningful as it appeared at the time. For a variety of reasons, not least that the credit rating agencies were paid by the very firms whose securities they were evaluating, toxic assets received top ratings. Too many investors got burned because they took the ratings seriously. The market for information worked quite poorly.

The costs of faulty ratings were borne not just by the investors in those securities but by society at large. This is the problem of systemic risk: when large, highly leveraged institutions go bust, they threaten to take the entire financial system with them. The failure of credit rating agencies had consequences well beyond those who purchased the toxic securities.

Every system of labeling in fact raises a higher-order governance question: To whom are the certifiers accountable, or who certifies the certifiers? Credit rating worked poorly in financial markets because credit rating agencies maximized their income and neglected their fiduciary duties to society. A complicated governance problem was "solved" by handing it over to private profit-seeking entities whose incentives weren't properly aligned with society's.

The problem with labeling is no less serious in the case of labor or environmental standards, where diverse coalitions of non-governmental organizations and private corporations have taken the lead in the face of governmental deadlock. All of the participants have their own agenda, with the result that the meaning the labels convey can become quite ambiguous. For example, "fair trade" labels denote products such as coffee, chocolates, or bananas that are grown in an environmentally sustainable manner and which pay the farmers a certain minimum price. This seems like a win-win. Consumers can sip their coffee knowing that they are contributing to alleviating poverty and safeguarding the environment. But does the consumer really know or understand what the "fair trade" label on her coffee means?

We have very little reliable information on how labeling efforts such as "fair trade" work out in practice. One of the few academic studies on the subject looked at coffee in Guatemala and Costa Rica and found very little interest on the part of growers in fair trade certification. This is quite surprising in light of the apparent advantages, most notably in terms of better prices. In reality, the price premium the growers received seems to have been low compared to what they could get from growing specialty coffees.

Often, the price was not high enough to cover the investments necessary to fit the requirements for certification. Moreover, the benefits did not necessarily flow to the poorest farmers, who are the landless indigenous growers.[19] Other reports suggest that only a tiny share of the price premium for fair trade coffee finds its way to the growers.[20]

Fair trade or other labeling programs like RugMark may be doing some good on the whole, but we should be skeptical about how informative these labels are and the likely magnitude of their effects. And what is true of NGO-led efforts is all the more true of corporate social responsibility. Corporations, after all, are motivated by the bottom line. They may be willing to invest in social and environmental projects if doing so buys them custom- ers' goodwill. Yet we shouldn't assume their motives align closely with those of society at large, nor exaggerate their willingness to advance societal agendas.

The most fundamental objection to labeling and other market- based approaches is that they overlook the *social* dimension of standard-setting. For example, the conventional approach to deal- ing with health and safety hazards calls for standards, not labeling. If labeling works so well, why don't we deal with these issues in the same way, by letting individuals decide how much risk they want to take? As far as I know, not even libertarian economists have pro- posed that the best way to deal with the problem of lead-tainted Chinese toys is to *label* Chinese-made toys as having uncertain or high lead content and let consumers choose according to their own preferences and health-hazard/price trade-offs. Instead, our natural instinct is to push for more regulation and better enforce- ment of existing standards. Even the U.S. toy industry has asked the federal government to impose mandatory safety-testing stan- dards for all toys sold in the United States.[21]

We prefer uniform, government-mandated standards in these cases for several reasons. We may be skeptical that consumers will have enough information to make the right choices or the capacity to process the information they have. We may believe in the importance of social goals and norms in addition to individual preferences. Even though a few people in our midst may be willing to sign on as indentured servants for a price, we are unlikely as a society to allow them to do so. Finally, individuals acting in their own best interest may create problems for the rest of society and as a consequence their freedom to choose may need to be restricted. Think again of the mess that the banks that invested in toxic assets created for the rest of us or how sweatshops can undermine employment conditions for others in the economy.

These reasons apply as much to social and economic issues as they do to health and safety risks. They suggest that labeling and certification will play only a limited role in addressing the governance challenges of the global economy.

The limits of global governance. Global governance offers little help in solving these challenges we have considered. We are dealing with problems rooted in deep divisions among different societies in terms of preferences, circumstances, and capabilities. Technical fixes don't help. Neither do networks of regulators, market-based solutions, corporate social responsibility, or transnational deliberation. At best, these new forms of governance provide a kind of global governance-light. They simply cannot carry the weight of a hyperglobalized world economy. The world is too diverse to be shoehorned into a single political community.

In the case of lead-tainted toys, most people would agree that the obvious and correct solution is to let the domestic standard prevail. The United States should determine its own health and safety standards, and allow only toys that satisfy those standards to be imported. If other countries want to have different standards, or are unable to match U.S. standards for practical reasons, they would be similarly entitled to their own variants. But they cannot expect to export their products freely to the United States unless they meet the U.S. standards. This approach enables countries to uphold their own regulations, even if it comes at the cost of barriers at the border.

Can we not apply the same principle to financial regulations, labor standards, or other areas of conflict arising from differences in national standards? We can, and we should.

Globalization and Identity Redux

In Nick Hornby's comic novel *Juliet, Naked* (2009), one of the main characters, Duncan, obsesses over an obscure and reclusive American rock musician named Tucker Crowe. Duncan's life revolves around Crowe: he lectures on him, organizes meetings and conventions, and has written an unpublished book on the great man. Initially, Duncan has few people nearby with whom he can share his passion. The nearest Tucker Crowe fan lives sixty miles away and Duncan can meet up with him only once or twice a year. Then the Internet comes along. Duncan sets up a Web site and makes contact with hundreds of equally passionate Tucker Crowe aficionados scattered around the world. As Hornby writes, "now the nearest fans lived in Duncan's laptop," and he could talk to them all the time.[22]

New information and communication technologies are bringing ordinary people like Duncan together around shared interests in ways that scholars including Peter Singer and Amartya Sen hope will shrink the world. Thanks to these global links, local attachments are becoming less important as transnational moral and political communities loom ever larger. Or are they?

Even though Duncan's story sounds familiar—we've all had similar transformations in our own lives thanks to the Internet— it doesn't tell us the full story. Do our global interactions really erode our local and national identities? Evidence from the real world presents a very different and quite surprising picture. Consider the case of Netville.

In the mid-1990s, a new housing development in one of the suburbs of Toronto engaged in an interesting experiment. The houses in this Canadian residential community were built from the ground up with the latest broadband telecommunications infrastructure and came with a host of new Internet technologies. Residents of Netville (a pseudonym) had access to high-speed Internet, a videophone, an online jukebox, online health services, discussion forums, and a suite of entertainment and educational applications.[23]

These new technologies made the town an ideal setting for nurturing global citizens. The people of Netville were freed from the tyranny of distance. They could communicate with anyone in the world as easily as they could with a neighbor, forge their own global links, and join virtual communities in cyberspace. They would begin, observers expected, to define their identities and interests increasingly in global, rather than local, terms.

What actually transpired was quite different. Glitches experienced by the telecom provider left some homes without a link to the broadband network. This allowed researchers to compare across wired and non-wired households and reach some conclusions about the consequences of being wired. Far from letting local links erode, wired people actually strengthened their existing local social ties. Compared to non-wired residents, they recognized more of their neighbors, talked to them more often, visited them more frequently, made many more local phone calls. They were more likely to organize local events and mobilize the community around common problems. They used their computer network to facilitate a range of social activities—from organizing barbecues to helping local children with their homework. Netville exhibited, as one resident put it, "a closeness that you don't see in many communities." What was supposed to have unleashed global engagement and networks had instead strengthened local social ties.

As powerful as information and communication technologies are, we should not assume that they will lead us down the path of global consciousness or transnational political communities. Distance matters. Our local attachments largely still define us and our interests.

The World Values Survey periodically polls random samples of individuals around the world on their attitudes and attachments. A recent round of surveys asked people in fifty-five countries about the strength of their local, national, and global identities. The results were similar across the world—and quite instructive. They reveal that attachment to the nation state overwhelms all other forms of identity. People see themselves primarily as citizens of their nation, next as members of their local community, and only last as "global citizens." The sole exceptions, where people identified more with the world than with their nation, were violence-ridden Colombia and tiny Andorra.[24]

These surveys uncover an important divide between elites and the rest of society. A strong sense of global citizenship tends to be confined, where it exists, to wealthy individuals and those with the highest levels of educational attainment. Conversely, attachment to the nation state is generally much stronger (and global identities correspondingly weaker) among individuals from lower social classes. This cleavage is perhaps not that surprising. Skilled professionals and investors can benefit from global opportunities wherever they may arise. The nation state and what it does matters a lot less to these people than it does to less mobile workers and others with fewer skills who have to make do with what's nearby. This opportunity gap reveals a certain dark side to the clamor for global governance. The construction of transnational political communities is a project of globalized elites attuned largely to their needs.

If Not Global Governance, Then What?

The new forms of global governance are intriguing and deserve further development, but ultimately they run up against some fundamental limits: political identities and attachments still revolve around nation states; political communities are organized domestically rather than globally; truly global norms have emerged only in a narrow range of issues; and there remain substantial differences across the world on desirable institutional arrangements. These new transnational mechanisms can take the edge off some contentious issues, but they are no substitute for real governance. They are insufficient to underpin extensive economic globalization.

We need to accept the reality of a divided world polity and make some tough choices. We have to be explicit about where one nation's rights and responsibilities end and another nation's begin. We cannot fudge the role of nation states and proceed on the assumption that we are witnessing the birth of a global political community. We must acknowledge and accept the restraints on globalization that a divided global polity entails. *The scope of workable global regulation limits the scope of desirable globalization.* Hyperglobalization cannot be achieved, and we should not pretend that it can.

Ultimately, this reality check can lead us to a healthier, more sustainable world order.

11

Designing Capitalism 3.0

Capitalism is unequaled when it comes to unleashing the collective economic energy of human societies. That great virtue is why all prosperous nations are capitalist in the broad sense of that term: they are organized around private property and allow markets to play a large role in allocating resources and determining economic rewards. Globalization is the worldwide extension of capitalism. Indeed, so intertwined has capitalism become with globalization that it is impossible to discuss the future of one without discussing the future of the other.

Toward Capitalism 3.0

The key to capitalism's durability lies in its almost infinite malleability. As our conceptions of the institutions needed to support markets and economic activity have evolved over the centuries, so has capitalism. Thanks to its capacity for reinvention, capitalism has overcome its periodic crises and outlived its critics, from Karl Marx on. Looking at capitalism from the prism of the global economy, we have observed in this book how these transformations occur.

Adam Smith's idealized market society required little more than a "night-watchman state." All that governments needed to do to ensure the division of labor was to enforce property rights, keep the peace, and collect a few taxes to pay for a limited range of public goods such as national defense. Through the early part of the twentieth century and the first wave of globalization, capitalism was governed by a narrow vision of the public institutions needed to uphold it. In practice, the state's reach often went beyond this conception (as when Bismarck introduced old-age pensions in Germany in 1889). But governments continued to see their economic roles in restricted terms. Let's call this "Capitalism 1.0."

As societies became more democratic and labor unions and other groups mobilized against capitalism's perceived abuses, a new, more expansive vision of governance gradually took hold. Antitrust policies that broke up large monopolies came first, spearheaded by the Progressive movement in the United States. Activist monetary and fiscal policies were widely accepted in the aftermath of the Great Depression. The state began to play an increasing role in providing welfare assistance and social insurance. In today's industrialized countries, the share of public spending in national income rose rapidly, from below 10 percent on average at the end of the nineteenth century to more than 20 percent just before World War II. In the wake of World War II, these countries erected elaborate social welfare states in which the public sector expanded to more than 40 percent of national income on average.

This "mixed-economy" model was the crowning achievement of the twentieth century. The new balance that it established between states and markets underpinned an unprecedented period of social cohesion, stability, and prosperity in the advanced economies that lasted until the mid-1970s. Let's call this "Capitalism 2.0."

Capitalism 2.0 went with a limited kind of globalization—the Bretton Woods compromise. The postwar model required keeping the international economy at bay because it was built for and operated at the level of nation states. Thus the Bretton Woods–

GATT regime established a "shallow" form of international economic integration, with controls on international capital flows, partial trade liberalization, and plenty of exceptions for socially sensitive sectors (agriculture, textiles, services) as well as developing nations. This left individual nations free to build their own domestic versions of Capitalism 2.0, as long as they obeyed a few simple international rules.

This model became frayed during the 1970s and 1980s, and now appears to have broken down irrevocably under the dual pressures of financial globalization and deep trade integration. The vision that the hyperglobalizers offered to replace Capitalism 2.0 suffered from two blind spots. One was that we could push for rapid and deep integration in the world economy and let institutional underpinnings catch up later. The second was that hyperglobalization would have no, or mostly benign, effects on domestic institutional arrangements. The crises—of both finance and legitimacy—that globalization has produced, culminating in the financial meltdown of 2008, have laid bare the immense size of these blind spots.

We must reinvent capitalism for a new century in which the forces of economic globalization are much more powerful. Just as Smith's lean capitalism (Capitalism 1.0) was transformed into Keynes's mixed economy (Capitalism 2.0), we need to contemplate a transition from the national version of the mixed economy to its global counterpart. We need to imagine a better balance between markets and their supporting institutions *at the global level*.

It is tempting to think that the solution—Capitalism 3.0—lies in a straightforward extension of the logic of Capitalism 2.0: a global economy requires global governance. But as we saw in the previous chapter, the global governance option is a dead end for the vast majority of nations, at least for the foreseeable future. It is neither practical nor even desirable. We need a different vision, one that safeguards the considerable benefits of a moderate globalization while explicitly recognizing the virtues of national diversity and the centrality of national governance. What we need, in effect, is an updating of the Bretton Woods compromise for the twenty-first century.

This updating must recognize the realities of the day: trade is substantially free, the genie of financial globalization has escaped the bottle, the United States is no longer the world's dominant economic superpower, and major emerging markets (China especially) can no longer be ignored or allowed to remain free riders on the system. We cannot return to some mythical "golden era" with high trade barriers, rampant capital controls, and a weak GATT—nor should we want to. What we can do is recognize that the pursuit of hyperglobalization is a fool's errand and reorient our priorities accordingly. What this means is laid out in this and the next chapter.

Principles for a New Globalization

Suppose that the world's leading policy makers were to meet again at the Mount Washington Hotel in Bretton Woods, New Hampshire, to design a new global economic order. They would naturally be preoccupied with the new problems of the day: global economic recovery, the dangers of creeping protectionism, the challenges of financial regulation, global macroeconomic imbalances, and so on. However, addressing these pressing issues requires rising above them to consider the soundness of global economic arrangements overall. What are some of the guiding principles of global economic governance they might agree on?

I present in this chapter seven commonsense principles. Taken together, they provide a foundation that would serve the world economy well in the future. The discussion in the present chapter stays at a general level. In the next chapter, I address the specific implications for some of the key challenges facing the world economy.

1. Markets must be deeply embedded in systems of governance.

The idea that markets are self-regulating received a mortal blow in the recent financial crisis and should be buried once and for all. As the experience with financial globalization demonstrates, "the magic of markets" is a dangerous siren song that can distract policy makers from the fundamental insight of Capitalism 2.0: markets and governments are opposites only in the sense that they form two sides of the same coin.

Markets require other social institutions to support them. They rely on courts and legal arrangements to enforce property rights and on regulators to rein in abuse and fix market failures. They depend on the stabilizing functions that lenders-of-last-resort and countercyclical fiscal policy provide. They need the political buy-in that redistributive taxation, safety nets, and social insurance programs help generate. In other words, markets do not create, regulate, stabilize, or sustain themselves. The history of capitalism has been a process of learning and relearning this lesson.

What is true of domestic markets is true also of global ones. Thanks to the trauma of the interwar period and the perspicacity of Keynes, the Bretton Woods regime sought a fine balance that did not push globalization beyond the ability of global governance to uphold it. We need a return to that same spirit if we are going to save globalization from its cheerleaders.

2. Democratic governance and political communities are organized largely within nation states, and are likely to remain so for the immediate future.

The nation state lives, and even if not entirely well, remains essentially the only game in town. The quest for global governance is a fool's errand, both because national governments are unlikely to cede significant control to transnational institutions and because harmonizing rules would not benefit societies with diverse needs and preferences. The European Union is possibly the sole exception to this truism, but the one that proves the rule.

Overlooking the inherent limits to global governance contributes to globalization's present frailties. We waste international cooperation on overly ambitious goals, ultimately producing weak results that go little beyond the lowest common denominator among major states. Current efforts at harmonizing global financial regulations, for example, will almost certainly end up there. When international cooperation does "succeed," it often spawns rules that reflect the preferences of the more powerful states and are ill-fitting to the circumstances of others. The WTO's rules on subsidies, intellectual property, and investment measures typify this kind of overreaching.

The pursuit of global governance leaves national policy makers with a false sense of security about the strength and durability of global arrangements. Bank regulators with a more realistic sense of the efficacy of Basel rules' impact on capital adequacy or the quality of U.S. credit rating practices would have paid more attention to the risks that their financial institutions at home were incurring.

Our reliance on global governance also muddles our understanding of the rights of nation states to establish and uphold domestic standards and regulations, and the maneuvering room they have for exercising those rights. The worry that this maneuvering room has narrowed too much is the main reason for the widespread concern about the "race to the bottom" in labor standards, corporate taxes, and elsewhere.

Ultimately, the quest for global governance leaves us with too little real governance. Our only chance of strengthening the infrastructure of the global economy lies in reinforcing the ability of democratic governments to provide those foundations. We can enhance both the efficiency and the legitimacy of globalization if we empower rather than cripple democratic procedures at home.

If in the end that also means giving up on an idealized, "perfect" globalization, so be it. A world with a moderate globalization would be a far better place to live in than one mired in the quixotic pursuit of hyperglobalization.

3. There is no "one way" to prosperity.

Once we acknowledge that the core institutional infrastructure of the global economy must be built at the national level, it frees up countries to develop the institutions that suit them best. Even today's supposedly homogenized industrial societies embrace a wide variety of institutional arrangements.

The United States, Europe, and Japan are all successful societies; they have each produced comparable amounts of wealth over the long term. Yet the regulations that cover their labor markets, corporate governance, antitrust, social protection, and even banking and finance have differed considerably. These differences enable journalists and pundits to anoint a succession of these "models"—a different one each decade—as the great success for all to emulate. Scandinavia was everyone's favorite in the 1970s; Japan became the country to copy in the 1980s; and the United States was the undisputed king of the 1990s. Such fads should not blind us to the reality that none of these models can be deemed a clear winner in the contest of "capitalisms." The very idea of a "winner" is suspect in a world where nations have somewhat different preferences— where Europeans, for example, would rather have greater income security and less inequality than Americans are used to living with, even if it comes at the cost of higher taxation.[1]

This surfeit of models suggests a deeper implication. Today's institutional arrangements, varied as they are, constitute only a *subset* of the full range of potential institutional possibilities. It is unlikely that modern societies have managed to exhaust all the useful institutional variation that could underpin healthy and vibrant economies.[2] We need to maintain a healthy skepticism toward the idea that a specific type of institution—a particular mode of corporate governance, social security system, or labor market legislation, for example—is the only type that works in a well-functioning market economy. The most successful societies of the future will leave room for experimentation and allow for further evolution of institutions over time. A global economy that recognizes the need for and value of institutional diversity would foster rather than stifle such experimentation and evolution.

4. Countries have the right to protect their own social arrangements, regulations, and institutions.

The previous principles may have appeared uncontroversial and innocuous. Yet they have powerful implications that clash with the received wisdom among boosters of globalization. One such implication is that we need to accept the right of individual countries to safeguard their domestic institutional choices. The recognition of institutional diversity would be meaningless if nations were unable to "protect" domestic institutions—if they did not have the instruments available to shape and maintain their own institutions. Stating principles clearly makes these connections transparent.

Trade is a means to an end, not an end in itself. Advocates of globalization lecture the rest of the world incessantly about how countries must change their policies and institutions in order to expand their international trade and become more attractive to foreign investors. This way of thinking confuses means for ends. Globalization should be an instrument for achieving the goals that societies seek: prosperity, stability, freedom, and quality of life. Nothing enrages WTO critics more than the suspicion that when push comes to shove, the WTO allows trade to trump the environment, human rights, or democratic decision making. Nothing infuriates the critics of the international financial system more than the idea that the interests of global bankers and financiers should come before those of ordinary workers and taxpayers.

Opponents of globalization argue that it sets off a "race to the bottom," with nations converging toward the lowest levels of corporate taxation, financial regulations, or environmental, labor, and consumer protections. Advocates counter that there is little evidence of erosion in national standards.

To break the deadlock we should accept that countries can uphold national standards in these areas, and can do so by raising barriers at the border if necessary, *when trade demonstrably threatens domestic practices enjoying broad popular support.* If globalization's advocates are right, then the clamor for protection will fail for lack of evidence or support. If they are wrong, there will be a safety valve in place to ensure that these contending values—the benefits of open economies and the gains from upholding domestic regulations—both receive a proper hearing in the domestic political debate.

The principle rules out extremism on both sides. It prevents globalizers from gaining the upper hand in cases where international trade and finance are a back door for eroding widely accepted standards at home. Similarly, it prevents protectionists from obtaining benefits at the expense of the rest of society when no significant public purpose is at stake. In less clear-cut cases where different values have to be traded off against each other, the principle forces internal deliberation and debate—the best way of handling difficult political questions.

One can imagine the questions a domestic political debate might raise. How much social or economic disruption does the trade in question threaten? How much domestic support is there for the practices, regulations, or standards at stake? Are the adverse effects felt by particularly disadvantaged members of society? How large are the compensating economic benefits, if any? Are there alternative ways of achieving the desired social and economic objectives without restricting international trade or finance? What does the relevant evidence—economic and scientific—say on all these questions?

If the policy process is transparent and inclusive, these kinds of questions will be generated naturally by the forces of competition among interest groups, both pro- and anti-trade. To be sure, there are no fail-safe mechanisms for determining whether the rules in question enjoy "broad popular support" and are "demonstrably threatened" by trade. Democratic politics is messy and does not always get it "right." But when we have to trade off different values and interests, there is nothing else to rely on.

Removing such questions from the province of democratic deliberation and passing them on to technocrats or international bodies is the worse solution. It ensures neither legitimacy nor economic benefits. International agreements *can* make an important contribution, but their role is to reinforce the integrity of the domestic democratic process rather than to replace it. I will return to this point in the next chapter.

5. Countries do not have the right to impose their institutions on others.

Using restrictions on cross-border trade or finance to uphold values and regulations at home must be sharply distinguished from using them to impose these values and regulations on other countries. Globalization's rules should not force Americans or Europeans to consume goods that are produced in ways that most citizens in those countries find unacceptable. Neither should they require nations to provide unhindered access to financial transactions that undercut domestic regulations. They also should not allow the United States or the European Union to use trade sanctions or other kinds of pressure to alter the way that foreign nations go about their business in labor markets, environmental policies, or finance. Nations have a right to difference, not to impose convergence.

In practice, upholding the first right may lead sometimes to the same consequence as upholding the second. Suppose that the United States decides to block imports from India made with child labor because of concern that such imports constitute "unfair competition" for domestically produced goods. Isn't that the same as imposing a trade sanction on India aimed at changing India's labor practices to make them look more like those in the United States? Yes and no. In both cases, India's exports are restricted, and the only way India can get unhindered access to the U.S. market is by converging toward U.S. standards. But intentions matter. While it is legitimate to protect our own institutions, it isn't equally legitimate to want to change others'. If my club has a dress code that requires men to wear ties, it is reasonable for me to expect that you will abide by these rules when you join me at dinner—no matter how much you hate wearing ties. But this doesn't give me the right to tell you how you should dress on other occasions.

*6. The purpose of international economic arrangements
must be to lay down the traffic rules for managing the interface
among national institutions.*

Relying on nation states to provide the essential governance functions of the world economy does not mean we should abandon international rules. The Bretton Woods regime, after all, did have clear rules, even though they were limited in scope and depth. A completely decentralized free-for-all would not benefit anyone; one nation's decisions can affect the well-being of others. An open global economy—perhaps not as free of transaction costs as hyperglobalizers would like, but an open one nonetheless— remains a laudable objective. We should seek not to weaken globalization, but to put it on a sounder footing.

The centrality of nation states means that the rules need to be formulated with an eye toward institutional diversity. What we need are traffic rules that help vehicles of different size and shape and traveling at varying speeds navigate around each other, rather than impose an identical car or a uniform speed limit on all. We should strive to attain the maximum globalization that is consistent with maintaining space for diversity in national institutional arrangements. Instead of asking, "What kind of multilateral regime would maximize the flow of goods and capital around the world?" we would ask, "What kind of multilateral regime would best enable nations around the world to pursue their own values and developmental objectives and prosper within their own social arrangements?" This would entail a significant shift in the mindset of negotiators in the international arena.

As part of this shift we can contemplate a much larger role for "opt-outs" or exit clauses in international economic rules. Any tightening of international disciplines should include explicit escape clauses. Such arrangements would help legitimize the rules and allow democracies to reassert their priorities when these priorities clash with obligations to global markets or international economic institutions. Escape clauses would be viewed not as "derogations" or violations of the rules, but as an inherent component of sustainable international economic arrangements.

To prevent abuse, opt-out and exit clauses can be negotiated multilaterally and incorporate specific procedural safeguards. This would differentiate the exercise of opt-outs from naked protectionism: countries withdrawing from international disciplines would be allowed to do so only after satisfying procedural requirements that have been negotiated beforehand and written into those same disciplines. While such opt-outs are not riskless, they are a necessary part of making an open international economy compatible with democracy. In fact, their procedural safeguards—calling for transparency, accountability, evidence-based decision making—would enhance the quality of democratic deliberation.

7. Non-democratic countries cannot count on the same rights
and privileges in the international economic order as democracies.

The primacy of democratic decision making lies at the foundation of the international economic architecture outlined so far.

It forces us to recognize the centrality of nation states, given the reality that democratic polities rarely extend beyond their boundaries. It requires us to accept national differences in standards and regulations (and therefore departures from hyperglobalization), because it assumes that these differences are the product of collective choices exercised in a democratic fashion. It also legitimizes international rules that limit domestic policy actions, as long as those rules are negotiated by representative governments and contain exit clauses that allow for and enhance democratic deliberation at home.

When nation states are not democratic, this scaffolding collapses. We can no longer presume a country's institutional arrangements reflect the preferences of its citizenry. Nor can we presume that international rules could apply with sufficient force to transform essentially authoritarian regimes into functional democracies. So non-democracies need to play by different, less permissive rules.

Take the case of labor and environmental standards. Poor countries argue that they cannot afford to have the same stringent standards in these areas as the advanced countries. Indeed, tough emission standards or regulations against the use of child labor can backfire if they lead to fewer jobs and greater poverty. A democratic country such as India can argue, legitimately, that its practices are consistent with the needs of its population. India's democracy is of course not perfect; no democracy is. But its civil liberties, freely elected government, and protection of minority rights insulate the country against claims of systematic exploitation or exclusion.[3] They provide a cover against the charge that labor, environmental, and other standards are inappropriately low. Non-democratic countries, such as China, do not pass the same prima facie test. The assertion that labor rights and the environment are trampled for the benefit of the few cannot be as easily dismissed in those countries. Consequently, exports of non-democratic countries deserve greater international scrutiny, particularly when they have costly ramifications—distributional or otherwise—in other countries.

This does not mean that there should be higher trade or other barriers against non-democratic countries across the board. Certainly not every regulation in such countries has adverse domestic effects. Even though China is an authoritarian regime, it has an exemplary economic growth record. And since countries trade to enhance their own well-being, blanket protectionism would not be in the interest of the importing countries in any case. Still, it would be legitimate to apply more stringent rules to authoritarian regimes in certain instances.

For example, there could be a lower hurdle for imposing restrictions on a non-democratic country's trade in cases where that trade causes problems in an importing country. If there is a requirement that compensation be paid to exporting countries when an escape clause is triggered, the requirement could be waived when the exporting country is non-democratic. And the burden of proof may need to be reversed in instances where an authoritarian regime seeks to exercise an opt-out—they should be required to demonstrate that the measure in question serves a real developmental, social, or other domestic purpose.

The principle of discrimination against non-democracies already has a place in the present trade regime. Duty-free market access to the United States under the African Growth and Opportunity Act of 2000 requires that the exporting country be democratic. When an African regime represses its political opposition or appears to rig an election, it is removed from the list of countries eligible for trade preferences.[4]

Universalizing this principle would no doubt be controversial. It is likely to be opposed both by trade fundamentalists and, more predictably, by authoritarian regimes. Nevertheless, it makes a lot of sense, especially in the context of the full set of principles considered here. Democracy, after all, *is* a global norm. It ought to be one of the cornerstone principles of the international trade regime, trumping non-discrimination when necessary.

What About the "Global Commons"?

There are a number of possible objections to the principles outlined here. I will address many of them in the next chapter, but I need to take up one major objection right away, as it derives from a fundamental misunderstanding. Some argue that the rules of a globalized economy cannot be left to individual nation states. Such a system, the objection goes, would greatly reduce international cooperation, and as each nation pursues its own narrow interests, the world economy would slide into rampant protectionism. Everyone would lose as a result.

The logic relies on a false analogy of the global economy as a global commons. To see how the analogy works (or rather fails), consider global climate change, the quintessential case of global commons. Ample and mounting evidence suggests that global warming is caused by atmospheric accumulations of greenhouse gases, primarily carbon dioxide and methane. What makes this a global rather than national problem, requiring global cooperation, is that such gases do not respect borders. The globe has a single climate system and it makes no difference where the carbon is emitted. What matters for global warming is the cumulative effect of carbon and other gases in the atmosphere, regardless of origin. If you want to avoid environmental catastrophe, you need everyone else to go along. One might say that all our economies are similarly intertwined, and no doubt that would be true to an important extent. An open and healthy world economy is a "public good" which benefits all, just like an atmosphere with low levels of greenhouse gases.

But there the parallel ends. In the case of global warming,

domestic restrictions on carbon emissions provide no or little benefit at home. There is a single global climate system, and my own individual actions have at best small effects on it. Absent cosmopolitan considerations, each nation's optimal strategy would be to emit freely and to free ride on the carbon controls of other countries. Addressing climate change requires that nation states rise above their parochial interests and work in concert to develop common strategies. Without international cooperation and coordination, the global commons would be destroyed.

By contrast, the economic fortunes of individual nations are determined largely by what happens at home rather than abroad. If open economy policies are desirable, it's because openness is in a nation's own self-interest—not because it helps others. Remember Henry Martyn's case for free trade: buying cheaper cotton textiles from India is just like technological progress at home. As we have seen repeatedly in this book, there are legitimate reasons why countries may want to stop at less than free trade. Barriers on international trade or finance may fortify social cohesion, avoid crises, or enhance domestic growth. In such instances, the rest of the world generally benefits. When trade barriers serve only to transfer income from some groups to others, at the cost of shrinking the overall economic pie, domestic rather than foreign groups bear the bulk of these costs.[5] In the global economy, countries pursue "good" policies because it is in their interest to do so. Openness relies on self-interest, not on global spirit. The case for open trade has to be made and won in the domestic political arena.

A few wrinkles complicate this picture. One is that large economies may be able to manipulate the prices of their imports and exports in ways that shift more of the gains from trade to themselves—think about the impact of OPEC on oil, for example. These policies certainly harm other nations and need to be subject to international disciplines. But today such motives are the exception rather than the rule. Foreign economic policies are shaped largely by domestic considerations, as they should be. Another wrinkle involves the adverse effects on others of large external imbalances—trade deficits or surpluses. These also need international oversight. I will address this issue when I turn to China's trade surplus in the next chapter.

The principles above leave plenty of room for international cooperation over these and other matters. But they do presume a major difference, when compared to other areas like climate change, in the degree of international cooperation and coordination needed to make the global system work. In the case of global warming, self-interest pushes nations to ignore the risks of climate change, with an occasional spur toward environmentally responsible policies when a country is too large to overlook its own impact on the accumulation of greenhouse gases. In the global economy, self-interest pushes nations toward openness, with an occasional temptation toward beggar-thy-neighbor policies when a large country possesses market power.[6] A healthy global regime has to rely on international cooperation in the first case; it has to rely on good policies geared toward the domestic economy in the second.

Applying the Principles

A common but misleading narrative shapes our collective understanding of globalization. According to this narrative, the world's national economies have become so inextricably linked that nothing short of a new kind of governance and a new global consciousness can address adequately the challenges we face. We share a common economic destiny, we are told. We have to rise up above our parochial interests, responsible leaders implore us, and devise common solutions to common problems.

This narrative has the ring of plausibility and the virtue of moral clarity. It also gets the main story wrong. What is true of climate change, say, or human rights—genuine areas of "global commons"—is not true of the international economy. The Achilles' heel of the global economy is not lack of international cooperation. It is the failure to recognize in full the implications of a simple idea: the reach of global markets must be limited by the scope of their (mostly national) governance. Provided the traffic rules are right, the world economy can function quite well with nation states in the driving seats.

12

A Sane Globalization

How might the principles proposed in the previous chapter work in practice? Is it possible to devise sensible rules that uphold these principles while preventing descent into international economic anarchy? And how would these rules address the kind of challenges that the world economy currently confronts?

This final chapter provides some answers by focusing on four key areas where the challenges are concentrated. I begin by applying my principles to the world's trade regime and show how they call for rules that differ significantly from those that trade negotiators have been pursuing in recent years. Next I turn to global finance and propose an approach that would allow different national regulations to co-exist side by side without undermining each other. The third area is labor migration, a phenomenon not discussed much in this book, but which can generate significant benefits if properly managed. Finally, I take up a question that is likely to produce the most important headache for the world economy in the years immediately ahead: how to accommodate China in the global economy.

Reforming the International Trade Regime

Our current trade strategy, centered on trade agreements to open markets, wastes a lot of political and negotiating capital for the prospect of meager economic gains. Worse still, it neglects the system's major defect, which is its lack of widespread support among ordinary people.

Today's challenge is no longer to open up the trade regime; that battle was fought in the 1960s and 1970s and has been decisively won. The infamous Smoot-Hawley Tariff of the 1930s has turned into a symbol of everything that can go wrong when nations turn their back on the world economy. "Protectionism" has become a dirty word. Import tariffs and other restrictions that governments impose on international trade have been reduced to the lowest levels the world has ever seen. Even though restrictions and subsidies continue to be important in some areas, especially in certain agricultural products (such as rice, sugar, and dairy products), world trade is remarkably free. As a result, the gains that we stand to reap from removing the remaining vestiges of protectionism are puny—much smaller than what the pundits and the financial press presume. One recent study estimates those benefits to rise to no more than one third of 1 percent of world GDP (and this at the end of a full decade).[1] Most other credible estimates are also in the same ball park.

Free trade advocates, including some economists, often obfuscate this point by touting the "hundreds of billions of dollars" of trade that would be created by this or that trade agreement. But what generates higher incomes, better jobs, and economic progress is not more trade as such. Shipping a T-shirt or a PC across the border is not what makes us better off. What makes us better off is the ability to consume those goods at lower cost and sell our products at better prices abroad. This is why we want to reduce man-made barriers to trade. Such gains are small at present, however, because the barriers are so low.[2]

Our challenge today is to render the existing openness sustainable and consistent with broader social goals. This requires a decisive shift in the focus of multilateral negotiations. When trade ministers get together, they should talk about expanding the maneuvering room for individual nations rather than narrowing it further through cuts in tariffs and subsidies. They should create the domestic space needed to protect social programs and regulations, renew domestic social contracts, and pursue locally tailored growth policies. They should be bargaining about policy space rather than market access. Such a reorientation would benefit rich and poor nations alike. Expanding policy space to accomplish domestic objectives does not negate an open, multilateral trade regime; it is a precondition for it.

The world's trade rules already allow nations to resort to "safeguards" in the form of higher import tariffs when a sudden surge in imports puts domestic firms in difficulty.[3] I would like to see the WTO's Agreement on Safeguards (which is a carryover from GATT) rewritten to expand policy space under a broader set of circumstances. A wider interpretation of safeguards would acknowledge that countries may wish to restrict trade or suspend WTO obligations—exercise "opt-outs"—for reasons other than a competitive threat to their industries. Distributional concerns, conflicts with domestic norms and social arrangements, prevention of the erosion of domestic regulations, or developmental priorities would be among such legitimate grounds.

Specifically, countries would be able to "violate" WTO rules when those rules threaten to undermine domestic labor and environmental standards or when they hamper the pursuit of sound development policies.[4] In effect, the agreement would be recast into an expanded Agreement on *Developmental and Social Safeguards*. A country that applies such a safeguard would have to satisfy a key procedural requirement: it would need to demonstrate that it followed democratic procedures in reaching the determination that the safeguard measure is in the public interest. The specific criteria might include transparency, accountability, inclusiveness, and evidence-based deliberation. This hurdle would replace the current agreement's "serious injury" test, which focuses largely on domestic firms' financial profitability.

WTO panels would still have jurisdiction, but on procedural rather than substantive grounds. They would examine the degree to which democratic requirements were fulfilled. Were the views of all relevant parties, including consumer and public interest groups, importers and exporters, civil society organizations, sufficiently represented? Was all relevant evidence, scientific and economic, brought to bear on the final determination? Was there broad enough domestic support in favor of the opt-out or safeguard in question? The panels may rule against a country because the internal deliberations excluded an interested party or relevant scientific evidence. But they would not be able to rule on the substantive claim—whether in fact the safeguard measure serves the public interest at home by furthering a domestic social purpose or promoting economic development at home. This echoes the procedural emphasis in the existing Agreement on Safeguards, although it greatly increases the scope of its application.[5]

The case in favor of economic openness must be made and won at home. A sustainable trade regime ultimately rests not on external constraints but on domestic political support. The proposed procedure would force a deeper and more representative public debate on the legitimacy of trade rules and on the conditions under which it may be appropriate to suspend them. The most reliable guarantee against abuse of opt-outs is informed deliberation at the national level. The requirements that groups whose incomes would be adversely affected by the opt-out—importers and exporters—participate in the deliberations, and that the domestic process balance the competing interests in a transparent manner, would minimize the risk of protectionist measures benefiting a small segment of industry at large cost to society. A safety valve that allows principled objections to free trade to prevail makes it easier to repress protectionist steam.

Even though domestic interests would presumably dominate the deliberations, the consequences for foreign countries would not be entirely overlooked. When social safeguards pose serious threat to poor countries, for example, non-governmental organizations and other groups may mobilize against the proposed opt-out, and those considerations may well outweigh ultimately the costs of domestic dislocations. A labor union may win protection when its members are forced to compete against workers abroad who toil in blatantly exploitative conditions. They are much less likely to carry the day against countervailing domestic interests when foreign working conditions reflect poor productivity rather than repression of rights. As the legal scholar Robert Howse notes, enhancing confidence in the ability of domestic deliberations to distinguish between legitimate domestic regulations and protectionist "cheating" should allay concern that domestic measures are purely protectionist. "Requiring that regulations be defensible in a rational, deliberative public process of justification may well enhance such confidence, while at the very same time serving, not frustrating, democracy."[6]

An extension of safeguards to cover environmental, labor, and consumer safety standards or developmental priorities at home— with appropriate procedural restraints against abuse—would increase the legitimacy and resilience of the world trading system and render it more development-friendly. It would breathe life into the principle that countries have the right to uphold national standards when trade undermines broadly popular domestic practices, by withholding market access or suspending WTO obligations if necessary. Advanced countries could seek temporary protection against imports originating from countries with weak enforcement of labor rights when these imports worsen working conditions at home. Poor nations might be allowed to subsidize industrial activities (and indirectly their exports) when those subsidies contribute to a broadly supported development strategy aimed at stimulating technological capabilities.

Current safeguard procedures require most-favored-nation treatment of exports, permit only temporary measures, and demand compensation from the country applying the safeguard. These need to be rethought in the context of the broader arrangement I am proposing. MFN treatment will often not make sense. If the safeguard is a reaction to labor abuses in a particular country, it is appropriate to direct the measure solely against imports from that country. Similarly, an ongoing abuse will require ongoing use of the safeguard. Instead of imposing temporary relief, it would be better to require periodic review or a sunset clause that could be revoked in case the problem continues. This way, trade restrictions or regulations that hamper other countries' interests are less likely to become ossified.

The issue of compensation is trickier. When a country adopts a safeguard measure, the logic goes, it revokes a "trade concession" it had previously granted to other countries in an internationally binding agreement. Those other countries are entitled to receive equivalent concessions or to revoke some of their own concessions in return. In a dynamic world with near-constant change, the nature of the concessions that a country grants to others cannot be predicted perfectly. This uncertainty turns international trade agreements into "incomplete contracts." When unforeseen developments change the value or cost of trade flows—because of new technologies on genetic engineering, say, or new values on the environment, or new understandings on desirable development strategy—who controls rights over those flows? The requirement of compensation places those rights squarely with the international trade regime; the exporter can continue to demand market access on the original terms. But we might just as legitimately argue that the value of the original concessions depends on the circumstances under which they were provided. Under this interpretation, an exporter could not claim a benefit that did not exist, nor the importer be forced to suffer a loss that was not originally contemplated, when the agreement was signed. This would bring control rights closer to nation states and sharply limit the amount of compensation that exporters could expect.

Authoritarian regimes would be subject to additional substantive requirements when resorting to opt-outs. Such countries may need to make an explicit social or developmental case to justify safeguard measures. They may need to demonstrate that the safeguard would effectively achieve a specified public purpose.

Authoritarian regimes likely will become easier targets for safeguard action by democratic nations when their exports cause problems in those nations. Even though some of their labor practices, for example, will be easy to justify, others may not be. Minimum wages that are significantly lower than in rich countries can be rationalized in the domestic debate by pointing to lower labor productivity and living standards. Lax child-labor regulations are often justified by the argument that it is not feasible or desirable to withdraw young workers from the labor force in a country with widespread poverty. In other cases, arguments like these carry less weight. Basic labor rights such as non-discrimination, freedom of association, collective bargaining, and prohibition of forced labor do not cost anything. Compliance with these rights does not harm, and indeed possibly benefits, economic development. Gross violations constitute exploitation of labor, and will open the door for safeguards in importing countries on the ground that they generate unfair distributional costs.

Generalizing the safeguards agreement in this fashion would have its risks. Critics will worry that the reduced scope for compensation will lower the value of trade agreements. They will be concerned that the new procedures put us on a "slippery slope" of protectionism. Such qualms have to be tempered by considering the abuse that occurs under the existing rules without great detriment to the system. If mechanisms explicitly designed to facilitate protectionist barriers, such as the anti-dumping rules of the GATT, have not destroyed the multilateral trade regime thus far, it is not clear why well-designed exit clauses would have consequences that are worse.

Less flexible rules do not necessarily make better ones. They increase the risk that governments will find their hands tied in circumstances where it would have been desirable for them to act. They may therefore reduce, rather than increase, the value of trade agreements and diminish the incentive to sign on to them.

Consider what happens if we continue on our current path. The Doha Round of trade negotiations, with which the world's trade officialdom remains preoccupied, focuses on reducing the remaining barriers at the borders, especially in agriculture. The round was launched in 2001 and has experienced one collapse after another. Despite all the hoopla that accompanies these negotiations, it is safe to say that the prospective gains from a successful completion of the Doha Round are quite small—even paltrier than the one third of 1 percent of world income that a movement to full liberalization would entail.

Of course, there may still be some big winners from the Doha agenda. In particular, cotton growers in West Africa would benefit substantially from the removal of subsidies in the United States, their incomes rising by up to 6 percent—not a small amount for farmers so close to the subsistence level.[7] On the other hand, poor urban consumers who do not grow their food and low-income food-importing countries would be hurt by the increase in the world price of agricultural commodities as rich country subsidies are phased out.[8]

Taken as a whole, Doha should be considered small potatoes. After the kind of progress achieved by export-oriented East Asian economies in recent decades, facing barriers even higher than those of today, no serious economist would argue that the existing restrictions on market access limit seriously the growth prospects of poor countries (or anyone else, for that matter). Indeed, the lack of political momentum behind Doha can be explained at least in part by the weak prospects of significant economic gains.

National borders *do* impose significant transaction costs on trade. However, these costs derive less from protectionism at the border than from differences in standards, currencies, legal systems, social networks, and so on. Squeezing large gains from the world trade regime would require extensive institutional surgery, going beyond conventional trade liberalization and reaching behind borders to harmonize national standards and regulations. Those gains would be quite ephemeral, as they would come at the expense of the benefits of institutional diversity and policy space. Such a strategy is of questionable merit; indeed, there is little appetite for it after the disappointments of the last GATT trade round (the Uruguay Round)—and for understandable reasons.

The Doha Round's troubles are indicative of the impasse in which the trade regime finds itself. They exemplify the problems of the prevailing low-return, high-cost strategy, which leaves the world economy straddling a choice between two unappetizing options. One possibility is that popular pressure will force governments to resort to unilateral protectionism outside existing rules, inviting retaliation from others. Nations will refuse to sign on to substantive trade agreements for fear that the commitments will severely undermine policy space. International cooperation will gradually erode. Another possibility is that the spirit of "deep integration" will ultimately prevail and governments will sign ever-constraining trade agreements. The room for institutional diversity will then shrink and the legitimacy of the trade regime and prospects for economic development will both suffer.

Either way, the "business as usual" approach poses a greater risk to globalization's health than the reforms I have outlined here. It may seem like a paradox, but it isn't: reempowering national democracies is a precondition for an open world economy, not an obstacle to it.

Regulating Global Finance

The subprime mortgage meltdown has laid bare the inadequacies of the prevailing approach to regulation—both nationally and internationally. Loopholes in the rules allowed financial entities to take on risks that endangered not only themselves but society at large. The fallout has unleashed a flurry of efforts to improve the stringency and soundness of financial regulation. The measures under discussion include tighter capital-adequacy standards, restrictions on leverage, caps on executive pay, rules that facilitate bank closures, broader disclosure requirements, greater regulatory oversight, and limits on bank size.

These efforts are marred by a big fudge. Policy makers pay lip service to regulatory diversity and the push and pull of domestic politics that lead major players like the United States and the European Union to design their own regulations. Yet these same policy makers press for regulatory harmonization, fearful that diverse regulations will raise transaction costs and impede financial globalization. As a senior U.S. Treasury official put it to a European audience, "we cannot go our own ways, deviating significantly from international standards or practices, and exposing global markets to the risk of fragmentation." Yet, he added, "[n]or should we impose standards on one another if we are not identical."[9] No one has articulated how to steer a sensible path between these competing objectives. The attempt to have one's cake and eat it too is not just misguided; it leaves the world economy exposed to exactly the kind of mishaps that almost brought it down.

For global governance enthusiasts, international cooperation has produced a few successes since the crisis. These fall far short of a real shift in authority away from national policy makers. A global regulator, say, or a world central bank remains as much a fantasy as ever. The changes are minor and somewhat cosmetic. Most notably, the Group of Seven, the rich country club which serves as the global economy's talking shop, has been effectively supplanted by the Group of Twenty, which includes in addition a number of major developing nations. The International Monetary Fund has received additional financial resources. The Financial Stability Board (previously Forum), an association of two dozen nations' regulators and central banks, has been given new monitoring responsibilities. The Basel Committee on Banking Supervision has been put to work on a new set of global principles for bank regulation, its third in barely more than two decades.

The real story of financial regulation is one of international discord rather than harmony. Domestic pressure is forcing national politicians to act quickly on financial reforms rather than wait for bankers to come up with globally harmonized rules.[10]

The fault lines among industrial countries fall along expected lines. With some important exceptions, continental Europeans tend to favor a more stringent approach, while the Americans and the British are wary of regulatory overreach that would cripple their financial industries. In 2009, the European Commission, prodded by Socialist parties, proposed extensive regulations on hedge funds and private equity firms that would restrict debt levels, impose capital requirements, require strict disclosure, and cap the pay of managers. These measures, which go well beyond American proposals and would apply also to any American firm that wants to do business in Europe, unleashed a flurry of U.S. lobbying in support of British efforts to water them down.[11] Similarly, the European Parliament approved broad regulations governing credit rating agencies in April 2009, drawing complaints from U.S.-based credit rating agencies about the additional costs the new requirements would impose. The French and Germans, joined this time by the British, have pushed for a global tax on cross-border financial transactions (a variant of the Tobin tax we saw earlier), only to be rebuffed by the American administration. Finally, Europeans have taken a much harder line on bankers' bonuses than Americans.

On other issues, it is the Americans who have led the way while the Europeans have resisted tighter controls. President Barack Obama has endorsed the so-called "Volcker rules," which would impose ceilings on bank size and prohibit banks trading on their own account. A watered-down version of some of these ideas eventually found its way to the financial reform bill that Congress passed in July 2010. The United States has also generally shown much greater appetite for raising banks' capital requirements than Europe.[12] In both instances, Europeans have accused the United States of going it alone and undermining international coordination.

We have to think of these differences not as aberrations from the norm of international harmonization, but as the natural consequences of varying national circumstances. In a world where national interests, perceived or real, differ, the desire to coordinate regulations can do more harm than good. Even when successful, it produces either weak agreements based on the lowest common denominator or tougher standards that may not be appropriate to all. It is far better to recognize these differences than to presume that they can be papered over given sufficient time, negotiation, and political pressure.

The principle we should apply here is the same one that we apply in the case of consumer safety. If another country wants to export us toys, it has to make sure that those toys pass our lead-content and other safety standards. Similarly, when a financial firm does business in our economy, it has to comply with our financial regulations, regardless of where it is based. That means it has to hold the same level of capital reserves as domestic firms, face the same disclosure requirements, and abide by the same trading rules. It's a simple principle: if you want to be part of our game, you have to play by our rules.

As Simon Johnson rightly asks, why should the United States be left hostage to European resistance when its lawmakers agree that capital requirements need to be increased or banks "too big to fail" need to be broken up?[13] It is better for the United States to go it alone, he argues, than be slowed down by "the glacial nature of international economic diplomacy, and the self-interest of the Europeans."

Take the example of capital requirements, where the United States wants tougher rules than Europe. Here is what Johnson proposes. If other nations don't raise their capital requirements, then their banks should not be allowed to enter the American market or do business with American banks unless those American banks carry extra cushions of capital reserves. U.S. banks and their executives would face criminal penalties if they violated these regulations. Johnson thinks this approach will bring the Europeans to heel and force them to match America's high standards to gain access to the world's largest and most sophisticated market.

Regardless of whether others follow suit, Johnson has the right idea. As he puts it, the United States should "stop worrying about what other countries might or might not do . . . [it should] establish high capital requirements in the US, and make this a beacon for safe and productive finance."[14] If the United States feels safer under a certain set of standards, it should be free to implement them—not in order to bring other nations into line, but because national interest demands it.

What is true of the United States is true of other nations as well. Even though other countries may not always have the power to force emulation by others, if they decide they want certain kinds of regulations they should feel empowered to institute them, even if this means imposing restrictions on cross-border finance. Just as in trade, a healthy global regime leaves space for national diversity in standards.

The fly in the ointment is that maintaining regulatory differences when finance can freely cross national boundaries is quite difficult. Banks and investment houses can simply move to jurisdictions with less onerous restrictions. Financial globalization in effect neutralizes differences in national regulations. This is what is known in the trade as "regulatory arbitrage," a race to the bottom in finance.[15]

For this reason, a commitment to regulatory diversity has a very important corollary: the need for restrictions on global finance. The rules of the game have to allow for restrictions on cross-border finance designed to counter regulatory arbitrage and protect the integrity of national regulations. Governments should be able to keep banks and financial flows out—not for financial protectionism but to prevent the erosion of national regulations. None of the leading governments has acknowledged this need explicitly to date, yet without such restrictions domestic regulations would have little effect and domestic firms would stand little chance to compete with financial services exported from lax jurisdictions. The domestic economy would remain hostage to the risks emanating from those transactions.

Hence a new global financial order must be constructed on the back of a minimal set of international guidelines and with limited international coordination.[16] The new arrangements would certainly involve an improved IMF with increased resources and a larger voice for developing nations. It might require an international financial charter with limited aims, focused on encouraging financial transparency, promoting consultation and information sharing among national regulators, and placing limits on jurisdictions (such as financial safe havens) that export financial instability. A small global tax on financial transactions (say on the order of one tenth of 1 percent) would generate tens of billions of dollars to address global challenges such as climate change or health pandemics at little economic cost.[17] But the responsibility for regulating leverage, setting capital standards, and supervising financial markets more broadly would rest squarely at the national level. Most important, the rules would explicitly recognize governments' right to limit cross-border financial transactions, insofar as the intent and effect are to prevent foreign competition from less strict jurisdictions from undermining domestic regulatory standards.

Deemphasizing international regulatory standards in favor of national ones would shift power away from technocrats to domestic groups, especially legislatures. It would politicize and democratize financial regulation.[18] Technocrats dominate the discussion in international bodies such as the Basel Committee or the Group of Twenty. Stronger democratic accountability to national parliaments would reduce the influence of such technocrats and base regulations on the preferences of a wider group of domestic constituencies. Many economists would consider politicization a big step back. But we might be allowed a measure of skepticism on this in view of the technocrats' dismal recent record. As Professor Nicholas Dorn of the Erasmus School of Law argues, "democratically-fuelled regulatory diversity is a safeguard against the recently experienced frenzy in global financial regulation and markets."[19]

For developing countries, these rules would have additional benefits. They would open up the policy space for them to manage international capital flows and prevent sudden stops and overvalued currencies. Excessive focus on international harmonization has sidelined the specific interests of emerging nations. As we have seen, financial integration can often have unexpected and adverse effects on these countries. Short-term capital flows wreak havoc with domestic macroeconomic management and aggravate adverse currency movements. "Hot money" can make it difficult for financially open economies like Brazil, South Africa, or Turkey to maintain a competitive currency, depriving them of a potent form of industrial policy. Prudent controls, managed in a countercyclical manner so as to deter excessive financial inflows in good times, are part and parcel of good economic policy. Their importance only grows in a world where the mood in global finance can swing from euphoria to gloom in short order. International bodies such as the IMF and the Group of Twenty must look sympathetically, rather than frown, on such controls.[20]

Of course, groups of like-minded countries that desire deeper financial integration would be free to harmonize their regulations, provided they do not use this as a cover for financial protectionism. One can imagine Europe taking this route and opting for a common regulator. East and Southeast Asian nations may eventually produce a regional zone of deep integration around an Asian monetary fund.

The rest of the world would have to live with a certain amount of financial segmentation—the necessary counterpart to regulatory diversity. That is as it should be. In a diverse world with divided sovereignty, it is the prospect of the deepening of financial globalization that should cause us to lose sleep.

Reaping the Benefits of Global Labor Flows

The problems in international trade and finance arise from too much globalization, not properly managed. By contrast, one large segment of the world economy is not globalized nearly enough. Further economic openness in the world's labor markets could potentially provide huge benefits, especially to the world's poor. Even a minor liberalization of the advanced countries' restrictions on the use of foreign workers would produce a large impact on global incomes. In fact, the gains would outstrip comfortably any other proposal currently on the table, including the entire package of trade measures being considered under the Doha Round of negotiations! Labor markets are the unexploited frontier of globalization.

It may seem surprising to suggest that labor markets are not sufficiently globalized. The news media are full of stories of foreign workers in rich lands, ranging from the inspiring to the terrifying: Indian software engineers in Silicon Valley, illegal Mexicans in

New York sweatshops, poorly treated Filipina maids in the Persian Gulf countries, or disgruntled North Africans in Europe. Human smuggling and trafficking in sex workers represent the especially ugly side of the global trade in labor. But the facts are incontrovertible. The transaction costs associated with crossing national borders are much larger in this segment of the world economy than in any other. Moreover, these costs are created for the most part by explicit government barriers at the border, namely, visa restrictions. They can be lowered at the stroke of a pen.

Consider the numbers. Wages for similarly qualified workers in poor and rich countries can differ by an order of magnitude; a worker could increase his income several-fold just by crossing the border. Straightforward comparisons of wages across nations are fraught with problems because it is difficult to tease out the effects of visa restrictions from other factors such as differences in skills, education, experience, or aptitude. A recent study which makes adjustments for these factors delivers some striking findings. The average Jamaican worker who moves to the United States would increase his earnings by at least twofold, a Bolivian or Indian by at least threefold, and a Nigerian by more than eightfold. To put these numbers in context, we can compare them to the mere 50 percent gain that a Puerto Rican worker can expect to make when she moves to New York City, which she is of course free to do, unlike other foreign counterparts.[21] Or we can compare them to differences across nations in the prices of goods or financial assets, which are again much smaller in magnitude (50 percent or less at most).

Labor markets are much more segmented internationally than any other market. This extreme segmentation, and the huge wage gaps it gives rise to, induces illegal migrants from low-income countries to take serious risks and endure extreme hardships in the hope of improving their incomes and the living standards of their families back home. The reason such large wage gaps persist is not difficult to fathom. The visa policies of rich countries allow limited numbers of workers from poor countries to move in legally and take up jobs in their economies. Moreover, these restrictions tend to favor, increasingly, the skilled and well-educated workers from abroad.

If the leaders of the advanced nations were serious about boosting incomes around the world and in doing so equitably, they would focus single-mindedly on reforming the rules that govern international labor mobility. Nothing else on their agenda—not Doha, not global financial regulation, not even expanding foreign aid—comes even close in terms of potential impact on enlarging the global pie. I am not talking about total liberalization. A complete, or even significant, reduction in visa restrictions in the advanced countries would be too disruptive. It would set off a mass migration that would throw labor markets and social policies in the advanced nations into disarray. But a small-scale program of expanded labor mobility would be manageable, and still generate very large economic gains for the migrant workers and their home economies.

Here is what I have in mind. Rich nations would commit to a *temporary* work visa scheme that would expand their total labor force by no more than 3 percent. Under the scheme, a mix of skilled and unskilled workers from poor nations would be allowed to fill jobs in the rich countries for a period of up to five years. To ensure that the workers return home at the end of their contracts, the programs would be supported by a range of carrots and sticks applied by both home and host countries. As the original migrants return home, a new wave of workers from the same countries would replace them.[22]

Such a system would produce an estimated gain of $360 billion annually for the world economy, a sum considerably greater than what an agreement to remove *all* remaining tariffs and subsidies in global trade in goods could deliver.[23] The bulk of this increase in income would accrue directly to citizens of developing nations—the poorest workers in the world. We wouldn't have to wait for the benefits to trickle down to them as is the case for trade and financial liberalization. Equally important, these numbers underestimate the overall gains since they do not account for the additional economic benefits that returnees would generate for their home countries. Workers who have accumulated know-how, skills, networks, and savings in rich countries could be true agents of change for their societies upon return. Their experience and investments would spark positive economic and social dynamics. The powerful contribution that former émigrés have made in getting software and other skill-intensive industries off the ground in India and Taiwan indicates the potential benefits of this plan.[24]

The sizable benefits of a temporary work visa program have to be considered against the backdrop of a series of objections. Many of these objections, arguments that the program would create a new underclass or that it would close the path to full citizenship for hardworking immigrants, are incomplete at best.[25] They ignore the benefits to the migrants' home economies of maintaining a revolving door that would diffuse the gains more widely. They overlook that the likely alternative to a temporary worker program is not greater immigration but sharply curtailed immigration. And they fail to recognize that workers from developing nations would queue up in droves for temporary jobs abroad, given their alternatives. However, two of the objections deserve closer scrutiny.

The first is that it will be difficult, if not impossible, to enforce the return of foreign workers to their home countries after their permits expire. This is a legitimate concern since many "guest worker" programs have in practice produced permanent immigrants, sometimes creating a large underclass of foreign-born residents left in ambiguous status (as in Germany and many other countries of Europe). On the other hand, past programs typically have offered few incentives for "temporary" workers to return, relying on little more than their willingness to abide by the terms of their visa. It comes as no surprise that many do not go home, given the huge wage gaps between home and host countries.

A workable temporary work visa program will need to offer clear carrots and sticks. To have a chance, these incentives will also need to apply to all parties—workers, employees, and home and host governments. One idea is to withhold a portion of workers' earnings in blocked accounts until the actual repatriation takes place. A migrant worker who overstays his visa would forfeit a large chunk of change. An enforced saving scheme like this would have the added benefit that migrant workers would return home with a sizable pool of resources to invest.

Perhaps more important, there could be penalties for home governments whose nationals failed to comply with the return requirement. For example, sending countries' worker quotas could be reduced in proportion to the numbers that fail to return: the larger the number of workers who overstay their visa, the fewer the number of temporary visas allotted in the next round. Sending countries that can successfully organize themselves to bring their migrant workers back home would benefit from a revolving door. Others would get shut out. That would create a strong incentive for the sending governments to provide a hospitable economic and political climate at home that would encourage their nationals' return. Democratic governments in particular would be under pressure from their voters, many of whom would be in line for future work permits, to ensure that their visa allotments do not shrink.

It is unlikely that any temporary visa program will work perfectly. A fair amount of experimentation will be required to get the details right; but we haven't tried hard or been imaginative enough to give up on the idea yet.

The second objection is that foreign workers would compete with the local workforce and drive wages down in the advanced economies. The degree to which immigrant labor displaces domestic labor remains a hotly contested issue among economists. Many analysts have concluded from the available evidence that immigration has negligible or even positive effects on wages. I will not enter that debate here, but simply grant the possibility that there may be negative effects. Even so, the kind of limited program I am advocating would depress domestic wages by a very small amount—by no more than 1 percent at most.[26]

Nevertheless, the reader can legitimately ask: How can you support such a program when you appear so concerned about the wage reductions that may arise from regular trade with low-income nations? Recall the argument made earlier in chapter Three when we discussed the ethical questions that trade raises when it generates domestic dislocations. Picking up on the analogy with technological progress, I concluded then that "legitimate" arguments against freer trade must pass one of two tests. First, the overall economic gains must remain small compared to the distributional "costs" that freer trade generates. Second, the trade in question must involve practices that violate prevailing norms and social contracts at home.

The distributional objection against a small temporary work visa program clears neither hurdle. As discussed, a program along the proposed lines would generate large net benefits relative to the redistribution it might cause, given the height of border barriers at present.[27] The foreign workers also would be employed at home, under the same labor standards and regulations that protect domestic workers. This invalidates any claim of unfair competition on the basis of a non-level playing field. If either of these assertions turns out to be invalid, opponents would then have a stronger case.

Whether a sufficiently broad domestic political consensus on temporary work visas can be reached in the advanced nations remains to be seen. The Comprehensive Immigration Reform Act of 2006 contained provisions that would have expanded a guest worker scheme in the United States, but the bill died an early death in Congress. An enlarged foreign worker presence clearly garners little enthusiasm in the United States or in Europe. In light of this, it would be easy to write such programs off as politically unrealistic.

That would be a mistake. Trade liberalization has never had a huge amount of domestic political support either. Imports from developing countries create the same downward pressure on rich country wages as immigration. Yet that has not stopped policy makers from bringing trade barriers down. Trade liberalization succeeded through a combination of political leadership, lobbying by exporters and multinational enterprises, and the ideas of economists. Temporary migration, by contrast, has rarely had a well-defined constituency in the advanced countries. The benefits are no smaller, but the beneficiaries are less clearly identifiable. It is only after a Mexican worker enters the United States and lands a job that his employer develops a direct stake in keeping him in the country and the worker himself can add his voice to the domestic debate. For their part, economists have remained excessively tolerant of the political realities that underpin the highly restrictive regime of international labor mobility, even as they decry the protectionist forces that block further liberalization of an already very open trading system.

Today, the global labor regime looks like the international trade regime in 1950—full of high barriers that prevent the world's economies from reaping substantial benefits. The transformation that the trade regime has undergone since that time gives hope that something similar might happen in the area of immigration as well. This will require an honest and clearsighted political debate that allows advocates to make the case for expanded labor mobility. Economists could play an important role in shaping that debate. They can explain the substantial benefits for rich and poor nations alike, and clarify that the gains from worker mobility are low-hanging fruit compared to the mere crumbs from further liberalization in trade and finance.

Accommodating China in the World Economy

China was globalization's greatest success story during the last quarter century. Yet it may prove to be the reason for its downfall during the next.

China embodies all the major challenges that the global economy must overcome. How do we reconcile an open economy with the distributional and adjustment difficulties that trade with low-cost countries raises? How do we address the adverse effects that such trade can have on the welfare states, labor markets, tax regimes, and other social arrangements of advanced nations? How do we help developing countries restructure their economies while retaining an open, rules-based world economy? How do we integrate a large authoritarian regime into a global economy where the major players are all democratic?

These difficulties are all rooted in the enormous institutional diversity that exists around the globe. There are few nations whose institutions are as idiosyncratic as China's or leave as large a footprint on the world's marketplace. The appropriate way to respond to these challenges is not through tighter international rules or coordination, as we so often hear. It is possible to provide all countries, *including* China, with greater room to run their economic and social policies, and do so in ways that reduce adverse effects across national borders.

China remains a poor country. Average income has risen very rapidly in recent decades, but still stands at between one seventh and one eighth the level in the United States—lower than in Turkey or Colombia and not much higher than in El Salvador or Egypt. While coastal China and major metropolises such as Shanghai and Guangzhou reflect tremendous wealth, large swathes of western China are mired in poverty. China is not a candidate to take over global economic leadership from the United States or become a global hegemon—at least not anytime soon. But its population of

1.3 billion and rapidly growing wealth ensure that it projects a very large image on the global screen.

China's economic rise has been a boon for the world economy for the most part. The incredible variety of manufactured goods—everything from toys to autos—that its factories churn out has been a veritable gift for consumers in the rest of the world, especially the poor for whom many of these products have become affordable for the first time. China also offers a beacon of hope for developing nations in Africa and elsewhere whose economic difficulties sometimes seem insurmountable. The country stands as the premier example of how the global economy can be leveraged for economic growth and poverty reduction—by combining exports with a domestically tailored strategy of economic diversification and institutional innovation.

But the picture is not all pretty. China and its trade partners have become embroiled in a growing number of trade disputes in recent years on product safety, patent and copyright infringement, government subsidies, dumping, currency manipulation, and market-access restrictions of various kinds. Imports from China have become a leading scapegoat for the stagnant median wages in the United States. China's huge trade surplus has led even sober economists such as Paul Krugman to complain that the country's "mercantilist" policies are costing the U.S. economy more than a million jobs.[28] And China is widely blamed for running roughshod over human rights and good governance in Africa in its quest for natural resources.

The conflict that poses the greatest threat in the near term concerns China's trade imbalance. The country's current account surplus (a broad measure of the excess of export receipts over imports) has risen to great heights in recent years, reaching an astounding 11 percent of GDP on the eve of the financial crisis in 2007 (from low single digits a decade ago). This imbalance increases global demand for goods produced in China at the cost of reducing it elsewhere, greatly complicating the economic recovery in the rest of the world. It has adverse effects on the health of manufacturing sectors everywhere but China. But the problem is not just an economic one. Historically, large trade imbalances have created fertile ground for protectionism. If China's trade surplus does not shrink, the United States likely will resort to trade barriers directed at Chinese exports, inviting retaliation from China and similar tactics from other countries. A major political backlash against China's trade and globalization in general will become a real possibility.

Has China's dependence on exports put the world economy on a collision course? Do we face a fundamental, irremovable conflict between China's development strategy, on the one hand, and economic and social stability in the rest of the world, on the other?

Not necessarily. A trade surplus is only an *incidental* consequence of China's growth strategy, more the result of our present global rules than of the inherent logic of that strategy. To see why, we must return briefly to the story of Chinese growth. The Chinese strategy relies on rapid structural change, which the government accomplishes by promoting industrialization together with continuous upgrading of the country's productive structure. Most of the economic activities that the government encourages are tradable, mainly manufactures. This strategy is perfectly compatible with balance on the external trade accounts as long as the increased supply of electronic products, steel, autos, and other manufactured goods that China's factories turn out is matched by increased demand in China for such goods—not necessarily product by product but in total.

Until very recently, the Chinese model worked this way. Even though the Chinese government has promoted manufacturing heavily since the 1980s, it did so through industrial policies—trade restrictions, investment incentives, subsidies, and domestic-processing requirements—that did not spill over into a trade imbalance.

Things began to change in the second half of the 1990s as the government prepared for membership in the World Trade Organization. It brought tariffs down sharply and phased out many of the subsidies and domestic-processing requirements to bring policies in line with WTO requirements. But the Chinese government wasn't about to give up on its growth strategy. To compensate for the decline in protection and direct support to manufacturing, it allowed the renminbi to become increasingly undervalued.[29]

A cheap domestic currency has the same economic effects as a subsidy on exports *combined with a tax on imports*. Unlike conventional industrial policy, it necessarily generates a trade surplus.[30] So China's membership in the WTO in December 2001 produced an unwelcome side effect: a precipitous rise in its trade surplus followed at just around the same time.

We can now better understand why the Chinese government resists so vehemently external pressure for the renminbi's appreciation. Such a policy would help reduce global imbalances, but it would also threaten China's economic growth. My own research suggests that China's growth might be reduced by 2 percentage points or more if the renminbi is allowed to appreciate sufficiently to eliminate its undervaluation.[31] A reduction of this magnitude would in turn bring growth below the 8 percent threshold that the Chinese leadership believes is necessary for the economy to generate sufficient employment and avoid social strife. Given the size and geopolitical importance of the country, anything that undermines China's political stability should be of great concern to the rest of the world as well.

Unlike the picture that the typical commentary in the Western press suggests, this is not a simple morality play, with the Chinese as the "bad guys." China's trade surplus threatens the world economy, but so does a significant slowdown in its growth.

Such is the conundrum that our present rules have produced. Many consider the WTO's ability to constrain the use of subsidies and other industrial policies a great achievement for the world economy. It was a Pyrrhic victory. Restricting industrial policies has forced China to resort to what is, for the rest of the world, a much inferior tool: currency undervaluation. Since the Chinese government has to buy dollars to prevent its currency from appreciating, it has also required China to accumulate more than $2 trillion in reserves—low-return U.S. Treasury bills and other assets for which the country has no conceivable use.[32] The paradox—more apparent than real—is that tighter global rules have led to worse global problems.

The right approach would be to leave China, and indeed all emerging nations, free to pursue their own growth policies. WTO restrictions on subsidies and other industrial policies should be suspended or subsumed under a general exception for developing nations. It would then be reasonable to expect that China and other emerging nations will pursue currency, financial, and macroeconomic policies that do not generate large trade imbalances. The quid pro quo would be this: you are entitled to your own growth strategy, but you also need to ensure that you do not produce large negative effects for the rest of the world in the form of trade surpluses. This would enable China to employ smart industrial policies in support of its employment and growth objectives without fear of WTO sanction. It would also allow China to let the renminbi appreciate without fear of adverse effects on growth. At the very least, it would eliminate the only sound justification for China's refusal to shrink its trade surplus.

As China moves toward balanced trade, the most significant immediate threat to the world economy will subside. But China's large and growing footprint in global markets will continue to render some of its trade problematic. As China continues its economic transformation and gains market share in ever more sophisticated products, we can be certain that this trade will generate persistent complaints from other countries about the undermining of domestic distributional bargains, labor standards, environmental regulations, or social norms. These complaints would have significantly greater traction in a world where China has a large trade surplus overall; but they will not disappear in its absence. China and the importing countries must respond appropriately.

In this book I have provided a way to think about these conflicts and separate the legitimate wheat from the "protectionist" chaff. I have also proposed an escape clause mechanism—an expanded safeguard agreement along with domestic procedures—that would be appropriate for handling them. China may think the flexibility that this new apparatus affords importing nations will excessively restrict its exports. Yet the Chinese government (along with the governments of other major emerging nations) must recognize a basic reality of the global economy. If China and other developing nations want their policy space, they will have to allow rich nations to have theirs as well. China has every right to maintain its distinctive institutions; but it cannot expect other nations to alter their own economic and social models under threat from Chinese competition. Furthermore, China's non-democratic political regime requires that its trade receive much greater scrutiny than the trade of other countries like Brazil, Turkey, or India.

Still, provided the proposed safeguard mechanism is designed well, the policies it sanctions will not do much damage to trade overall. Its consequences will be a small price for exporters to pay for preserving an open global economy overall. China will have to take the trade restraints it experiences under this mechanism in stride—not as instances of protectionism that it needs to fight tooth and nail, but as necessary exercises in system maintenance.

Ultimately, the world economy must reconcile the big differences in China's cultural, social, and political system with the Western values and institutions that have dominated it to date. Americans and Europeans might assume that economic growth will make China more Western: liberal, capitalist, and democratic. But as the British scholar and journalist Martin Jacques reminds us, there is little reason to believe in such convergence.[33] China has distinctive views, rooted in its long history, on the organization of the economy, society, and government, and on the proper relationships among them. As China gains economic power, it will advocate for a world order that better reflects these views.

The resulting tensions will not be easy to manage. But the challenge will be considerably easier to handle under global rules that respect diversity and minimize the need for international fetters than under rules that maximize reliance on coordination and common standards. These rules need not be underpinned by a single hegemon (whether the United States or China) and they will provide for greater stability in the world economy as the U.S role inevitably wanes.[34] That emphasis should suit China as well. The humiliations the country suffered during the nineteenth century at the hands of Britain and other imperialist powers have made the Chinese leaders great believers in national sovereignty and non-interference in domestic affairs. A light global touch would be consistent with those values.

Final Words

Read any book, article, or op-ed on the future of globalization, or listen to any statesman on the subject, and you will quickly feel crushed under the burden of weighty problems. Will we manage to coax enough international cooperation out of the political leaders of major nations? Will we succeed in erecting the structures of global governance that the world economy needs? How do we convince the rank and file of the world economy that economic globalization is good for them, and not a force for inequality and insecurity? What will happen to the global economy as the economic might of the United States recedes? Will China become the new global hegemon, and if so, how will that transform the international order?

These questions are enough to give one a headache. But they derive from faulty premises: that hyperglobalization is desirable (or unavoidable) and that reempowering nation states would unleash forces that would severely damage the world economy. They make our task needlessly complicated.

We can and should tell a different story about globalization. Instead of viewing it as a system that requires a single set of institutions or one principal economic superpower, we should accept it as a collection of diverse nations whose interactions are regulated by a thin layer of simple, transparent, and commonsense traffic rules. This vision will not construct a path toward a "flat" world—a borderless world economy. Nothing will. What it will do is enable a healthy, sustainable world economy that leaves room for democracies to determine their own futures.

A Bedtime Story for Grown-ups

Once upon a time there was a little fishing village at the edge of a lake. The villagers were poor, living off the fish they caught and the clothing they sewed. They had no contact with the other inland villages, which were miles away and reached only after days of travel through a dense forest.

Life for the villagers took a turn for the worse when the stock of fish in the lake plummeted. Villagers responded by working harder, but they were caught in a vicious cycle. The scarcer the fish got, the longer the hours that each fisherman spent on the lake, which in turn depleted the fish stock at an even faster rate.

The villagers went to the village shaman and asked for help. He shrugged and said, "What is our council of elders for? They sit around all day and do nothing but gossip. They should solve this problem." "How?" the villagers asked. "Simple," he said. "The council should set up a fishermen's cooperative that decides how much fish each man can catch in a month. The fish stock will be renewed and we will not run into this problem in the future."

The council of elders did as the shaman suggested. The villagers weren't happy that the elders told them how to run their business, but they understood the need for the restraint. In no time, the lake was overflowing with fish.

The villagers returned to the shaman. They bowed in front of him and thanked him for his wisdom. Just as they were leaving, the shaman said: "Since you seem to be interested in my help, would you like me to give you another idea?" "Of course," the villagers cried in unison.

"Well," the shaman said. "Isn't it crazy that you all have to spend so much of your time sewing your own clothes when you could buy much better and cheaper ones from the villages on the other side of the forest? They aren't easy to get to, but you would only have to make the trip once or twice a year."

"Oh, but what can we sell in return?" asked the villagers. "I hear the people inland love dried fish," said the shaman.

And that is what the villagers did. They dried some of their fish and started to trade with the villages on the other side of the forest. The fishermen got rich on the high prices they received while the price of garments in the village dropped sharply.

Not all villagers were happy. Those who did not own a boat and whose livelihood depended on the garments they sewed were caught in a squeeze. They had to compete with the cheaper and higher-quality garments brought in from the other villages and had a harder time getting their hands on cheap fish. They asked the shaman what they should do.

"Well, this is another problem for the council of elders to solve," said the shaman. "You know how every family has to make a contribution during our monthly feast?" "Yes," they replied. "Well, since the fishermen are now so much richer, they should make a bigger contribution and you should make less."

The council of elders thought this was fair and they asked the fishermen to increase their monthly contribution. The fishermen weren't thrilled, but it seemed like a sensible thing to do to avoid discord in the village. Soon the rest of the village was happy, too.

The shaman meanwhile had another idea. He said: "Imagine how much richer our village could be if our traders did not have to spend days traveling through the dense forest. Imagine how much more trade we could have if there was a regular road through the forest." "But how?" asked the villagers. "Simple," said the shaman. "The council of elders should organize work brigades to cut through the forest and lay down a road."

Before long, the village was connected to the other villages by a paved road that cut down on travel time and cost. Trade expanded and the fishermen got even richer, but they didn't neglect to share their riches with the other villagers at feast time.

As time passed, however, things turned sour. The road gave villagers from beyond the forest easy access to the lake and allowed them to take up fishing, which they did in droves. Since neither the council nor the fishermen's cooperative could enforce the fishing restrictions on outsiders, the fish stock began to deplete rapidly again.

The new competition also cut into the earnings of the local fishermen. They began to complain about the feast tax being too onerous. "How can we compete effectively with the outsiders who are not subject to similar requirements?" they asked in desperation. Some local fishermen even made a habit of absenting themselves from the village on feast days—the road had made it easy to come and go—and evaded their obligations altogether. This made the rest of the villagers furious.

It was time for another trip to the shaman. The village held a long and boisterous meeting at which each side argued its case passionately. All agreed that the situation was unsustainable, but the proposed solutions varied. The fishermen wanted a change in the rules that would reduce their contributions to the monthly feasts. Others wanted an end to the fish trade with outsiders. Some even asked to blockade the road with boulders so that no one could enter or leave the village.

The shaman listened to these arguments. "You have to be reasonable and compromise," he said after some thought. "Here is what I suggest. The council of elders should place a tollbooth at the entrance to the access road, and everyone who comes in and out should pay a fee." "But this will make it more costly for us to trade," the fishermen objected. "Yes, indeed," the shaman replied. "But it will also reduce overfishing and make up for the loss in contributions at the feasts. And it won't cut off trade altogether," he added, pointing with his head to the villagers who wanted to block the road.

The villagers agreed that this was a reasonable solution. They walked out of the meeting satisfied. Harmony was restored to the village.

And everyone lived happily ever after.

NOTES

Introduction

1 This article was eventually published in 2009. See Dani Rodrik and Arvind Subramanian, "Why Did Financial Globalization Disappoint?" *IMF Staff Papers*, vol. 56, no. 1 (March 2009), pp. 112–38.

1. Of Markets and States

1 For the early history of what became known as the Hudson's Bay Company, see Beckles Willson, *The Great Company* (Toronto: Copp, Clark Company, 1899).

2 The Garraway's coffeehouse was itself the product of globalization, of course, coffee having made its way from the Near East to Europe during the sixteenth century. Coffeehouses spread like mushrooms in England during the second half of the seventeenth century and became popular gathering places for social and business purposes. See Deborah Hale, "The London Coffee House: A Social Institution" (April 2003), available online at http://www.rakehell.com/article.php?id=206. A fictionalized but highly informative account of the coffee trade during the seventeenth century, centered on Amsterdam, is provided in David Liss, *The Coffee Trader* (New York: Random House, 2003).

3 The online Canadian Encyclopedia is a good source on the voyage of the *Nonsuch* and other information related to Hudson's Bay Company. See http://www.thecanadianencyclopedia.com/index.cfm?PgNm= ArchivedFeatures&Params=A256.

4 The full text of the charter is available at http://www.solon.org/

Constitutions/Canada/English/PreConfederation/hbc_charter_1670
.html.

5 Peter C. Newman, *Empire of the Bay: An Illustrated History of the Hudson's Bay Company* (New York: Viking/Madison Press, 1989), p. 39.

6 Converted to 2009 U.S. dollars with help from Lawrence H. Officer, "Five Ways to Compute the Relative Value of a UK Pound Amount, 1830 to Present," MeasuringWorth, 2008. http://www.measuringworth.com/ukcompare/.

7 One percent versus 0.4 percent per annum, respectively. See Kevin H. O'Rourke and Jeffrey G. Williamson, "After Columbus: Explaining Europe's Overseas Trade Boom, 1500–1800," *Journal of Economic History*, vol. 62, no. 2 (June 2002), pp. 417–55.

8 Following Zeng He's famous voyages to East Africa in the early fifteenth century, the Chinese emperors inexplicably banned such intercontinental expeditions.

9 Ronald Findlay and Kevin H. O'Rourke, *Power and Plenty: Trade, War, and the World Economy in the Second Millennium* (Princeton and Oxford: Princeton University Press, 2007), p. 146.

10 This summary of their argument is taken from Eric Williams, *From Columbus to Castro: The History of the Caribbean 1492–1969* (New York: Random House, 1984), pp. 138–39.

11 George Bryce, *The Remarkable History of the Hudson's Bay Company*, 3rd ed. (London: Sampson Low, Marston & Co., 1910), pp. 22–23.

12 Quoted in Newman, *Empire of the Bay*, p. 165.

13 The actual quote is: "This division of labour, from which so many advantages are derived, is not originally the effect of any human wisdom, which foresees and intends that general opulence to which it gives occasion. It is the necessary, though very slow and gradual consequence of a certain propensity in human nature which has in view no such extensive utility; the propensity to truck, barter, and exchange one thing for another"—Adam Smith, *An Enquiry into the Nature and Causes of the Wealth of Nations* (1776), Bk. I, chap. 2.

14 See David R. Cameron, "The Expansion of the Public Economy: A Comparative Analysis," *American Political Science Review*, vol. 72, no. 4 (December 1978), pp. 1243–61.

15 Vito Tanzi and Ludger Schuknecht, *Public Spending in the 20th Century: A Global Perspective* (Cambridge: Cambridge University Press, 2000), chap. 1.

16 Dani Rodrik, "Why Do More Open Economies Have Bigger Governments?" *Journal of Political Economy*, vol. 106, no. 5 (October 1998), pp. 997–1032. For an update on these findings, see Giuseppe Bertola and

Anna Lo Prete, "Openness, Financial Markets, and Policies: Cross-Country and Dynamic Patterns," Unpublished paper, University of Torino, November 2008.

17 Jeffrey Immelt, "A Consistent Policy on Cleaner Energy," *Financial Times*, June 29, 2005, quoted in Daniel W. Drezner, *All Politics Is Global: Explaining International Regulatory Regimes* (Princeton: Princeton University Press, 2007), p. 44.

18 Some idea about the terms of trade offered to the Indians can be obtained by noting that in one year (1676) the value of merchandise exported from England by the Hudson's Bay Company was a mere £650 compared to £19,000 for the value of the furs imported—Willson, *The Great Company*, p. 215. Even with transport and other costs, this enabled a hefty profit for the company.

2. The Rise and Fall of the First Great Globalization

1 See Kevin H. O'Rourke and Jeffrey G. Williamson, "Once More: When Did Globalisation Begin?" *European Review of Economic History*, 8 (2004), pp. 109–17, for estimates of the growth rate of world trade during different historical eras.

2 John Morley, *The Life of Richard Cobden* (London: T. Fisher Unwin, 1905), p. 711. Quoted in the Wikipedia entry http://en.wikipedia.org/wiki/Cobden-Chevalier_Treaty.

3 The indispensable source on nineteenth-century tariff history is Paul Bairoch, "European Trade Policy, 1815–1914," in Peter Mathias and Sydney Pollard, eds., *The Cambridge Economic History of Europe*, Vol. 8: *The Industrial Economies: The Development of Economic and Social Policies* (Cambridge: Cambridge University Press, 1989), pp. 11–161.

4 Ibid., p. 138.

5 Southern interests had managed to insert a clause in the U.S. Constitution that prohibits the taxation of exports. They had failed to anticipate the "Lerner theorem," posited by the late economist Abba Lerner, which states that import tariffs are identical to export taxes with respect to their economic consequences.

6 Robert O. Keohane, "Associative American Development, 1776–1861: Economic Development and Political Disintegration," in John G. Ruggie, ed., *The Antinomies of Interdependence* (New York: Columbia University Press, 1983), p. 48.

7 One relevant comparison is provided by the experience of Latin America, whose economies remained dependent on large-scale plantation agriculture and authoritarian control mechanisms over the local popu-

lation. As Engerman and Sokoloff have convincingly argued, this goes far to explain why these economies never developed high-quality representative institutions and good systems of governance. The same point was also made earlier by Barrington Moore, Jr., who speculated that a Southern victory in the Civil War would have left the country "in the position of some modernizing countries today, with a latifundia economy, a dominant antidemocratic aristocracy, and a weak and dependent commercial and industrial class unable and unwilling to push forward toward political democracy." See Stanley L. Engerman and Kenneth L. Sokoloff, "Factor Endowments, Institutions and Differential Paths of Growth Among New World Economies: A View from Economic Historians of the United States," in Stephen Huber, ed., *How Latin America Fell Behind* (Stanford, CA: Stanford University Press, 1997); Barrington Moore, Jr., *Social Origins of Dictatorship and Democracy: Lord and Peasant in the Making of the Modern World* (Boston: Beacon Press, 1966), p. 153, quoted in Keohane, "Associative American Development," p. 73.

8 See Bairoch, "European Trade Policy," who provides a range of estimates.

9 Ibid., pp. 88–90.

10 And even then, as John Nye reminds us, British enthusiasm for free trade did not extend to a few non-manufactures such as wine, on which tariffs remained high—John V. C. Nye, "The Myth of Free-Trade Britain," March 3, 2003, available at http://www.econlib.org/library/Columns/y2003/Nyefreetrade.html.

11 Cited in Bairoch, "European Trade Policy," p. 84.

12 This is a mercantilist fallacy that free traders, strangely enough, will often hijack whenever it suits their purpose. For example, Samuel Brittan cites approvingly the first part of the Gladstone quote in his critique of contemporary "fair traders," excluding the mercantilist justification—Brittan, "Free Trade versus 'Fair Trade'," Remarks at Foreign Policy Centre meeting with Hilary Benn, January 10, 2005, available online at http://www.samuelbrittan.co.uk/spee39_p.html. A particularly jarring instance was the argument used by some of the proponents of NAFTA that it would increase U.S. employment because of its positive effects on the U.S. trade balance with Mexico. See Gary Clyde Hufbauer and Jeffrey J. Schott, *NAFTA: An Assessment*, rev. ed., Peterson Institute for International Economics, Washington, DC, October 1993.

13 Niall Ferguson, *Empire: The Rise and Demise of the British World Order and the Lessons for Global Power* (New York: Basic Books, 2003), p. xxi.

14 Kris James Mitchener and Marc Weidenmier, "Trade and Empire," Working Paper 13765, National Bureau of Economic Research, Cambridge, MA, January 2008, p. 2. These authors do not find any statisti-

cally significant difference between the British and other empires with respect to their trade-promoting effects.

15 John Gallagher and Ronald Robinson, "The Imperialism of Free Trade," *Economic History Review*, new series, vol. 6, no. 1 (1953), pp. 1–15: "in any particular region, if economic opportunity seems large but political security small, then full absorption into the extending economy tends to be frustrated until power is exerted upon the state in question. Conversely, in proportion as satisfactory political frameworks are brought into being in this way, the frequency of imperialist intervention lessens and imperialist control is correspondingly relaxed" (p. 6).

16 One troy ounce equals 480 grains of gold, so one grain is equivalent to 0.0021 ounces.

17 See Barry Eichengreen, *Globalizing Capital: A History of the International Monetary System*, 2nd ed. (Princeton and Oxford: Princeton University Press, 2008), p. 29.

18 The relationship among the key central bankers of the interwar period is the subject of Liaquat Ahamed's *Lords of Finance: The Bankers Who Broke the World* (New York: Penguin, 2009).

19 Eichengreen, *Globalizing Capital*, chap. 2.

20 John Maynard Keynes, *The Economic Consequences of the Peace* (London: Macmillan, 1919), p. 11.

21 The speech ends as follows: "Having behind us the producing masses of this nation and the world, supported by the commercial interests, the laboring interests and the toilers everywhere, we will answer their demand for a Gold Standard by saying to them: You shall not press down upon the brow of labor this crown of thorns, you shall not crucify mankind upon a cross of gold." The "them" in question are the bankers and other northeastern interests. See http://en.wikipedia.org/wiki/Cross_of_gold_speech.

22 The efficacy of reputation in sustaining international lending continues to be debated about economists and political scientists. For a recent evaluation, which suggests reputation can be quite effective, see Michael Tomz, *Reputation and International Cooperation: Sovereign Debt across Three Centuries* (Princeton: Princeton University Press, 2007).

23 Quoted in Gallagher and Robinson, "The Imperialism of Free Trade," pp. 4–5.

24 David J. Mentiply, "The British Invasion of Egypt, 1882," March 23, 2009, available online at http://www.e-ir.info/?p=615.

25 Kris James Mitchener and Marc Weidenmier, "Empire, Public Goods, and the Roosevelt Corollary," *Journal of Economic History*, vol. 65, no. 3 (September 2005), pp. 658–92.

26 Quoted in Ahamed, *Lords of Finance*, p. 231.

27 Ibid., p. 220. My account of the interwar period relies heavily on Aha-med's fascinating book.

28 Laura Beers, "Education or Manipulation? Labour, Democracy, and the Popular Press in Interwar Britain," *Journal of British Studies*, 48 (January 2009), p. 129.

29 Ibid.

30 Findlay and O'Rourke, *Power and Plenty*, p. 451.

31 The classic study of this experience is Albert O. Hirschman's *National Power and the Structure of Foreign Trade* (Berkeley: University of California Press, 1980, first published 1945).

32 Findlay and O'Rourke, *Power and Plenty*, Table 8.3. As these authors note (p. 467) there is evidence that countries in the periphery that resorted to protection recovered sooner from (or were less affected by) the Great Depression.

33 See Barry Eichengreen and Doug Irwin, "The Protectionist Tempta-tion: Lessons from the Great Depression for Today," VoxEU.org, March 17, 2009, http://voxeu.org/index.php?q=node/3280.

34 Jeffry Frieden, "Will Global Capitalism Fall Again?" Presentation for Bruegel's Essay and Lecture Series. Brussels, June 2006, available online at www.people.fas.harvard.edu/~jfrieden/Selected%20Articles/Misc_Works/GlobalCapFallAgainWebversion.pdf.

3. Why Doesn't Everyone Get the Case for Free Trade?

1 See the discussion in Andrea Maneschi, "The Tercentenary of Henry Martyn's *Considerations Upon the East-India Trade*," *Journal of the History of Economic Thought*, vol. 24, no. 2 (2002), pp. 233–49. An excellent his-tory of the evolution of free trade doctrine can be found in Douglas A. Irwin, *Against the Tide: An Intellectual History of Free Trade* (Princeton: Princeton University Press, 1996).

2 P. J. Thomas, *Mercantilism and the East India Trade* (London: P. S. King & Son, 1926), Appendix B.

3 Henry Martyn, *Considerations Upon the East-India Trade* (1701), p. 32, reprinted in John R. McCulloch, ed., *Early English Tracts on Commerce* (Cambridge: Cambridge University Press, 1954), pp. 541–95.

4 Paul A. Samuelson, "The Way of an Economist," in P. A. Samuelson, ed., *International Economic Relations: Proceedings of the Third Congress of the International Economic Association* (London: Macmillan, 1969), pp. 1–11, quoted at http://www.wto.org/english/res_e/reser_e/cadv_e.htm. The mathematician in question was Stanislaw Ulam.

5 Frank W. Taussig, "Abraham Lincoln on the Tariff: A Myth," *Quarterly Journal of Economics*, vol. 28, no. 4 (August 1914), pp. 814–20.

6 World Values Survey online database (http://www.worldvaluessurvey .org/).

7 This can be seen in the cross-tabs that World Values Survey makes available online—ibid.

8 Anna Maria Mayda and Dani Rodrik, "Why Are Some Individuals (and Countries) More Protectionist Than Others?" *European Economic Review*, 49 (August 2005), pp. 1393–1430.

9 So Adam Smith was not correct when he famously wrote, in defense of free trade, that "What is prudence in the conduct of every private family, can scarce be folly in that of a great kingdom"—Smith, *The Wealth of Nations*, Bk. IV, chap. 2.

10 Regulatory decisions on new technologies can have large economic impacts on particular groups, just like trade policies. In October 2009, for example, when the Food and Drug Administration issued a negative judgment on a drug meant to treat osteoporosis in postmenopause women, the stock of the company that makes the drug fell by more than 2 percent. See Andrew Pollack, "F.D.A. Says No, for Now, to an Amgen Bone Drug," *New York Times*, October 19, 2009; http://www.nytimes .com/2009/10/20/business/20amgen.html?_r=1&ref=business.

11 Lori G. Kletzer, "Job Displacement," *Journal of Economic Perspectives*, vol. 12, no. 1 (Winter 1998), pp. 115–36.

12 Wolfgang F. Stolper and Paul A. Samuelson, "Protection and Real Wages," *Review of Economic Studies*, 9 (1941), pp. 58–73. The theorem has a number of assumptions, some of which are more restrictive than others, but its central intuition is quite robust.

13 Another common mistake is to presume that even if some people lose from trade, most people must gain. See Robert Driskill, "Deconstructing the Argument for Free Trade," Unpublished paper, February 2007, who interestingly uses as an illustration a *New York Times* profile which ascribes (wrongly) that view to me!

14 The models that do not generate distributional conflict tend to rely on rather special assumptions. For example, it is possible for trade based on scale economies to generate all-around gains, but this obtains only if the trading countries are sufficiently similar in factor endowments and technological capabilities. This scenario may apply to two rich countries, but it would not apply to trade between advanced and developing countries. Similarly, it is possible for trade not to generate distributional conflict when the goods being imported are "non-competing"—that is, there is no domestic production that is displaced. But a common reason why domestic production has disappeared is that import competition has driven it out of existence in an earlier period.

15 Dani Rodrik, "The Rush to Free Trade in the Developing World: Why

So Late? Why Now? Will It Last?" in S. Haggard and S. Webb, eds., *Voting for Reform: Democracy, Political Liberalization, and Economic Adjustment* (New York: Oxford University Press, 1994).

16 As is shown in Rodrik, ibid., we need two other pieces of information besides tariffs to compute this ratio: the import demand elasticity and the share of imports in GDP. For the purposes of this exercise, I have assumed (generously) values of –2 and 0.2, respectively, for these two parameters.

17 Technically, the reason for this is that the efficiency loss from tariffs rises with the square of the tariff, while the distributive effects are linear.

18 See Antoine Bouët, "The Expected Benefits from Trade Liberalization: Opening the Black Box of Global Trade Modeling," *Food Policy Review*, no. 8, International Food Policy Research Institute, Washington, DC, 2008 (http://www.ifpri.org/sites/default/files/publications/pv08. pdf). This study estimates that the U.S. economy would reap a total gain of 0.1 percent of GDP by 2015 as a consequence of a complete move to free trade in the world, with the bulk of the benefits coming from other nations' liberalization rather than the United States' own move to free trade.

19 For example, the article I mentioned in a previous chapter on the complementarity between states and markets ("Why Do More Open Economies Have Bigger Governments?") was published in the flagship journal of the Economics Department at the University of Chicago— the seat of free market orthodoxy if there ever was one. Similarly, a paper I wrote calling into question the widely held view that freer trade has promoted growth around the world was published in a publication of the National Bureau of Economic Research, the premier network for applied economists—Francisco Rodriguez and Dani Rodrik, "Trade Policy and Economic Growth: A Skeptic's Guide to the Cross-National Evidence" in Ben Bernanke and Kenneth S. Rogoff, eds., *Macroeconomics Annual 2000* (Cambridge, MA: MIT Press for NBER, 2001).

20 Driskill, "Deconstructing the Argument for Free Trade," p. 6.

21 Ibid., p. 2.

4. Bretton Woods, GATT, and the WTO

1 John Maynard Keynes, "National Self-Sufficiency," *The Yale Review*, vol. 22, no. 4 (June 1933), pp. 755–69. This is the article in which the following famous quote appears: "I sympathize, therefore, with those who would minimize, rather than with those who would maximize, economic entanglement among nations. Ideas, knowledge, science, hospitality,

travel—these are the things which should of their nature be international. But let goods be homespun whenever it is reasonably and conveniently possible, and, above all, let finance be primarily national."

2 Raymond Mikesell, *The Bretton Woods Debates: A Memoir* (Princeton: Princeton Dept. of Economics, International Finance Section, Essays in International Finance, no. 192, 1994).

3 John Ruggie has called this the "embedded liberalism" compromise. See John G. Ruggie, "International Regimes, Transactions, and Change: Embedded Liberalism in the Postwar Economic Order," *International Organization*, vol. 36, no. 2 (Spring 1982), pp. 379–415. I will return to Ruggie's ideas below.

4 John G. Ruggie, "Multilateralism: The Anatomy of an Institution," *International Organization*, vol. 46, no. 3 (1992), pp. 561–98.

5 These rounds of negotiations were initially small affairs, taking less than a year to complete. The Uruguay Round, which was the round that created the WTO, took eight years to complete. See http://www.wto.org/english/thewto_e/whatis_e/tif_e/fact4_e.htm.

6 Indeed, quantitative studies have a hard time explaining the postwar expansion of trade, without placing a lot of emphasis on economic growth itself. The declines in tariffs and transport costs clearly do not go far enough on their own. See Andrew K. Rose, "Why Has Trade Grown Faster Than Income?" Board of Governors of the Federal Reserve System, International Finance Discussion Papers no. 390, November 1990.

7 Ruggie, "International Regimes," p. 393.

8 Peter A. Hall and David W. Soskice, eds., *Varieties of Capitalism: The Institutional Foundations of Capitalism* (Oxford and New York: Oxford University Press, 2001).

9 Thomas L. Friedman's *The Lexus and the Olive Tree: Understanding Globalization* (New York: Farrar, Straus & Giroux, 1999), captures the ethos of this era extremely well.

10 Susan Esserman and Robert Howse, "The WTO on Trial," *Foreign Affairs*, vol. 82, no. 1 (January–February 2003), pp. 130–31.

11 The story of the U.S.-Europe dispute over trade in hormone-treated beef is told in Charan Devereux, Robert Z. Lawrence, and Michael D. Watkins, *Case Studies in U.S. Trade Negotiations*, Vol. 2: *Resolving Disputes* (Washington, DC: Institute for International Economics), chap. 1.

12 Mike Moore, *A World Without Walls: Freedom, Development, Free Trade and Global Governance* (New York: Cambridge University Press, 2003), p. 114. See also my review of this book—Dani Rodrik, "Free Trade Optimism: Lessons from the Battle in Seattle," *Foreign Affairs*, vol. 82. no. 3 (May–June 2003), pp. 135–40.

13 Recent estimates suggest that removing all government barriers to trade would yield global "welfare" gains of the order of a mere 0.3 percent of world GDP, an effect that would be barely noticeable in practice. See Bouët, "The Expected Benefits from Trade Liberalization."

14 The travails of the Doha Development Round are chronicled in Paul Blustein, *Misadventures of the Most Favored Nations* (New York: Public Affairs, 2009).

15 Robert Z. Lawrence, *Regionalism, Multilateralism, and Deeper Integration* (Washington, DC: Brookings Institution, 1996).

16 "Krugman's Conundrum—Economics Focus," *The Economist*, April 19, 2008, p. xx. The Krugman study is Paul Krugman, "Trade and Wages, Reconsidered," *Brookings Papers on Economic Activity* (Spring 2008), pp. 103–37.

17 I had taken a different position in this debate, arguing that there were many channels through which globalization could imperil the incomes and economic security of the low-paid. See Dani Rodrik, *Has Globalization Gone Too Far?* (Washington, DC: Institute for International Economics, 1997). The empirical studies available at the time had looked at only a few of those channels and therefore had been too quick to dismiss popular concern about trade. The tendency of economists at the time was to dismiss these arguments. Even worse, books like mine could be dangerous because they would end up providing "ammunition to the barbarians," as Krugman himself warned me in a personal communication before my book was published.

18 Wage inequality has stopped growing in the lower half of the distribution, while it keeps increasing in the top half. The gap in wages between production and non-production (e.g., managerial and supervisory) workers has come down since 2000.

19 Christian Broda and John Romalis, "Inequality and Prices: Does China Benefit the Poor in America?" University of Chicago Graduate School of Business, March 2008.

20 See the discussion by Douglas Irwin, Larry Katz, and Robert Lawrence that follows Paul Krugman's essay in the *Brookings Papers on Economic Activity* (Spring 2008), pp. 138–54.

21 As measured by the import-penetration ratio.

22 The source for this information is Avraham Ebenstein, Ann Harrison, Margaret McMillan, and Shannon Phillips, "Estimating the Impact of Trade and Offshoring on American Workers Using the Current Population Surveys," National Bureau of Economic Research, Working Paper 15107, Cambridge, MA, June 2009.

23 Lawrence Summers, "America Needs to Make a New Case for Trade," *Financial Times*, April 27, 2008 (http://www.ft.com/cms/s/0/0c185e3a-

1478-11dd-a741-0000779fd2ac.html); and Summers, "A Strategy to Promote Healthy Globalization," *Financial Times*, May 4, 2008 (http://www.ft.com/cms/s/0/999160e6-1a03-11dd-ba02-0000779fd2ac.html?nclick_check=1).

24 Summers, "America Needs to Make a New Case."

25 Alan Blinder, "Offshoring: The Next Industrial Revolution," *Foreign Affairs*, vol. 85, no. 2 (March–April 2006), pp. 113–28.

26 Ibid., p. 119.

27 Jagdish Bhagwati, "Does the U.S. Need a New Trade Policy?" *Journal of Policy Modeling*, 31 (July–August 2009), pp. 509–14.

28 There is a simple explanation for why compensation ex post is never quite credible ex ante. Before a trade agreement is passed, export interests want to minimize opposition from labor and other groups worried about adverse effects, and hence will promise programs such as adjustment assistance to blunt the opposition. But once the agreement is passed, the winners have much less incentive to keep the losers happy. So the promised adjustment assistance will become underfunded and ineffective over time. The history of U.S. trade adjustment assistance has followed this logic, which is why labor unions are rarely mollified these days by promises of expanded adjustment assistance.

5. Financial Globalization Follies

1 I served for several years as research coordinator for the Group of Twenty-Four, a developing country caucus group within the IMF. The group's plenary gathering during the IMF annual meetings was emblematic of the treatment ministers from developing nations, save for a few among them, typically received. The World Bank president and the IMF managing director would stroll in at the beginning of the meeting, shake a few hands, read their prepared remarks, and then promptly depart. Their seats would then be filled by Bank and Fund officials several grades their junior, charged with the task of listening to (suffering through?) the presentations by the developing nations themselves.

2 Quoted in Rawi Abdelal, *Capital Rules: The Construction of Global Finance* (Cambridge, MA: Harvard University Press, 2007), p. 156. Abdelal provides an excellent account of the 1997 meetings and the run-up to them.

3 Communiqué of the Interim Committee of the Board of Governors of the IMF, IMF Press Release #97–44, September 21, 1997 (http://www.imf.org/external/np/sec/pr/1997/pr9744.htm).

4 Stanley Fischer, "Capital Account Liberalization and the Role of the

IMF," Presentation at the Seminar on Asia and the IMF, Hong Kong, September 19, 1997 (http://www.iie.com/fischer/pdf/Fischer144.pdf).

5 Stanley Fischer, "Globalization and Its Challenges," *American Economic Review*, vol. 93, no. 2 (May 2003), p. 14. As we shall see when we turn to trade and growth, the evidence on trade liberalization that Fischer refers to was itself quite problematic.

6 See Rudiger Dornbusch, "It's Time for a Financial Transactions Tax," *International Economy* (August–September 1996), and Dornbusch, "Capital Controls: An Idea Whose Time Is Past," in Stanley Fischer, et al., *Should the IMF Pursue Capital-Account Convertibility?* Essays in International Finance, no. 207, Princeton University, May 1998. My own views at the time are evident in the title of an article included in the same collection as the second Dornbusch piece. See Rodrik, "Who Needs Capital-Account Convertibility?" in Fischer et al., *Should the IMF Pursue Capital-Account Convertibility?*

7 Rodrik, "Who Needs Capital-Account Convertibility?" p. 55.

8 In an article with the headline "ASEAN's Sound Fundamentals Bode Well for Sustained Growth" in International Monetary Fund, *IMF Survey*, November 25, 1996. Quoted in Jonathan Kirshner, "Keynes, Capital Mobility and the Crisis of Embedded Liberalism," *Review of International Political Economy*, vol. 6, no. 3 (Autumn 1999), pp. 313–37.

9 Dani Rodrik, "Governing the World Economy: Does One Architectural Style Fit All?" in Susan Collins and Robert Lawrence, eds., *Brookings Trade Forum: 1999* (Washington, DC: Brookings Institution, 2000).

10 For an elaboration of the Sachs argument, see Steven Radelet and Jeffrey Sachs, "The Onset of the East Asian Financial Crisis." in Paul Krugman, ed., *Currency Crises*, (Chicago: University of Chicago Press for the NBER, 2000). The story of the Asian financial crisis and the debates around it is well told in Paul Blustein, *The Chastening: Inside the Crisis That Rocked the Global System and Humbled the IMF* (New York: Public Affairs, 2001).

11 Arthur I. Bloomfield, "Postwar Control of International Capital Movements," *American Economic Review*, vol. 36, no. 2, Papers and Proceedings of the Fifty-eighth Annual Meeting of the American Economic Association (May 1946), p. 687.

12 John Maynard Keynes, "Activities 1941–1946: Shaping the Post-war World, Bretton Woods and Reparations," in D. Moggridge, ed., *The Collected Writings of John Maynard Keynes*, Vol. 26 (Cambridge: Cambridge University Press, 1980), p. 17.

13 Abdelal, *Capital Rules*, p. 48.

14 See Eichengreen, *Globalizing Capital*, p. 119, and the studies cited therein.

15 Barry Eichengreen, "From Benign Neglect to Malignant Preoccupation: U.S. Balance-of-Payments Policy in the 1960s," National Bureau of Economic Research, Working Paper 7630, March 2000.

16 Jeffry Frieden provides a nice account. See Jeffry A. Frieden, *Global Capitalism: Its Fall and Rise in the Twentieth Century* (New York: W. W. Norton, 2006), chap. 15.

17 This could be done, for example, by manipulating the timing of payments for (ostensibly) trade transactions.

18 See Eric Helleiner, "Explaining the Globalization of Financial Markets: Bringing States Back," *Review of International Political Economy*, vol. 2, no. 2 (Spring 1995), pp. 315–41.

19 Ibid.

20 Ibid.

21 This account draws heavily on Abdelal, *Capital Rules*, chaps. 4 and 5.

22 Cited in ibid., p. 63.

23 The forerunner of the OECD was the Organization for European Economic Co-operation (OEEC), established in 1948 to administer U.S. aid to Europe in the context of the Marshall Plan.

24 Abdelal, *Capital Rules*, pp. 106ff. It is striking in each of these cases how positive the OECD view was on the likely effects of capital flows, just months before financial crises struck.

25 As estimated by the Bank of International Settlements. See http://www.forex-brokerage-firms.com/news/currency-markets-rises.htm.

26 James Tobin, "A Proposal for Monetary Reform," *Eastern Economic Journal*, vol. 4, nos. 3–4 (July–October 1978), pp. 153–59.

27 Lord Turner, chairman of the U.K. Financial Services Authority, raised an outcry in August 2009 when he expressed support for a global Tobin tax. This was the first time that a major policy maker from the United States or Britain, the two leading centers of global finance, has come out in favor of the tax.

28 Luc Leaven and Fabian Valencia, "Systemic Bank Crises: A New Database," International Monetary Fund, Working Paper WP/08/224, September 2008.

29 Guillermo A. Calvo, "Explaining Sudden Stops, Growth Collapse and BOP Crises: The Case of Distortionary Output Taxes," in his *Emerging Capital Markets in Turmoil: Bad Luck or Bad Policy?* (Cambridge, MA: MIT Press, 2005).

30 Laeven and Fabian, "Systemic Bank Crises," p. 25.

31 Charles P. Kindleberger, *Manias, Panics and Crashes: A History of Financial Crises* (New York: Basic Books, 1989).

32 Carmen M. Reinhart and Kenneth S. Rogoff, "This Time Is Different: A Panoramic View of Eight Centuries of Financial Crises," Unpublished

paper, Harvard University, April 16, 2008, p. 7 (http://www.economics
.harvard.edu/faculty/rogoff/files/This_Time_Is_Different.pdf).

33 Research at the IMF has shown that the volatility of consumption in the
developing economies rose under financial globalization—M. Ayhan
Kose, Eswar S. Prasad, and Marco E. Terrones, "Growth and Volatil-
ity in an Era of Globalization," *IMF Staff Papers*, vol. 52, Special Issue
(September 2005). The absence of a positive relationship between capi-
tal inflows and economic growth is shown in Eswar Prasad, Raghuram
G. Rajan, and Arvind Subramanian, "Foreign Capital and Economic
Growth," *Brookings Papers on Economic Activity*, 1 (2007), pp. 153–209.

6. The Foxes and Hedgehogs of Finance

1 Isaiah Berlin, *The Hedgehog and the Fox: An Essay on Tolstoy's View of History*
(New York: Simon & Schuster, 1953).

2 Using economists' jargon, this distinction corresponds to the difference between first-best and second-best economic analysis. The hedgehog applies first-best principles while the fox applies second-best tools.

3 Stanley Fischer, "Capital Account Liberalization and the Role of the
IMF," September 19, 1997, http://www.imf.org/external/np/speeches/
1997/091997.htm.

4 Frederic S. Mishkin, *The Next Great Globalization: How Disadvantaged
Nations Can Harness Their Financial Systems to Get Rich* (Princeton: Princeton University Press, 2006).

5 Two prominent economists who are strong supporters of globalization
but have expressed doubts on the wisdom of freeing up capital flows are
Jagdish Bhagwati and Martin Wolf.

6 Frederic S. Mishkin, "Why We Shouldn't Turn Our Backs on Financial
Globalization," *IMF Staff Papers*, vol. 56, no. 1 (2009), pp. 150ff.

7 Quoted at http://www.imf.org/external/np/sec/mds/1996/MDS9611
.htm.

8 Mishkin, "Why We Shouldn't Turn Our Backs," p. 106.

9 Michael Lewis, "The End," Portfolio.com, Nov. 11, 2008 (http://www
.portfolio.com/news-markets/national-news/portfolio/2008/11/11/
The-End-of-Wall-Streets-Boom?print=true#).

10 James Tobin, "A Proposal for International Monetary Reform," *Eastern
Economic Journal*, 4 (July–October 1978), pp.153–59.

11 The Tobin tax rate that is contemplated usually lies in the vicinity of
0.10 to 0.25 percent. Consider, e.g., a tax of 0.10 percent. For a specula-
tor to be willing to pay this tax on a very short term transaction that he
plans to undo within a day, he must expect a return from the transaction of at least 0.20 percent on a daily basis (so that he can more than

cover the tax on the round trip), or 7.4 percent on an annual basis. The tax would be prohibitive for any return differential below that threshold. Therefore it would curb financial transactions in pursuit of small short-term returns and would allow interest rates to diverge in different jurisdictions.

12 See Joseph E. Stiglitz, *Globalization and Its Discontents* (New York: W. W. Norton, 2002).

13 Jagdish Bhagwati, "The Capital Myth: The Difference Between Trade in Widgets and Dollars," *Foreign Affairs*, vol. 77, no. 3 (May–June 1998), pp. 7–12.

14 Jagdish Bhagwati, *In Defense of Globalization* (New York: Oxford University Press, 2004), p. 239.

15 M. Ayhan Kose, Eswar Prasad, Kenneth Rogoff, and Shang-Jin Wei, "Financial Globalization: A Reappraisal," *IMF Staff Papers*, vol. 56, no. 1 (April 2009), pp. 8–62.

16 Louise Story, Landon Thomas, Jr., and Nelson D. Schwartz, "Wall St. Helped to Mask Debt Fueling Europe's Crisis," *New York Times*, February 13, 2010 (http://www.nytimes.com/2010/02/14/business/global/14debt.html?emc=eta1).

17 The story comes via Ragnar Nurkse, a leading economist of the interwar era, and is quoted in Frieden, *Global Capitalism: Its Fall and Rise in the Twentieth Century*, p. 197.

18 The best evidence for this comes, somewhat paradoxically, from research done at the IMF. See M. Ayhan Kose, Eswar S. Prasad, and Marco E. Terrones, "Growth and Volatility in an Era of Globalization," *IMF Staff Papers*, vol. 52, Special Issue (September 2005).

19 "Crisis may be worse than Depression, Volcker says," Reuters, February 20, 2009 (http://uk.reuters.com/article/idUKN2029103720090220).

20 Craig Torres, "Bernanke Says Crisis Damage Likely to Be Long-Lasting," Bloomberg News Service, April 17, 2009.

21 David A. Moss, "An Ounce of Prevention: Financial regulation, moral hazard, and the end of 'too big to fail,'" *Harvard Magazine* (September–October 2009) (http://harvardmagazine.com/2009/09/financial-risk-management-plan?page=0,1).

22 Enrque G. Mendoza and Vincenzo Quadrini, "Did Financial Globalisation Make the US Crisis Worse?" VoxEU.org, November 14, 2009 (http://voxeu.org/index.php?q=node/4206).

23 And not just financial havens. The reason that AIG's credit-default swap operations were based in London is that this was a much less heavily regulated environment than New York.

24 Simon Johnson, "The Quiet Coup," *The Atlantic* (May 2008) (http://www.theatlantic.com/doc/200905/imf-advice).

25 Johnson and I had often taken stands on the opposite sides of the argument, while remaining friends and respectful of each other's views. Johnson had been critical of my argument that capital controls had helped Malaysia avoid an even worse downturn during the Asian financial crisis. When my skeptical views on financial globalization appeared in the financial press, Johnson was quick with his letters to the editor taking me and my co-author to task for underselling the benefits of free capital flows and for overlooking the "collateral benefits" argument in their favor. These letters, one in *The Economist* and the other in the *Financial Times*, are reproduced on the IMF Web site at http://www .imf.org/external/np/vc/2008/030608.htm and http://www.imf.org/ external/np/vc/2008/050108.htm. As late as October 2007, Johnson was reluctant, as the chief economist of the IMF, to recommend stronger financial regulation because he thought it was unclear whether the problems in financial markets required more or *less* regulation. See Transcript of a Press Briefing by Simon Johnson, Economic Counsellor and Director of the IMF's Research Department, on the Analytic Chapters of the World Economic Outlook, Washington, DC, October 10, 2007 (http://www.imf.org/external/np/tr/2007/tr071010.htm).

26 Tim Fernholz, "The Unlikely Revolutionary," *The American Prospect*, online, April 22, 2009 (http://www.prospect.org/cs/articles?article= the_unlikely_revolutionary).

27 A number of good articles and books have recently underscored this point. See in particular Barry Eichengreen, "The Last Temptation of Risk," *The National Interest*, April 30, 2009; John Cassidy, *How Markets Fail: The Logic of Economic Calamities* (New York: Farrar, Straus & Giroux, 2009); and Yves Smith, *ECONned: How Unenlightened Self Interest Undermined Democracy and Corrupted Capitalism* (New York: Palgrave/ Macmillan, 2010).

28 In February 2010, the IMF published a little-noticed policy note which contained a remarkable admission. Under certain conditions, the IMF's economists wrote, capital controls are "justified" to deal with capital inflows. So the IMF too has come a long way from its enthusiastic embrace of finance fetishism during the 1990s. Perhaps the foxes are winning after all. See Jonathan D. Ostry, et al., "Capital Inflows: The Role of Controls," IMF Staff Position Note, February 19, 2010.

7. Poor Countries in a Rich World

1 These figures are in 1994 dollars. Here is how they are arrived at. The median "poor" country has a per capita income of $868 and an income share for the top decile of 35 percent. Therefore the average income of

a rich person in a poor country is $10 \times 868 \times 0.35 = \$3{,}039$. The median "rich" country has a per capita income of $\$34{,}767$ and an income share for the bottom decile of 2.7 percent. Therefore the average income of a poor person in a rich society is $10 \times 34{,}767 \times 0.027 = \$9{,}387$.

2 Angus Maddison, *Growth and Interaction in the World Economy: The Roots of Modernity* (Washington, DC: American Enterprise Institute, 2004), Table 2.

3 Lant Pritchett. "Divergence, Big Time" *Journal of Economic Perspectives*, vol. 11, no. 3 (Summer 1997), pp. 3–17.

4 Angus Maddison, *The World Economy: A Millennial Perspective* (Paris: OECD Development Centre, 2001).

5 Daron Acemoglu, Simon Johnson, and James A. Robinson, "The Colonial Origins of Comparative Development: An Empirical Investigation," *American Economic Review*, vol. 91, no. 5 (December 2001), pp. 1369–1401. See also Stanley L. Engerman and Kenneth L. Sokoloff, "Factor Endowments, Institutions and Differential Paths of Growth Among New World Economies: A View from Economic Historians of the United States," in Stephen Huber, ed., *How Latin America Fell Behind* (Stanford, CA: Stanford University Press, 1997).

6 Şevket Pamuk and Jeffrey G. Williamson, "Ottoman De-Industrialization 1800–1913: Assessing the Shock, Its Impact, and the Response," National Bureau of Economic Research, Working Paper 14763, March 2009.

7 Jeffrey G. Williamson, "Globalization and Under-development in the Pre-Modern Third World," The Luca d'Agliano Lecture, Turin, Italy, March 31, 2006.

8 Oded Galor and Andrew Mountford, "Trading Population for Productivity: Theory and Evidence," *Review of Economic Studies*, vol. 75, no. 4 (October 2008), pp. 1143–1179.

9 I am referring here to manufacturing output levels in per capita terms.

10 Paul Bairoch, "International Industrialization Levels from 1750 to 1980," *Journal of European Economic History*, 11 (Spring 1982), pp. 269–310.

11 The tale of the contrasting paths of Argentina and the United States is told in Alan Beattie, *False Economy: A Surprising Economic History of the World* (New York: Riverhead Books, 2009), chap. 1.

12 Ichirou Inukai and Arlon R. Tussing, "Kogyo Iken: Japan's Ten Year Plan, 1884," *Economic Development and Cultural Change*, vol. 16, no. 1 (October 1967), p. 53.

13 For varying accounts of the role played by the state and private industry in the takeoff of cotton spinning in Japan, see W. Miles Fletcher, "The Japan Spinners Association: Creating Industrial Policy in Meiji Japan,"

Journal of Japanese Studies, vol. 22, no. 1 (Winter 1996), pp. 49–75, and Gary Saxonhouse, "A Tale of Japanese Technological Diffusion in the Meiji Period," *Journal of Economic History*, vol. 34, no. 1 (March 1974), pp. 149–65.

14 *Japan as Number One: Lessons for America*, the title of a bestselling book of the 1980s, captures well the aura of its manufacturing prowess at the time—Ezra F. Vogel, *Japan as Number One: Lessons for America* (Cambridge, MA: Harvard University Press, 1979).

15 The story of Japan's drive to get the World Bank to pay more attention to the Japanese model is told in Robert Wade, "Japan, the World Bank, and the Art of Paradigm Maintenance: *The East Asian Miracle* in Political Perspective," *New Left Review*, 217 (May–June 1996), pp. 3–36.

16 My views on the report were written up in Dani Rodrik, "King Kong Meets Godzilla: The World Bank and the East Asian Miracle," in Albert Fishlow, et al., *Miracle or Design? Lessons from the East Asian Experience*, Overseas Development Council, Policy Essay No. 11, Washington, DC, 1994.

17 My interpretation of these two countries' takeoff is in Dani Rodrik, "Getting Interventions Right: How South Korea and Taiwan Grew Rich," *Economic Policy*, 20 (1995), pp. 55–107. The two best books on the subject remain Robert Wade, *Governing the Market: Economic Theory and the Role of Government in East Asian Industrialization* (Princeton: Princeton University Press, 1990), and Alice H. Amsden, *Asia's Next Giant: South Korea and Late Industrialization* (New York: Oxford University Press, 1989).

18 See Shaohua Chen and Martin Ravallion, "China Is Poorer Than We Thought, But No Less Successful in the Fight Against Poverty," World Bank, Policy Research Working Paper No. 4621, Washington, DC, May 2008.

19 Sebastian Heilmann, "Policy Experimentation in China's Economic Rise," *Studies in Comparative International Development*, vol. 43, no. 1 (Spring 2008), pp. 1–26.

20 Lawrence J. Lau, Yingyi Qian, and Gerard Roland, "Reform Without Losers: An Interpretation of China's Dual-Track Approach to Transition," *Journal of Political Economy*, vol. 108, no. 1 (February 2000), pp. 120–43.

21 Yingyi Qian, "How Reform Worked in China," in Dani Rodrik, ed., *In Search of Prosperity: Analytic Narratives of Economic Growth* (Princeton: Princeton University Press, 2003).

22 Dani Rodrik, "What's So Special About China's Exports?" *China & World Economy*, vol. 14. no. 5 (September–October 2006), pp. 1–19.

23 John Sutton, "The Auto-Component Supply Chain in China and India:

A Benchmarking Study," Unpublished paper, London School of Economics, 2005.

24 Jean-François Huchet characterizes China's policies as of the mid-1990s thus: "China's technological acquisition strategy is clear: It allows foreign firms access to the domestic market in exchange for technology transfer through joint production or joint ventures"—Huchet, "The China Circle and Technological Development in the Chinese Electronics Industry," in Barry Naughton, ed., *The China Circle: Economics and Electronics in the PRC, Taiwan, and Hong Kong* (Washington, DC: Brookings Institution Press, 1997), p. 270.

25 See ibid., and Kenneth L. Kraemer and Jason Dedrick, "Creating a Computer Industry Giant: China's Industrial Policies and Outcomes in the 1990s," Center for Research on Information Technology and Organizations, UC Irvine, 2001.

26 Dic Lo and Thomas M. H. Chan, "Machinery and China's Nexus of Foreign Trade and Economic Growth," *Journal of International Development*, vol. 10, no. 6 (1998), pp. 733–49.

27 See Dani Rodrik, "The Real Exchange Rate and Economic Growth," *Brookings Papers on Economic Activity*, 2 (2008).

28 Josh Lerner, *Boulevard of Broken Dreams: Why Public Efforts to Boost Entrepreneurship and Venture Capital Have Failed—and What to Do About It* (Princeton: Princeton University Press, 2009), p. 42. Lerner documents the role of public funding and military contracts in helping Silicon Valley get started, providing a useful counterweight to the mythology that the high-tech start-ups around Stanford University were the product of free markets alone.

8. Trade Fundamentalism in the Tropics

1 James E. Meade, *The Economic and Social Structure of Mauritius* (London: Methuen & Co., 1961), p. 3.

2 Ibid., p. 26.

3 Arvind Subramanian, *Trade and Trade Policies in Eastern and Southern Africa*, International Monetary Fund, Occasional Paper 196, Washington, DC, 2001.

4 See Arvind Subramanian and Devesh Roy, "Who Can Explain the Mauritian Miracle? Meade, Romer, Sachs, or Rodrik?" in Rodrik, ed., *In Search of Prosperity: Analytic Narratives on Economic Growth*, p. 228. For case studies of partnerships between domestic groups and foreign investors, see R. Lamusse, "Mauritius," in Samuel M. Wangwe, ed., *Exporting Africa: Technology, Trade, and Industrialization in Sub-Saharan Africa*

(London and New York: UNU/INTECH Studies in Technology and Development, Routledge, 1995), chap. 12.

5 There were a few exceptions, of course. Peter T. Bauer was the leading contrarian, arguing for a small state. See Bauer, *Economic Analysis and Policy in Under-developed Countries* (Cambridge: Cambridge University Press, 1957).

6 For John Williamson's own account of how the Washington Consensus was developed and of its evolution over time, see Williamson, "A Short History of the Washington Consensus," Peterson Institute for International Economics, Washington, DC, September 2004, available online at http://www.iie.com/publications/papers/williamson0904-2.pdf.

7 Jeffrey D. Sachs and Andrew M. Warner, "Economic Reform and the Process of Global Integration," *Brookings Papers on Economic Activity*, 1 (1995), pp. 1–95.

8 "We therefore argue against the notion of a low-income 'development trap' since open trade policies (and correlated market policies) are available to even the poorest countries," Sachs and Warner wrote (ibid., p. 52, n. 73).

9 My own critique of the Sachs and Warner study can be found in Francisco Rodríguez and Dani Rodrik, "Trade Policy and Economic Growth: A Skeptic's Guide to the Cross-National Evidence," in Bernanke and Rogoff, eds., *Macroeconomics Annual 2000*.

10 This interpretation is based on a number of conversations I had with Sachs subsequently.

11 What Sachs and Warner considered "open" policies on import tariffs and quotas were in fact remarkably protective by today's standard—so protective that few countries were classified as "closed" on account of their import tariffs or quantitative restrictions on imports. The real work in the classification was done by two other indicators: the black market premium for foreign currency, a measure of macroeconomic imbalance more than anything else, and an indicator for the presence of state monopoly in exports, the coverage of which was restricted to African countries. See Rodríguez and Rodrik, "Trade Policy and Economic Growth," for details.

12 Anne O. Krueger, "Trade Policy and Economic Development: How We Learn," *American Economic Review*, vol. 87, no. 1 (March 1997), p. 11.

13 So a senior U.S. Treasury economist could admonish the Mexican government to work harder to bring crime levels down, "because such high levels of crime and violence may drive foreign investors away." See Dani Rodrik, "Trading in Illusions," *Foreign Policy* (March–April 2001), p. 55.

14 The paper I was presenting was Rodríguez and Rodrik, "Trade Policy

and Economic Growth." Subsequent research by others has shown that tariffs on manufactures or on high-skill products can indeed promote economic growth. See Sybille Lehmann and Kevin H. O'Rourke, "The Structure of Protection and Growth in the Late 19th Century," *Review of Economics and Statistics* (forthcoming); and Nathan Nunn and Daniel Trefler, "The Structure of Tariffs and Long-Term Growth," *American Economic Journal—Macroeconomics* (forthcoming).

15 For example, it was common to argue that East Asian export subsidies simply offset the effects of import protection, resulting in near–free trade conditions. Similarly, price "distortions" in East Asia and elsewhere were rarely directly compared. If they were, it would be obvious that East Asian governments had not been on the side of angels. One of the bibles of the revisionists, a book project undertaken for the OECD, calculated an index of price distortion for a number of countries so as to compare their trade regimes in an objective manner. Among the countries included were Taiwan, the archetypal outward-oriented country, and Mexico, a leading case of inward-looking development. When one looks at the evidence in the OECD study closely, one finds that the average level of intervention in manufacturing seems to have been higher in Taiwan than it was in Mexico. See Ian M. D. Little, Tibor Scitovsky, and Maurice Scott, *Industry and Trade in Some Developing Countries* (London: Oxford University Press, 1970), Table 5.2.

16 When both inputs and outputs are valued at world prices. This is called "producing negative value added."

17 Enrique Cardenas, Jose Antonio Ocampo, and Rosemary Thorp, *An Economic History of Twentieth-Century Latin America*, Vol. 3: *Industrialization and the State in Latin America: The Postwar Years* (London: Palgrave, 2000), p. 16. The post-1990 growth rate comes from the World Bank's World Development Indicators online database.

18 See Barry P. Bosworth and Susan M. Collins, "The Empirics of Growth: An Update," *Brookings Papers on Economic Activity*, 2 (2003), Table 1.

19 Kalpana Kochhar, et al., "India's Pattern of Development: What Happened, What Follows?" *Journal of Monetary Economics*, vol. 53, no. 5 (July 2006), pp. 981–1019.

20 John Williamson, "Did the Washington Consensus Fail?" Outline of Speech at the Center for Strategic and International Studies, Washington, DC, November 6, 2002, online at http://www.iie.com/publications/papers/paper.cfm?ResearchID=488. The term "damaged brand" was used in Moisés Naím, "Washington Consensus: A Damaged Brand," *Financial Times*, October 28, 2002. British prime minister Gordon Brown officially pronounced the death of the Washington Consensus in early 2009.

21 Sachs and Warner, "Economic Reform," p. 44.

22 See Dani Rodrik, "Growth Strategies," in Philippe Aghion and Steven Durlauf, eds., *Handbook of Economic Growth*, Vol. 1A (Amsterdam: North-Holland, 2005).

23 Jeffrey Sachs's more recent worldview is captured in Jeffrey D. Sachs, et al., "Ending Africa's Poverty Trap," *Brookings Papers on Economic Activity*, 1 (2004).

24 Anoop Singh, et al., *Stabilization and Reform in Latin America: A Macroeconomic Perspective on the Experience Since the Early 1990s*, IMF Occasional Paper, Washington, DC, February 2005, p. xiv.

25 Anne O. Krueger, "Meant Well, Tried Little, Failed Much: Policy Reforms in Emerging Market Economies," Remarks at the Roundtable Lecture at the Economic Honors Society, New York University, New York, March 23, 2004.

26 Arvind Panagariya, "Think Again—International Trade," *Foreign Policy* (November–December 2003).

27 Hernando de Soto, *The Mystery of Capital* (New York: Basic Books, 2000).

28 Muhammad Yunus, *Banker to the Poor: Micro-Lending and the Battle Against World Poverty* (New York: Public Affairs, 2003).

29 William Easterly, *The White Man's Burden: Why the West's Efforts to Aid the Rest Have Done So Much Ill and So Little Good* (New York: Penguin, 2006).

30 This approach, called "the Growth Diagnostics framework," was developed by Ricardo Hausmann, Andres Velasco, and myself. It was subsequently applied to a large number of different settings. See Hausmann, Rodrik, and Velasco, "Growth Diagnostics," in Joseph Stiglitz and Narcis Serra, eds., *The Washington Consensus Reconsidered: Towards a New Global Governance* (New York: Oxford University Press, 2008). Some of the country applications can be found online at http://ksghome.harvard.edu/~drodrik/Growth_Diagnostics_Index.html.

31 In other words, it leads to overvaluation of the home currency. See Rodrik and Subramanian, "Why Did Financial Globalization Disappoint?" pp. 112–38.

32 Atul Kohli, "Politics of Economic Liberalization in India," *World Development*, vol. 17, no. 3 (1989), pp. 305–28.

33 Dani Rodrik and Arvind Subramanian, "From 'Hindu Growth' to Productivity Surge: The Mystery of the Indian Growth Transition," *IMF Staff Papers*, vol. 52, no. 2 (2005).

34 The project was led by my Harvard colleague Ricardo Hausmann. For background and discussion on South Africa's problems, see Dani

Rodrik, "Understanding South Africa's Economic Puzzles," *Economics of Transition*, vol. 16, no. 4 (2008), pp. 769–97. The full set of papers prepared for this project can be found in http://www.cid.harvard.edu/southafrica/.

35 For further elaboration, see Ricardo Hausmann, Dani Rodrik, and Charles F. Sabel, "Reconfiguring Industrial Policy: A Framework with an Application to South Africa," Center for International Development, Working Paper No. 168, Harvard University, May 2008. We may have exaggerated the novelty of our ideas. Meade himself was quite clear about the importance of the government–private-sector dialogue. The Industrial Development Corporation that he recommended was designed in part to stimulate the kind of strategic collaboration we had in mind for South Africa—See Meade, *The Economic and Social Structure of Mauritius*, p. 30.

36 See the speech by Rob Davies, minister of trade and industry, Budget Vote Address in Parliament delivered in Cape Town on June 30, 2009; available online at http://www.politicsweb.co.za/politicsweb/view/politicsweb/en/page71656?oid=134655&sn=Detail.

37 Alexander Hamilton, *Report on Manufactures*, Communication to the House of Representatives, December 5, 1791.

9. The Political Trilemma of the World Economy

1 See the interview with Domingo Cavallo at http://www.pbs.org/wgbh/commandingheights/shared/pdf/int_domingocavallo.pdf.

2 This account draws on Dani Rodrik, "Reform in Argentina, Take Two: Trade Rout," *The New Republic*, January 14, 2002, pp. 13–15.

3 Cavallo would later argue that the true culprit was loose fiscal policy in the years preceding the crisis. See the interview cited in note 1. From a narrow economic perspective, he may well be right. With enough fiscal austerity, price deflation, and belt-tightening, the Argentine economy would have been able to service external debts and maintain financial market confidence. The question is whether this is a sensible way to run an economy. Is it reasonable, or even desirable, to expect that the political system will deliver these drastic measures when needed (that is, when times are already tough) just to satisfy foreign creditors?

4 Thomas L. Friedman, *The Lexus and the Olive Tree* (New York: Anchor Books, 2000), pp. 104–06.

5 In a famous decision issued in 1905 (*Lochner v. New York*), the U.S. Supreme Court struck down a New York State law restricting the maximum hours of work for bakery employees. The New York statute was

"an illegal interference," the justices wrote, "with the right of individuals, both employers and employees, to make contracts regarding labor upon such terms as they may think best." See Michael J. Sandel, *Democracy's Discontent: America in Search of a Public Philosophy* (Cambridge, MA: Harvard University Press, 1996), p. 41. It wasn't until the 1930s, following Franklin D. Roosevelt's threat to pack the Court with sympathetic jurists, that the Supreme Court reversed course and upheld a minimum wage law for women in 1937 (*West Coast Hotel Co. v. Parrish*). This decision opened the way for subsequent legislation regulating employment practices including maximum work hours—Rodrik, *Has Globalization Gone Too Far?* Institute for International Economics, Washington, DC, 1997, p. 36.

6 Dani Rodrik, "Democracies Pay Higher Wages," *Quarterly Journal of Economics*, vol. 114, no. 3 (August 1999), pp. 707–38.

7 "Transcript of First Presidential Debate," September 9, 2008, at http://www.cnn.com/2008/POLITICS/09/26/debate.mississippi .transcript/#cnnSTCText.

8 Scott A. Hodge and Andre Dammert, "U.S. Lags While Competitors Accelerate Corporate Income Tax Reform," *Fiscal Fact No. 184*, Tax Foundation, August 2009, http://www.taxfoundation.org/files/ff184 .pdf.

9 Michael P. Devereux, Ben Lockwood, and Michela Redoano, "Do Countries Compete Over Corporate Tax Rates?" *Journal of Public Economics*, vol. 92, nos. 5–6 (June 2008), pp. 1210–1235.

10 Michael J. Trebilcock and Robert Howse, *The Regulation of International Trade*, 3rd ed. (New York: Routledge, 2005), p. 517.

11 In a similar case in 2006, the WTO also ruled against EU restrictions on genetically modified food and seeds, finding fault once again with the adequacy of EU scientific risk assessment.

12 Emma Aisbett, Larry Karp, and Carol McAusland, "Regulatory Takings and Environmental Regulation in NAFTA's Chapter 11," Unpublished paper, University of California at Berkeley, February 10, 2006.

13 For an inventory of cases brought under Chapter 11 of NAFTA, see the Public Citizen Web site: http://www.citizen.org/documents/Ch11Cases Chart-2009.pdf.

14 Luke Peterson and Alan Beattie, "Italian Groups Challenge Pretoria Over BEE," *Financial Times*, March 9, 2007.

15 Since these zones commonly provide differential benefits to exporting firms, it is easy to find them in violation of WTO's subsidy rules. Some developing nations have benefited from a delay of the entry into force of these restrictions on subsidies.

16 For a prescient article on the costs of WTO's patent rules, see Arvind Subramanian, "Putting Some Numbers on the TRIPs Pharmaceutical Debate," *International Journal of Technology Management*, vol. 10, nos. 2–3 (1995).

17 Richard R. Nelson, "The Changing Institutional Requirements for Technological and Economic Catch Up," Unpublished paper, Columbia University, June 2004.

18 Henrik Horn, Petros C. Mavroidis, and André Sapir, "Beyond the WTO? An Anatomy of EU and US Preferential Trade Agreements," Bruegel Blueprint 7, Bruegel Institute, Brussels, 2009.

19 For more elaboration and examples, see Dani Rodrik, *One Economics, Many Recipes: Globalization, Institutions and Economic Growth* (Princeton: Princeton University Press, 2007), chap. 4.

20 Robert O. Keohane, Stephen Macedo, and Andrew Moravcsik, "Democracy-Enhancing Multilateralism," *International Organization*, 63 (Winter 2009), pp. 1–31. See also Robert Howse, "Democracy, Science and Free Trade: Risk Regulation on Trial at the World Trade Organization," *Michigan Law Review*, 98 (June 2000).

21 In a few cases (such as the U.S.-Peru trade agreement of 2006), labor groups have managed to "balance" those interests by introducing labor standards clauses into bilateral or regional trade agreements. For reasons I will discuss in subsequent chapters, this can compound the problems. Pressure from U.S. trade unions is as unlikely to serve the interests of other countries as pressure from U.S. multinationals.

10. Is Global Governance Feasible?

1 African Development Bank and World Tourism (not Trade) Organization, respectively.

2 See http://voxeu.org/index.php?q=node/2544.

3 See Jeffrey Garten, "The Case for a Global Central Bank," Yale School of Management, posted online, September 21, 2009, at http://ba.yale.edu/news_events/CMS/Articles/6958.shtml.

4 Carmen Reinhart and Kenneth Rogoff, "Regulation Should Be International," *Financial Times*, November 18, 2008 (http://www.ft.com/cms/s/0/983724fc-b589-11dd-ab71-0000779fd18c.html?nclick_check=1).

5 David Epstein and Sharyn O'Halloran, *Delegating Powers: A Transaction Cost Politics Approach to Policy Making Under Separate Powers* (Cambridge and New York: Cambridge University Press, 1999).

6 Anne-Marie Slaughter, *A New World Order* (Princeton and Oxford: Princeton University Press, 2004).

7 John G. Ruggie, "Reconstituting the Global Public Domain—Issues, Actors, and Practices," *European Journal of International Relations*, 10 (2004), pp. 499–531.

8 There is a parallel debate in international law on whether it is possible to institute effective legal norms and practices at the global level in the absence of global government. See, e.g., Jeffrey L. Dunoff and Joel P. Trachtman, eds., *Ruling the World?: Constitutionalism, International Law, and Global Governance* (Cambridge and New York: Cambridge University Press, 2009), and Eric Posner, *The Perils of Global Legalism* (Chicago: University of Chicago Press, 2009), in addition to the work of Anne-Marie Slaughter already cited. The case against "global legalism" is stated succinctly by Posner, who argues that without legal institutions—legislators, enforcers, and courts—law cannot control behavior.

9 Joshua Cohen and Charles F. Sabel, "Global Democracy?" *International Law and Politics*, 37 (2005), p. 779.

10 Ibid., p. 796.

11 Peter Singer, *One World: The Ethics of Globalization* (New Haven: Yale University Press, 2002), p. 12.

12 Amartya Sen, *Identity and Violence: The Illusion of Destiny* (New York: W. W. Norton, 2006).

13 Amartya Sen, *The Idea of Justice* (Cambridge, MA: Harvard University Press, 2009), p. 143.

14 See Cohen and Sabel, "Global Democracy," and Charles F. Sabel and Jonathan Zeitlin, "Learning from Difference: The New Architecture of Experimentalist Governance in the EU," *European Law Journal*, vol. 14, no. 3 (May 2008), pp. 271–327.

15 Stephen Castle, "Compromise with Britain Paves Way to Finance Rules in Europe," *New York Times*, December 2, 2009 (http://www.nytimes.com/2009/12/03/business/global/03eubank.html?_r=1&sudsredirect=true).

16 The decision to send Greece to the IMF caused a certain amount of controversy within the European Union since, unlike the other two countries, Greece is a member of not only the European Union but also of the Eurozone. Ultimately, insistence on this score by German chancellor Angela Merkel overcame opposition from French president Nicolas Sarkozy and the European Central Bank president Jean-Claude Trichet.

17 See "After Severe Recession, Stabilization in Latvia," IMF Survey online, February 18, 2010, http://www.imf.org/external/pubs/ft/survey/so/2010/CAR021810A.htm.

18 The national regulators that negotiate these international agreements have their own interests, of course, and they enter into agreements

in part as a counterweight to domestic political pressures. See David Andrew Singer, *Regulating Capital: Setting Standards for the International Financial System* (Ithaca, NY: Cornell University Press, 2007).

19 Colleen E. H. Berndt, "Is Fair Trade in Coffee Production Fair and Useful? Evidence from Costa Rica and Guatemala and Implications for Policy," Mercatus Policy Series, Policy Comment No. 11, George Mason University, June 2007.

20 Andrew Chambers, "Not So Fair Trade," *The Guardian*, December 12, 2009. (http://www.guardian.co.uk/commentisfree/cif-green/2009/dec/12/fair-trade-fairtrade-kitkat-farmers).

21 See "Toy Makers Seek Standards for U.S. Safety," *New York Times*, September 7, 2007 (http://www.nytimes.com/2007/09/07/business/07toys.html?_r=2).

22 Nick Hornby, *Juliet, Naked* (New York: Penguin, 2009).

23 This account is based on Keith Hampton, "Netville: Community On and Offline in a Wired Suburb," in Stephen Graham, ed., *The Cybercities Reader* (London: Routledge, 2004), pp. 256–62. I owe the reference to this study to Nicholas A. Christakis and James H. Fowler, *Connected: The Surprising Power of Our Social Networks and How They Shape Our Lives* (New York: Little, Brown, 2009).

24 The data that I summarize here come from the World Values Survey databank at http://www.worldvaluessurvey.org/services/index.html.

11. Designing Capitalism 3.0

1 For a detailed statistical analysis of differences between European and American attitudes toward inequality, see Alberto Alesina, Rafael Di Tella, and Robert MacCulloch, "Inequality and Happiness: Are Europeans and Americans Different?" *Journal of Public Economics*, vol. 88, nos. 9–10 (August 2004), pp. 2009–42.

2 This argument is developed in Roberto Mangabeira Unger, *Democracy Realized: The Progressive Alternative* (London and New York: Verso, 1998).

3 There is a very large literature on the comparative economic performance of democracies versus non-democracies. This literature suggests that democratically governed economies tend to outperform authoritarian regimes on a number of dimensions: they are better at adjusting to external shocks, they provide greater stability and predictability, and they produce better social indicators and distributional outcomes. The results on long-term growth performance are more mixed, but the more recent evidence suggests that democracies have the edge there as well. See José Tavares and Romain Wacziarg, "How Democracy Affects

Growth," *European Economic Review*, vol. 45, no. 8 (August 2001), pp. 1341–1379; Dani Rodrik, "Participatory Politics, Social Cooperation, and Economic Stability," *American Economic Review, Papers and Proceedings* (May 2000); Dani Rodrik, "Democracies Pay Higher Wages," *Quarterly Journal of Economics* (August 1999); Dani Rodrik and Romain Wacziarg, "Do Democratic Transitions Produce Bad Economic Outcomes?" *American Economic Review, Papers and Proceedings*, vol. 95, no. 2 (May 2005), pp. 50–55; and Elias Papaioannou and Gregorios Siourounis, "Democratization and Growth," *Economic Journal*, vol. 118, no. 10 (2008), pp. 1520–51.

4 In December 2009, three countries—Guinea, Niger, and Madagascar—were removed from the list for lack of progress toward democratic practices. Mauritania was reinstated following democratic elections.

5 A good example is agricultural protection in the developed countries. The costs are paid primarily by consumers and taxpayers in those same developed countries.

6 In the language of economics, the global climate is a "pure" public good whereas an open economy is a private good, from the standpoint of individual nations, with some external effects on others.

12. A Sane Globalization

1 Antoine Bouët, "The Expected Benefits of Trade Liberalization for World Income and Development," Food Policy Review No. 8, International Food Policy Research Institute, Washington, DC, 2008. These estimates refer to the standard gains from freeing up trade, and neglect the second-best considerations we encountered earlier that might make trade restrictions economically beneficial in certain products for low-income countries.

2 It is a law of economics that the efficiency losses from taxes and other restrictions on economic activity are close to zero when they are small and rise with the *square* of the tax or restriction.

3 Currently the Agreement on Safeguards allows a temporary increase in trade restrictions under a fairly narrow set of conditions. It requires a domestic determination that increased imports "cause or threaten to cause serious injury to the domestic industry," that a cause-and-effect relationship between the import surge and injury be firmly established, and that injury not be attributed to imports if there are multiple causes for it. The safeguard measures must apply to all exporters of the product. However, safeguards cannot be applied to developing country exporters unless their share of imports of the product concerned is above a threshold. A country applying safeguard measures generally

has to compensate the affected exporters by providing "equivalent concessions."

4 This discussion is based on Dani Rodrik, *Has Globalization Gone Too Far?* and Rodrik, "The Global Governance of Trade As If Development Really Mattered," United Nations Development Program, New York, 2001.

5 This is what the existing agreement says: "A Member may apply a safeguard measure only following an investigation by the competent authorities of that Member pursuant to procedures previously established and made public in consonance with Article X of the GATT 1994. This investigation shall include reasonable public notice to all interested parties and public hearings or other appropriate means in which importers, exporters and other interested parties could present evidence and their views, including the opportunity to respond to the presentations of other parties and to submit their views, inter alia, as to whether or not the application of a safeguard measure would be in the public interest. The competent authorities shall publish a report setting forth their findings and reasoned conclusions reached on all pertinent issues of fact and law."

6 Howse's argument is developed in the context of risk regulation, but is valid more broadly. Robert Howse, "Democracy, Science, and Free Trade: Risk Regulation on Trial at the World Trade Organization," *Michigan Law Review*, vol. 98, no. 7 (June 2000), p. 2357.

7 Julian M. Alston, Daniel A. Sumner, and Heinrich Brunke, "Impacts of Reductions in US Cotton Subsidies on West African Farmers," Oxfam America, June 21, 2007 (http://www.oxfamamerica.org/pub lications/impacts-of-reductions-in-us-cotton-subsidies-on-west-afri can-cotton-producers/).

8 Unfortunately, there has been much obfuscation on this issue by Doha's advocates, who have tried to present an overly rosy scenario for the global poverty impact of the trade round. Removal of subsidies in the rich countries will raise the world prices of agricultural commodities. While this is good news for poor producers in the countryside (such as cotton farmers in West Africa), it is bad news for poor consumers in urban areas who do not grow their own food. The impact on poverty therefore is differentiated and depends on whether the poor are mostly urban or rural. See Dani Rodrik, "Food Prices and Poverty: Confusion or Obfuscation?" http://rodrik.typepad.com/dani_rodriks_ weblog/2008/05/food-prices-and.html.

9 "The Global Crisis Response and the Role of US-EU Cooperation," Remarks by Mark Sobel, Assistant Secretary of U.S. Department of Treasury for International Monetary and Financial Policy to the Euro-

pean Forum of Deposit Insurers at the Fédération Bancaire Française, June 29, 2009 (http://www.treas.gov/press/releases/tg196.htm). See also Marcus Walker and Stephen Fidler, "IMF Chief Urges Coordinated Finance Rules," *Wall Street Journal,* January 30, 2010, p. A11.

10 See Christine Harper and Simon Kennedy, "Politicians Can't Wait for Bankers Urging Caution on Regulation," Bloomberg News Service, February 1, 2010 (http://www.bloomberg.com/apps/news?pid=20601170&sid=aBY2eGclTyqg).

11 Alistair MacDonald, "U.S. Enters Europe's Fund Debate; Washington Joins U.K. in Lobbying EU for Less Stringent Regulations," *Wall Street Journal,* July 27, 2009, p. C3.

12 In December 2009, the Basel Committee agreed on a package of reforms that, among other things, would phase out the use of "hybrid" capital which European banks rely on as part of their capital requirements. It also proposed new rules on bank leverage and liquidity, countercyclical capital buffers, and new risk weightings to reflect counterparty credit risk. But the quantitative limits on capital, leverage, and liquidity that banks have to abide by were left unclear. Some of these proposals were further refined in a broad package proposed in July 2010. See Patrick Jenkins, "Bank Capital Rules Face Overhaul," *Financial Times,* December 17, 2009.

13 Simon Johnson, "Was the G20 Summit Actually Dangerous?" September 26, 2009, http://baselinescenario.com/2009/09/26/was-the-g20-summit-actually-dangerous/#more–5085.

14 Ibid.

15 Bankers are indeed quick to make this point when they are threatened by tighter regulations. In an October 2009 interview with the *Financial Times*, the chairman of Barclays warned about adverse implications for Britain's financial sector if "regulators are too rigorous in their implementation of a global crackdown on bonuses and capital requirements while other nations, such as the US, are lax." "There is the real risk of regulatory arbitrage," he added. "This is a global financial system. It is fungible. So I am very concerned there should be a level playing field." See http://www.ft.com/cms/s/0/47fd0f82-bc23-11de-9426-00144feab49a.html.

16 These ideas were first outlined in Dani Rodrik, "A Plan B for Global Finance," *The Economist,* March 12, 2009.

17 There is much debate among economists about whether a tax of this sort would also serve to curb destabilizing short-term speculation. If applied globally, it would certainly reduce the volume of short-term transactions on currency exchanges. Whether this would curtail more

flows of the destabilizing kind versus flows of the stabilizing kind is unclear. And a small tax certainly would not do much to prevent runs on countries of the type that took place during the Asian financial crisis, since the effects of the tax would be overwhelmed by the expectation of large capital gains. What is indisputable is that such a tax would mobilize considerable resources, given the large base. It would have negligible efficiency costs at worst, at the levels typically considered.

18 Nicholas Dorn, "Financial Market Systemic Regulation: Stability through Democratic Diversity," VoxEU.org, December 18, 2009, http://www.voxeu.org/index.php?q=node/4411.

19 Ibid.

20 See Dani Rodrik, "The IMF Needs Fresh Thinking on Capital Controls," Project Syndicate column, November 11, 2009 (http://www.project-syndicate.org/commentary/rodrik37), and Arvind Subramanian and John Williamson, "Put the Puritans in Charge of the Punchbowl," *Financial Times*, February 11, 2009 (http://www.ft.com/cms/s/0/a0c04b34-c196-11de-b86b-00144feab49a.html?nclick_check=1).

21 The figures are from Michael A. Clemens, Claudio E. Montenegro, and Lant Pritchett, "The Place Premium: Wage Differences for Identical Workers Across the U.S. Border," Unpublished paper, Harvard Kennedy School of Government, July 2008.

22 I discuss these ideas in Dani Rodrik, "Globalization for Whom?" *Harvard Magazine* (July–August 2002) (http://harvardmagazine.com/2002/07/globalization-for-whom.html), and Rodrik, "Feasible Globalizations," in Michael Weinstein, ed., *Globalization: What's New?* (New York: Columbia University Press, 2005). My Harvard colleague Lant Pritchett has developed them further in his *Let Their People Come: Breaking the Gridlock on Global Labor Mobility* (Washington, DC: Center for Global Development, 2006). For a legal scholar's perspective on these issues, see Joel P. Trachtman, *The International Law of Economic Migration: Toward the Fourth Freedom* (New York: Upjohn Institute, 2009).

23 The global gains from a full movement to free trade in goods would be around $100 billion—see Bouët, cited in note 1. The estimate on gains from labor mobility comes from World Bank, *Global Economic Prospects 2006*, Washington, DC, 2005.

24 See Devesh Kapur and John McHale, "Sojourns and Software: Internationally Mobile Human Capital and High-Tech Industry Development in India, Ireland, and Israel," in Ashish Arora and Alfonso Gamberdella, eds., *From Underdogs to Tigers: The Rise and Growth of the Software Industry in Some Emerging Market Eocnomies* (New York: Oxford University Press, 2005, pp. 236–74, and Annalee Saxenian, *Local and*

Global Networks of Immigrant Professionals in Silicon Valley (San Francisco: Public Policy Institute of California, 2002). For a detailed study of the impact of the Indian diaspora on the country's political and economic development, see Devesh Kapur, *Diaspora, Development, and Democracy: The Domestic Impact of International Migration from India* (Princeton and Oxford: Princeton University Press, 2010).

25 See the discussion on this question at http://rodrik.typepad.com/dani _rodriks_weblog/2007/05/the_new_york_ti.html.

26 The World Bank (*Global Economic Prospects 2006*) estimates a reduction in advanced country wages of 0.5 percent under a program that increases migration by 3 percent of the receiving countries' labor force. An earlier study, by Terri Louise Walmsley and L. Alan Winters, calculates that real wages in the United States would fall by 0.6–0.8 percent— Walmsley and Winters, "Relaxing the Restrictions on the Temporary Movements of Natural Persons: A Simulation Analysis," CEPR Discussion Paper No. 3719, London, 2003. The benchmark elasticity used by George Borjas in his analysis of the wage effect of immigration (–0.3) produces a similar estimate: -0.3×3 percent $= -0.9$ percent. See George J. Borjas, "The Analytics of the Wage Effects of Immigration," Harvard Kennedy School of Government, August 2009.

27 The simulations I referred to earlier assume that much of these benefits would accrue to foreign nationals. But the work visas can be administered in ways that retain some of these gains in the labor-importing countries. The issue here is who captures the wage differential between the home and host countries. Suppose, e.g., that the host government auctions the limited visas to domestic businesses or labor contractors who wish to bring workers from abroad. This would result in the bulk of the "rents" being captured by the host government rather than the workers themselves. Any conceivable distribution of the gains is possible with imaginative design of the visa allotment scheme.

28 Paul Krugman, "Chinese New Year," *New York Times*, December 31, 2009.

29 See Dani Rodrik, "The Real Exchange Rate and Economic Growth," *Brookings Papers on Economic Activity* (Fall 2008).

30 For the technically minded, here is a bit more explanation. An import tariff or export subsidy will have the effect, on impact, of improving the trade balance. However, this can be offset (and will be offset, unless the government actively intervenes) by an appreciation of the (real) exchange rate. The appreciation of the real exchange rate does not fully neutralize the stimulating effect of the original tariff or subsidy policies, as long as domestic demand for tradables responds positively

to the appreciation (which makes the relative price of tradables lower). Therefore, industrial policy combined with real exchange rate appreciation can promote the production of tradables without affecting the trade balance. See Dani Rodrik, "Growth After the Crisis," in *Globalization and Growth: Implications for a Post-Crisis World*, Commission on Growth and Development, Washington, DC, 2010.

31 This would be an appreciation of around 25 percent. See Dani Rodrik, "Making Room for China in the World Economy," VoxEU.org, December 17, 2009, http://voxeu.org/index.php?q=node/4399.

32 What links the two is that the Chinese government has to buy dollars in order to prevent the renminbi from appreciating.

33 Martin Jacques, *When China Rules the World: The End of the Western World and the Birth of a New Global Order* (New York: Penguin, 2009).

34 Stephen S. Cohen and Bradford DeLong express concern about the implications for global economic stability of the loss in the relative economic standing of the United States. See their work *The End of Influence: What Happens When Other Countries Have the Money* (New York: Basic Books, 2010).

ACKNOWLEDGMENTS

A very long list of friends, critics, and co-conspirators have been subjected over the years to earlier versions of the arguments in this book and have responded with reactions that have helped shape my thinking. These comments may not always have saved me from the errors that the more critical among them have found in my thinking, but I hope they have at least allowed me to state my views with greater sensitivity to these differences.

With apologies to those I may have forgotten, I want to thank Daron Acemoglu, Philippe Aghion, Abhijit Banerjee, Jagdish Bhagwati, Nancy Birdsall, George Borjas, François Bourguignon, Susan Collins, Avinash Dixit, Bill Easterly, Barry Eichengreen, Ron Findlay, Jeff Frankel, Richard Freeman, Jeff Frieden, Gene Grossman, Ricardo Hausmann, Gerry Helleiner, Elhanan Helpman, Peter Kenen, Bob Keohane, Tarun Khanna, Robert Lawrence, Frank Levy, Justin Lin, Jose Antonio Ocampo, Lant Pritchett, Jim Robinson, John Ruggie, Jeffrey Sachs, Mike Spence, T. N. Srinivasan, Nick Stern, Joe Stiglitz, Arvind Subramanian, Larry Summers, Robert Unger, and Andres Velasco. A word of special thanks to Avinash Dixit, a model "fox" who will always represent for me the best in the economic profession.

Three individuals in this list played a particularly important role in the preparation of this book. Jeff Frieden, Robert Lawrence, and Arvind Subramanian read the manuscript in its entirety and gave me very valuable feedback in addition to correcting many errors of fact or judgment. Aside from many other useful suggestions, Jeff Frieden saved me from misusing baseball analogies and from mistranslations from Latin.

I must confess to being disappointed by the initial response I received from Drake McFeely, my editor at W. W. Norton, when I sent him my first two draft chapters: "Let's talk before you write another word." These are two pretty darn good chapters, I thought! But Drake was right, and the gentle prodding I received from him on matters small and large, as well as Brendan Curry's detailed suggestions, made this a much better book—even in my eyes! It has been a great privilege to work with them. Scott Moyers of the Wylie Agency read carefully every incarnation of this work, from the initial proposal to the final product. He has been a tremendous source of support and good judgment.

Words cannot express my gratitude to my family: my wife Pınar Doğan who is my greatest source of support and whom I am extraordinarily lucky to have as my life partner; my son Deniz who is too young to have a firm opinion on this book but loves me nonetheless; my daughter Odile who drew supply and demand curves long before she understood what they meant; and my daughter Delphine who doesn't hold it against me that she didn't get to design the book's cover. My brother İzel has always been there for me, along with Nita and their extended family. The memory of my father Vitali Rodrik has been a constant companion all these years, always spurring me to do better. Last but not least, I want to acknowledge my great debt to my mother Karmela Rodrik. If I can write half-decent prose, she knows where it comes from. I love you all.

I have dedicated this book to Çetin Doğan, my father-in-law. As I write these words, he remains imprisoned in Turkey on false and fabricated charges, along with scores of others who served with him. I hope justice will have long been done by the time this book is out.

INDEX

Abdelal, Rawi, 99
accountability, 217, 226, 254, 265
 of global governance, 202, 203,
   212–13
adjustment assistance, 19, 88, 295n
advanced economies, 135–37, 182
 customized capitalism in, 74–75
 fertility rates in, 141
 floating currencies and, 97
 GATT and, 71, 75
 IMF and, 90
 imperialism and, 26
 living standards of, 165, 166
 oil shocks (1970s) and, xvii, 101
 poor in, 135–36
 product certification and labeling
   for, 224–25
 prosperity in, xvi, xvii, 234
 reform of international trade
   regime and, 255–56
 size of government in, 16, 17
 subprime mortgage crisis and, xi,
   118–19, 127
 temporary work visas and, 268–72,
   316n
 see also specific countries
affirmative action, 198
Africa, 82, 158, 198, 204–5, 274, 304n
 import-substituting
   industrialization in, 168, 169,
   205
 mercantilism and, 11

 mineral economies of, 140
 Sachs in, 171
 sub-Saharan, 146, 169
 see also West Africa; *specific countries*
African Growth and Opportunity Act
   (2000), 248
African National Congress, 180
Agreement on Developmental and
   Social Safeguards, 253–54
Agreement on Intellectual Property
   Rights (TRIPS), 199
Agreement on Safeguards, WTO,
   253, 254, 312n–13n
Agreement on Sanitary and
   Phytosanitary (SPS) Measures,
   WTO, 80, 195, 196
agriculture, 169, 204, 235
 in Argentina, 82, 142
 in China, 150–51, 178
 GATT and, 72, 75, 76, 77
 genetically modified crops and, 54
 in Mauritius, 160, 161
 price declines in, 37, 67
 quotas for, 72, 78, 150
 in South Africa, 180
 subsidies for, 78, 81, 82, 252, 258,
   313n
 in Taiwan, 146
 tariffs and, xiv, 30, 72, 78
 WTO and, 77, 78, 82–83, 258
 see also farmers
AIG, xiii, 299n

Index

329

Industrial Revolution in, 138, 139
Martyn's views on free trade
benefits to, 48–50
English East India Company
(Governor and Company of
Merchants of London Trading
into the East Indies), 7–8,
12–13, 32, 48
environment, 240, 241
exploitation of, xiii, 53, 58
global governance and, 211
global warming and, 247–48, 249
regulation of, 79, 198, 277
U.S policy on, 79
environmental standards, 22, 54, 226,
227, 245
reform of the international trade
regime and, 253, 255
equilibrium, macroeconomic, 96
equity, 53, 84, 114, 115
Bretton Woods and, 70, 72
Esserman, Susan, 78–79
ethics, 41, 213, 214, 271
Ethiopia, 82
EU, see European Union
euro, 124, 215, 219, 220
Eurodollar market, 102
Europe, 46, 89, 98–99, 100, 141, 239,
272
capital controls and, 99, 102–3
capital flows in, 128
financial crisis in (1990s), 108
financial regulation in, 260–63,
266
foreign-born underclass in, 269
Indonesia's exports to, 220–25
see also Continental Europe;
Western Europe; specific
countries
European Central Bank, 215
European Commission, 103, 196, 215,
261
European Constitution, 215
European Council, 216
European Economic Community, 99
European Parliament, 215, 216, 261
European Union (EU), 81, 103, 124,
189, 199, 242, 308n
Doha Round and, xiv, 82
experimentalist governance of,
216–17

financial regulation and, 260, 261
global governance and, 203, 214–
20, 238
governance gaps in, 218–19, 310n
hormone-treated beef and, 79–80,
195–97, 293n
tax competition and, 194
Eurozone, 124, 220, 310n
exchange controls, 40
exchange rates, 40, 121, 157
appreciation of, 316n–17n
fixed, see fixed exchange rates
fixed but adjustable, 98
floating, 97, 100–101, 104–7
export-processing zones (EPZs), 162,
163, 177, 198–99
exports, 8, 29, 31, 78, 145
of China, 85, 152–55, 181, 220–24,
227, 228, 274, 275
of developing countries, 72, 77,
84–85, 125, 146, 147, 148, 162–
63, 168, 169, 170, 272, 304n
of India, 242–43
of Indonesia, 220–25
of Japan, 73, 75, 142
of Mauritius, 162–63, 168
of non-democratic countries,
245–46
subsidies for, 148, 154, 155, 177,
198, 256, 305n, 308n, 316n
externalities:
negative, 53
positive, 53, 157
extractive model, 140

fair trade, 31, 288n
labeling and, 226–27
Fannie Mae, xiii
farmers, xiii, 30, 45, 67, 142
in China, 150–51
fair trade labeling and, 226–27
poor, xiii, 83, 258
price deflation and, 37
fascists, 46
federalism, global, 202–3
Federal Reserve, xiii, 36, 42, 127,
129
Federal Reserve Act (1913), 36
Ferguson, Niall, 32
fertility rates, 141, 162
Finance Ministry, Japanese, 144

Index